Between Nihilism and Politics

SUNY series in Contemporary Italian Philosophy
Silvia Benso and Brian Schroeder, editors

Between Nihilism and Politics

The Hermeneutics of Gianni Vattimo

Edited by Silvia Benso
and Brian Schroeder

Published by State University of New York Press, Albany

© 2010 State University of New York

All rights reserved

Printed in the United States of America

No part of this book may be used or reproduced in any manner whatsoever without written permission. No part of this book may be stored in a retrieval system or transmitted in any form or by any means including electronic, electrostatic, magnetic tape, mechanical, photocopying, recording, or otherwise without the prior permission in writing of the publisher.

For information, contact State University of New York Press, Albany, NY
www.sunypress.edu

Production by Diane Ganeles
Marketing by Anne M. Valentine

Library of Congress Cataloging-in-Publication Data
Between nihilism and politics : the hermeneutics of Gianni Vattimo / edited by Silvia Benso and Brian Schroeder.
    p. cm. — (SUNY series in contemporary Italian philosophy)
  Includes bibliographical references and index.
  ISBN 978-1-4384-3285-4 (hardcover : alk. paper)
  ISBN 978-1-4384-3284-7 (pbk. : alk. paper)
  1. Vattimo, Gianni, 1936– I. Benso, Silvia. II. Schroeder, Brian.
  B3654.V384B48 2010
  195—dc22
                                                                2010007176

10 9 8 7 6 5 4 3 2 1

Contents

List of Abbreviations   *vii*

Introduction   *1*
    BRIAN SCHROEDER

Part One.
Hermeneutics and Nihilism

1. The Experiment of Nihilism: Interpretation and Experience of Truth in Gianni Vattimo   15
    GAETANO CHIURAZZI

2. Vattimo's Theory of Truth   33
    FRANCA D'AGOSTINI

3. Vattimo's Hermeneutics as a Practice of Freedom   47
    DAVID WEBB

4. Weak Thought and the Recovery of Reason   63
    ROBERT T. VALGENTI

5. *Beyond* Interpretation? On Some Perplexities Following upon Vattimo's "Turn" from Hermeneutics   79
    PETER CARRAVETTA

Part Two.
Metaphysics and Religion

6. Metaphysics, Violence, and Alterity in Gianni Vattimo   *101*
    EDISON HIGUERA AGUIRRE

7. Thinking the Origin, Awaiting Salvation   *121*
    CLAUDIO CIANCIO

8. Postmodern Salvation: Gianni Vattimo's Philosophy of Religion   *135*
    GIOVANNA BORRADORI

9. Secularization as a Post-Metaphysical Religious Vocation:
   Gianni Vattimo's Post-Secular Faith   *149*
   EDUARDO MENDIETA

Part Three.
Politics and Technology

10. Philosophy and Politics at the End of Metaphysics   *167*
    JAMES RISSER

11. Deciding to Bear Witness: Revolutionary Rupture and
    Liberal Continuity in Weak Thought   *183*
    LUCA BAGETTO

12. Emancipation and the Future of the Utopian:
    On Vattimo's Philosophy of History   *203*
    SILVIA BENSO

13. "Postmodernity as the Ontological Sense of Technology"
    and Democratic Politics   *221*
    ERIK M. VOGT

14. What's Wrong with Biotechnology? Vattimo's Interpretation
    of Science, Technology, and the Media   *241*
    MARTIN G. WEISS

    Contributors   *257*

    Index   *261*

List of Abbreviations

(Translations of passages from Vattimo's volumes not yet translated into English are the editors' unless otherwise noted).

AC   *After Christianity*. Translated by Luca D'Isanto. New York: Columbia University Press, 2002.

AD   *The Adventure of Difference: Philosophy after Nietzsche and Heidegger*. Translated by C. P. Blamires and T. Harrison. Cambridge: Polity Press, 1993.

ADG *After the Death of God*. Edited by Jeffrey W. Robbins. New York: Columbia University Press, 2007.

AS   *Al di là del soggetto. Nietzsche, Heidegger e l'ermeneutica*. Milan: Feltrinelli, 1981.

B   *Belief*. Translated by Luca D'Isanto and David Webb. Cambridge: Polity Press, 1997.

BI   *Beyond Interpretation: The Meaning of Hermeneutics for Philosophy*. Translated by David Webb. Cambridge: Polity Press, 1997.

DN *Dialogue with Nietzsche*. Translated by William McCuaig. New York: Columbia University Press, 2005.

EC   *Ecce comu. Come si ri-diventa ciò che si era*. Rome: Fazi, 2007.

EI   *Etica dell'interpretazione*. Turin: Rosenberg & Sellier, 1989.

EM *The End of Modernity: Nihilism and Hermeneutics in Postmodern Culture*. Translated by Jon R. Snyder. Baltimore: Johns Hopkins University Press, 1988.

FR   *The Future of Religion*. With Richard Rorty. Edited by Santiago Zabala. New York: Columbia University Press, 2005.

IH   *Introduzione a Heidegger*. Rome-Bari: Laterza, 1971.

N   *Nietzsche: An Introduction.* Translated by Nicholas Martin. Stanford: Stanford University Press, 2002.

NE *Nihilism and Emancipation: Ethics, Politics, and Law.* Edited by Santiago Zabala and translated by William McCuaig. New York: Columbia University Press, 2004.

PD *Il pensiero debole.* With Pier Aldo Rovatti. Milan: Feltrinelli, 1983.

R   *Religion.* With Jacques Derrida. Stanford: Stanford University Press, 1998.

SM *Il soggetto e la maschera. Nietzsche e il problema della liberazione.* Milan: Bompiani, 1974.

TS *The Transparent Society.* Translated by David Webb. Cambridge: Polity Press, 1992.

VRF *Vocazione e responsabilità del filosofo.* Edited by Franca D'Agostini. Genoa: Il Melangolo, 2000.

Introduction

One of Italy's leading contemporary philosophers for more than forty years, Gianni Vattimo has exercised a significant effect on contemporary debates in hermeneutics, political philosophy, and religious thought. A student of Luigi Pareyson at the University of Turin, under whose guidance he wrote a dissertation on Aristotle, Vattimo found his own philosophical ground during the course of his studies with Karl Löwith and Hans-Georg Gadamer at the University of Heidelberg, during which time he translated into Italian Gadamer's magnum opus, *Wahrheit und Methode* [*Truth and Method*], thus launching the interest in philosophical hermeneutics in Italy.

Refusing the path of phenomenological thought advanced by Gadamer's mentor Martin Heidegger and the later French reception of phenomenology, Vattimo formulated his own variant of hermeneutic philosophy that put the question of nihilism at center stage, drawing on the works of Heidegger and Gadamer, but now adding Nietzsche to this company as a hermeneutical thinker. In short, Vattimo proposes a radical hermeneutic ontology in which he essentially equates being and language, insofar as individual beings, and even the world, are defined and understood in light of their disclosure or appearance in the multiplicity of linguistic openings delivered by the text, in all its diverse forms, as it has been transmitted and received by and in the history of ideas. Moreover, Vattimo proposes that nihilism has a positive, affirmative aspect, without the acknowledgment of which the transformative, creative potential of hermeneutic thinking cannot be realized, and the problems of onto-theological metaphysics identified by Nietzsche and Heidegger never adequately overcome.

Vattimo's principal contribution, the concept of "weak thought" (*il pensiero debole*), first announced in 1983 in a groundbreaking and highly influential volume of the same name he coedited with Pier Aldo Rovatti, remains an important starting point for key discussions in Continental philosophy and offers one of the most lucid and far-reaching alternatives to Derridean deconstruction and Deleuzo-Guattarian poststructuralism. The "weakness" of weak thought is actually a positive reading of nihilism predicated on the rejection of the "strong" aspects of traditional metaphysical positions that are grounded on a correspondence theory of truth and reality, wherein concepts are equated with the existence of objective realities, be it forms or essences in the Platonist sense or the Being of God. The positive connotation of weak thought lies in its realization and affirmation of the present condition of existence, characterized by the increasing erosion of the traditional metaphysical and rational foundations of modernism. While this is indeed an expression of nihilism, he argues throughout the corpus of his work that nihilism need not be construed solely or at least primarily as reactive and destructive. Vattimo announces an "optimistic" or affirmative nihilistic phase of intellectual and cultural realization that will lead to an actual ethical social and political transformation. In the present postmodern scenario of rapidly changing values, belief systems, geopolitical boundaries, and epistemological foundations, Vattimo's weak thought represents an approach that attempts to move beyond the confining structures of modernity while nevertheless preserving and building on certain forms of critique located in modernity.

Weak thought, however, does not represent a simple refusal of certain metaphysical principles. Rather, weak thought understands itself in full continuity with the Western metaphysical tradition, but now replacing the certainty of metaphysical concepts with the Nietzschean observation that there are no facts, only interpretations. In this sense, weak thought can be construed as postmetaphysical and not simply another manifestation of the culmination of metaphysics, such as one encounters in Heidegger's interpretation of Nietzsche's philosophy.

Supplementing the body of philosophical reflection made possible after the "death of God" and the subsequent exposure of nihilism is arguably the central problem of contemporary metaphysics, ethics, and politics. Vattimo's work is nothing short of an attempt to rescue philosophy and thinking itself from its own nihilistic awareness through a recovery or saving of that which has always been at the heart of the Western philosophical project—namely, the hermeneutic dimension of thinking that Nietzsche, among others, reveals after the death of God as being the fundamental project of philosophy per se. This radical thinking of the nineteenth century is conjoined with that of the twentieth century, the philosophy of difference, to produce a new approach to interpretation that both releases thinking from the metaphysical and epistemological constraints of modern and pre-modern thought, while at the same time allows the positive, critical aspects of previous philosophies to flourish in a new, critical manner.

Vattimo's work has provoked intense reaction, both positive and negative, in Italy and Europe ever since the controversial thesis of weak thought advanced the notion of a positive construal of nihilism and called into question the importance of philosophy itself. In a time of postmodern reconfiguration, Vattimo's lifelong work offers a viable path out of the morass of a deconstructed, foundationless metaphysics to positions that enable the thinking of new ethical and political possibilities. A long and arduous undertaking, this is precisely the road that must be trod in order to overcome the nihilism of the late modern, techno-scientific paradigm that is increasingly enfolding the horizon of future possibility, a horizon that in many respects is stripping away human freedom and autonomy, and threatening what remains of the environing world with the plastic and ultimately sterile veneer of manufactured reality.

The book is divided into three main parts: "Hermeneutics and Nihilism," "Metaphysics and Religion," and "Politics and Technology." Gaetano Chiurazzi's chapter, "The Experiment of Nihilism: Interpretation and Experience of Truth in Gianni Vattimo," leads off the volume. According to Chiurazzi, Vattimo's definition of hermeneutics as "a philosophical theory of the interpretative character of every experience of truth" needs to be understood in relation to the nexus of hermeneutics and nihilism, which Vattimo has posited since his earlier works. Chiurazzi considers Vattimo's contention that truth is an *event*, that is, a transforming occurrence. Insofar as it is transformative, such an event has an *experiential* character. Moreover, this transformation is connected to an interpretative work (that is, a work of reconstruction of meaning) that is also emancipatory in the sense of *Verwindung*. Hermeneutics is therefore a praxis and annihilates itself as simple theory. Chiurazzi clarifies this last point through a discussion of Nietzsche's doctrine of the eternal recurrence, which is understood, following Vattimo's remarks, as theory of the relation between truth and experience.

In "Vattimo's Theory of Truth," Franca D'Agostini notes that in *The End of Modernity* Vattimo suggests that truth should be seen in a rhetorical rather than logical perspective. Since "there is no truth," properly and strictly speaking what we call "truth" is an intersubjective agreement on some topics of common use. When we inquire into truth, D'Agostini argues, we are in fact exploring the nature and extension of our agreement. Vattimo points out that friendship is the foundation of truth, so Aristotle's saying "*magis amica veritas*" should be reverted: friendship should be preferred to truth. D'Agostini examines this particular version of combined pragmatism and coherentism, which significantly also combines Nietzsche's early writing "On Truth and Lie in an Extra-Moral Sense" and the Christian theory of truth. Vattimo's view, however, can easily be misunderstood. By associating truth and friendship, logic and rhetoric, one may be inclined to assert the primacy of the latter over the former terms. It all depends on how the two concepts involved are constructed. What D'Agostini calls Vattimo's "theory of truth" is based (via Heidegger) on assuming friendship as the context of relevance of truth: there is no (question of) truth if we are not interested in agreement. Consequently, D'Agostini claims, rhetoric (in a particular sense) is the right perspective in considering "truth" as a concept of philosophical analysis. Logical truth is based on constructed domains or worlds, but philosophical truth regards the (truthful-friendly) ways of constructing these domains or worlds.

Heidegger recognizes that ontology has an ontic foundation. Developing a reading in which this foundation cannot be definitively overcome, whereupon ontology remains implicated in the concreteness of everyday existence, is the task that David Webb sets in "Vattimo's Hermeneutics as a Practice of Freedom." For Heidegger, Webb argues, this implication still leaves the ontological thinking attendant on a prior opening, the truth of Being, to which it must respond. While Vattimo shares this understanding of the truth of Being, his emphasis on the breakdown of the strong structures of metaphysical thought gives rise to an interpretative practice in which thinking can be genuinely transformative—a practice of freedom. In this respect Vattimo goes beyond Heidegger, and in doing so he also places in question Heidegger's insistence on the priority of ontology over ethics. Webb focuses on this idea of thinking as a transformative practice of freedom in an attempt to clarify its conditions and the relation between thinking and the matter of thinking involved in it. Noting that despite his long history of political activism Vattimo provides little in the way of an account of power, Webb explores the extent to which his understanding of thinking as a transformative practice calls for such an account.

In the 1980s Vattimo introduced the idea that hermeneutics had become a sort of *koine* or general idiom of Western culture. Vattimo is not, however, making a theoretical or descriptive claim here, claims Robert T. Valgenti in "Weak Thought and the Recovery of Reason." Rather, as much of his work over the past two decades bears out, Vattimo's statement reads more like a diagnosis and prescription. Recovery from this illness requires, above all, an assessment of philosophy's role within the recovery so that it can, Vattimo writes, "redefine itself in a more coherent and rigorous way, rediscovering its original inspiration (namely the Heideggerian meditation on metaphysics and its destiny)." And while this recovery embraces the "irrational" elements of the history of metaphysics interpreted as the occurrence of nihilism, for Vattimo "the truth is rather that hermeneutics can defend its theoretical validity only to the precise degree that the interpretative reconstruction of history is a rational activity—in which, that is, one can argue, and not only intuit, *fühlen, einfühlen* etc." Valgenti argues that a persistent theme in Vattimo's philosophical hermeneutics—from the publication of *Il pensiero debole* to his most recent work in *Nihilism and Emancipation*—is the meaning and scope of a rational justification of the project of hermeneutics as the philosophy of late modernity. To this end, Valgenti recovers and reconstructs the central theses of Vattimo's theoretical arguments, as well as those of his critics, in an attempt to present the force (and flaws) of the reasons behind his brand of philosophical hermeneutics.

Vattimo's thinking in the 1960s and 1970s was marked strongly by his studies and reflection on Nietzsche and Heidegger, in which the relationship "I-world" was unquestionably couched in terms of interpretation, as *Verstehen*. In the 1980s Vattimo gave an original twist to the hermeneutic tradition with his idea of weak thought, which allowed him to recover the traditions of both, dialectics and difference, but in which the linguisticality of understanding was still the key factor. This is further developed in his *Etica dell'interpretazione* (1989) insofar as interpretation, in virtue of its being dialogical, interpersonal, or community-oriented, must give preeminence to neither epistemology nor even ontology, but rather to ethics. In the 1990s, however, Vattimo signals a more radical turn with *Beyond Interpretation* and *Belief*, in which the idea of a secular sense of *pietas* is elaborated. These works dovetail in his more recent *After Christianity*, which is, according to Peter Carravetta, the most problematic, as it seems to suggest a radical, antitheometaphysical revision of Christianity (like the untenability of Christ, son of a transcendent God) and yet hold that all our thinking cannot but be influenced by the tradition of Christian thought, and the point at which it is configured today, in *our* age, the postmetaphysical world. In "*Beyond* Interpretation? On Some Perplexities Following upon Vattimo's 'Turn' from Hermeneutics," Carravetta explores the paradoxes of Vattimo's thought at the beginning of the twenty-first century, and its implications for a theory of interpretation.

Part Two, "Metaphysics and Religion," opens with Edison Higuera's "Metaphysics, Violence, and Alterity in Gianni Vattimo." According to

Higuera, Vattimo's weak thought relates to a Nietzschean-Heideggerian tradition that considers "reason" as the source of the violence exerted in the Western world on behalf of the truth. Thinkers such as Adorno, Levinas, and Derrida have evinced the connection that exists between metaphysics and violence. Vattimo echoes the vivacious denunciations launched by contemporary thought against the "violent essence of metaphysics." Metaphysics is a synonym of violence when it claims to have reached *the* "truth as conformity." Within metaphysical thought, truth is in fact identified with first principles, immutable axioms, the certainty of the doubting ego, and so on. When truth becomes the possession of one single individual, therefore, it dangerously translates into a source of violence, because it reduces the other to a silent being. Higuera seeks to expose the reasons that explain the "logical" nexus between metaphysics and violence in order to understand why, in Vattimo's words, "all metaphysical categories . . . are violent categories," and to show the ways that one must proceed to overcome the violence inherent to metaphysics.

In "Thinking the Origin, Awaiting Salvation," Claudio Ciancio engages Vattimo's relationship to Heidegger's and Levinas' thinking. In his conception of the origin, Ciancio explains, Vattimo refers to Heidegger and yet his position is fundamentally different. In Heidegger, the origin is the end of a cyclical return and not of a linear process of weakening. Moreover, whereas Vattimo thinks a process of the weakening of God, the Heideggerian god is a god that withdraws. In the process of distancing from the origin, Vattimo finds the presence of an emancipatory intention. In this, Ciancio argues that there is an ethical note, such as one finds in the thought of Levinas, that is completely absent from the destinal vision of history belonging to Heidegger. Ciancio proposes a thinking of the origin as both unity and alterity, and turns to Schelling's philosophy and the phenomenon of love as a possible way to address Vattimo's later emphasis on charity.

Giovanna Borradori, in "Postmodern Salvation: Gianni Vattimo's Philosophy of Religion," draws the reader's attention to a startling claim that runs through Vattimo's original contributions to the philosophy of religion: In the age of the death of God, secularization is the constitutive trait of authentic religious experience. In pronouncing the words "I am . . . the truth," Christ turned divine and metaphysical truth into a human and mortal construct. For Vattimo, secularization is thus the innermost core of Christian theology. In dialogue with two twentieth-century philosophical heretics, Jacques Derrida and Richard Rorty, Borradori discusses Vattimo's notion of salvation as *kenosis*, an "emptying" of individual will in the face of the defining challenges of the postmodern condition: democratic politics, social pluralism, information technology, and globalization. While traditional Christian calls to silence the will have been aimed at intensifying one's receptivity of God, assumed both as the ontological principle of reality and the guarantor of the original meaning of the sacred text, Vattimo's focus, she maintains, is to enhance one's spiritual receptivity of others. Borradori sees Vattimo's conviction that the possibility of a spiritual connection to others, particularly the marginalized and disenfranchised ones, depends on attitudes of buoyancy, humility, and leniency, rather than gravity, arrogance, and justice, as striking an especially relevant chord in the post-9/11 world, both in Europe and the United States.

Vattimo's weak thought is an unmistakable and avowed form of post-metaphysical thinking, claims Eduardo Mendieta in "Secularization as a Post-Metaphysical Religious Vocation: Gianni Vattimo's Post-Secular Faith." The consequences of such a post-metaphysical stance for philosophy have been variously studied, assessed, exegeted, and either vilified or celebrated. What has not been properly considered, argues Mendieta, are the consequences of such post-metaphysical stance toward both theology and religion. At least since the early 1990s, when Vattimo and Derrida coedited a volume entitled *Religion*, Vattimo has explored these consequences in at least three incisive and provocative books: *Belief, After Christianity*, and *The Future of Religion* (this last one is a collection of two short papers and an interview between Vattimo and Rorty). Considering Vattimo's espousal of a post-secular view of faith and religion, or a stance that is "beyond atheism and theism," Mendieta attempts to reconstruct Vattimo's views on religion and theology. He then considers Vattimo's similarities and differences with Derrida's own articulation of a religious without a religion stance. Mendieta brings Vattimo's unique combination of the post-metaphysical and the post-secular into dialogue with Jürgen Habermas' similar trajectory from the post-metaphysical to the post-secular, and concludes with a consideration of Vattimo's post-secular faith as it relates to Europe and the West in general.

The third and final part of the book, "Politics and Technology," leads off with James Risser's chapter, "Philosophy and Politics at the End of Metaphysics," which begins by considering Vattimo's question in "Philosophy, Metaphysics, Democracy": What becomes of the relationship of philosophy to politics in a world in which, as the result of both the end of metaphysics and the expansion of democracy, we cannot think of politics in terms of truth? Within this question, Risser argues, one can readily see much of Vattimo's philosophical project of weak thought where the end of metaphysics signals philosophy's inability to discover essences and provide a foundation for truth. In response to his own question, Vattimo states that philosophy at the end of metaphysics becomes political thought in the form of an "ontology of actuality." Not to be confused with the Hegelian idea of philosophy as the expression of an age, the task of philosophy at the end of metaphysics is merely an interpretation of an epoch that "offers politics a certain vision of the ongoing historical process" and a certain interpretation of its positive potential, judged solely on its arguable choices from within the process itself. While Vattimo acknowledges that, given the existing relation between politics and philosophy, there is an enormous distance between even this form of philosophy and politics, an ontology of actuality may at least contribute to the advent of democracy in philosophical thought. What Vattimo appears to be arguing for, Risser submits, echoes not only Rorty's notion of philosophy as the "conversation of humanity," but also Gadamer's idea of the transformation of the theoretical life of philosophy into the hermeneutical communicative event. Proposing to explore the implications of Vattimo's ontology of actuality in two directions, Risser considers first the way in which an ontology of actuality is able to carry out in its own way emancipatory interests that would in fact enhance the relationship between philosophy and politics. This leads to a consideration of the character of interpretation that would be given over to democratic discourse within an ontology of actuality in order to reveal the limits of the relation between philosophy and politics.

In "Deciding to Bear Witness: Revolutionary Rupture and Liberal Continuity in Weak Thought," Luca Bagetto argues that weak thought has paid no attention to the polemic against neo-Kantianism within which Heidegger's thinking developed. Thus it has itself ended up understanding the *a priori* in a neo-Kantian (albeit historico-social and supra-subjective) way as a mentalistic shaping of beings. Beings give themselves to us from out of our epochal way of ordering the phenomena. Here is born, in Vattimo, a theory of political representation that is founded on an immanent cultural continuity and on the refusal of all transcendent element up to the reduction of the political space to a testimony of the consciousness immanent to it. It is as if the action of political representation were to find its own tribunal in the consciousness of cultural history, and not in its own responsibility toward the transcendent of the common space.

The connections between Vattimo's theoretical commitment to history (and the political) and the concrete project of emancipation, which inspires the content of his philosophy, are explored in Silvia Benso's chapter, "Emancipation and the Future of the Utopian: On Vattimo's Philosophy of History." Benso inquires whether Vattimo is a utopian thinker, with the intention of assessing the kind of philosophy of history that supports Vattimo's overall position. Ultimately, underlying the question of the utopian is the question of the possibility of the future and its unexpected nature; that is, whether there is a place for ruptures, breaks, and discontinuities—some form of radical alterity, of which the future and the utopian would be a mark, interrupting the process of historical thinking—in Vattimo's epochal thinking. The issue is whether the new is a matter of radical novelty (as, for example, in messianism), or the consequence and the consignment of a legacy, in which case it does not properly exist as new. In other words, is revolution or reformism at work in Vattimo's philosophy? Benso concludes that the continuity of resistance and not the eschatological discontinuity of the utopian revolution leads Vattimo's political agenda and his philosophy of history.

Vattimo's account of contemporary forms of technology presents a novel standpoint within the tradition of Continental philosophy, insofar as he interprets technology not in terms of a closure of our horizon of thinking, but rather in terms of a pluralization of possibilities for thought and action. Although his point of departure for thinking technology is Heidegger's notion of *Ge-stell*, Vattimo claims, contra Heidegger, that the *Ge-stell* constitutes not so much the danger of quasi-totalitarian closure, but rather harbors the potential for a "weakening" of reality in that the former metaphysical "objectivity" of reality is dissolved into multiple mediatic realities. In "'Postmodernity as the Ontological Sense of Technology' and Democratic Politics," Erik M. Vogt contends that, for Vattimo, contemporary media technologies enact and testify to the new freedom(s) of a groundless, post-metaphysical life-world. Moreover, the general mediatization of "reality" contains within itself a plural democratic politics (that Vattimo develops, for instance, in *Nihilism and Emancipation*). Although Vattimo's novel interpretation of technology is intriguing, Vogt inquires about the possible price that has to be paid for this celebration of the democratic structure of mediatic reality. Vogt takes recourse to the work of Slavoj Žižek in order to assess the question of whether there is any place in Vattimo's thought for the (Lacanian) Real, and thus for some of the more problematic effects generated by a mediatic world that supposedly consists only of endless interpretations.

Like Nietzsche and Husserl, Vattimo shares the view that there is no "real world" hidden behind our interpretations, because our interpretations are the appearance, that is, the being of reality. According to Vattimo, our interpretations are not based on any kind of hidden substratum or Kantian *Ding an sich*. The productivity of Vattimo's starting point becomes clear, claims Martin Weiss in "What's Wrong with Biotechnology? Vattimo's Interpretation of Science, Technology, and the Media," when we look at two phenomena, which Vattimo's position opens to completely new possibilities of interpretation: science and technology. Following from Gadamer's hermeneutics, one might think that only the *Geisteswissenschaften* can access hermeneutic truth, understood as interpretation within a historical horizon, whereas the natural sciences are unable to get away from the idea of truth as *adaequatio intellectus et rei*. But Vattimo, following Heidegger, argues that modern technology need not lead to the reification and solidification of phenomena. Rather, he says, the straight striving of modern science for absolute availability and predictability turns over into absolute incalculability, because in the attempt to control nature, science dissolves its object into interpretations. According to Vattimo, philosophy's fight against the natural sciences in the name of hermeneutics is anachronistic, because today the straight natural sciences are the most striking argument against reification. Similarly, Heidegger says that the quest for total control finally leads to radical uncontrollability, and that in this phenomenon we could perhaps experience *Sein* itself, understood as the act of appearing. Weiss takes up Vattimo's proposal for a revaluation of science and technology, no longer seen as the realm of reification, but as an outrider of the nihilistic postmodern insights that the world has became a fable, that there is no objective truth, but only interpretations. This is especially true if one looks at the astonishing possibilities given with biotechnologies. Thus the dissolution of (normative) human nature, due to genetics, pharmacology, and prosthetics, can be interpreted as an aspect of the more general weakening of Being, argues Weiss, which according to Vattimo characterizes postmodernity.

While the name and thought of Gianni Vattimo is familiar to European philosophers, theologians, cultural and political theorists, and even the general public, in North America he is comparatively little known outside the domain of Continental philosophy. Yet he is the author of some thirty-three books and coauthor of another seven, of which sixteen have been translated and published in English (an excellent bibliography including secondary works can be found in Santiago Zabala's recently edited volume, *Weakening Philosophy*) and is regarded by many as one of today's most original and influential thinkers (if not the most, as another leading Italian philosopher, Pier Aldo Rovatti, attests). Moreover, Vattimo is a genuinely public intellectual—something that is painfully absent in American society. A former member of the European Parliament from 2000 to 2005, Vattimo recently retired in the spring of 2009 from his position as Professor of Theoretical Philosophy at the University of Turin, yet he still regularly writes commentaries for *La Stampa*, a major Italian newspaper in Turin, appears frequently on television talk shows, and continues to publish philosophical works. In many respects, Vattimo serves as a model for what the academic thinker can and arguably should be.

This volume is the first collection of chapters in English that deals directly with Vattimo's philosophy from a purely *critical* perspective. More than just interpretations of Vattimo's thinking, the chapters are also expressions of the new impetus given to hermeneutic philosophy by weak thought. While Vattimo's thinking represents a continued and consistent engagement of the themes and figures first addressed in his early writing, his later efforts mark a distinctive broadening of his philosophy, wherein the relationship between politics and religion becomes more prominent in his attempt to address the problem of nihilism in Western thought and culture.

BRIAN SCHROEDER
Ivrea, Italy and Rochester, New York

Part One

Hermeneutics and Nihilism

1

The Experiment of Nihilism

Interpretation and Experience of Truth in Gianni Vattimo

GAETANO CHIURAZZI

Hermeneutics and Nihilism

In an essay contained in *The End of Modernity*, Vattimo offers what can be considered as the cornerstone in his philosophical proposal: the nexus between hermeneutics and nihilism.[1] This nexus is theorized in relation to the way in which, in the fundamental text of contemporary philosophical hermeneutics—specifically, in Hans-Georg Gadamer's *Truth and Method*—the problem of the truth is posed from out of the experience of art. For Vattimo, this experience has a peculiar nihilistic undertone because it is the experience of an "ungrounding" (*sfondamento*) in which one experiences the loss of cogency and continuity of one's own world. That is, one experiences that dimension of historicity that for Gadamer joins artistic and historical experiences, but that for Vattimo is still thought in excessively cumulative and even substantialist (in Hegel's sense) terms. In truth, such a nihilistic dimension is not absent from Gadamer's analysis either; inspired by Hegel's concept of *Erfahrung*, he emphasizes the negative moment that destabilizes the certainties of the subject and induces it to a readjustment of its worldview.

Taking into account such an ungrounding, destructive effect, one can say that every experience of truth *requires* an interpretation, and therefore that truth *is* interpretation. In its ungrounding feature, the experience of truth is the experience of an interruption of meaning (*senso*). The subsequent need for integration is not, however, mere assimilation or mirroring; nor can it be, because it translates itself into the modification of the world of the one who has such an experience. The conception of truth as conformity of the proposition to the thing is thus overcome in favor of a "more comprehensive notion founded on the concept of *Erfahrung*, that is, on experience as a modification that the subject undergoes when it encounters something that truly has relevance for it" (EM 123).

Ten years after, the relation between nihilism and hermeneutics is resumed by Vattimo in *Beyond Interpretation*[2] in the attempt at defining positively the hermeneutic meaning of the concept of truth. The general framework of the book is expressed in the first chapter, titled "The Nihilistic Vocation of Hermeneutics" (BI 1–14). Here Vattimo manifests his discomfort toward the ecumenical physiognomy that hermeneutics has taken up in the contemporary philosophical scenario, which on the one hand has turned hermeneutics into a sort of *koinè* of Western culture (this fact had been positively considered in a 1980s essay),[3] and on the other hand risks excessively diluting its meaning and neutralizing its philosophical import. Such import lies in its "nihilistic vocation," as Vattimo reasserts. The nihilistic vocation is not entirely explicit, though, in the definition that in these pages Vattimo offers of hermeneutics as "the philosophical theory of the interpretative character of every experience of truth" (BI 7). Contrary to what one might be led to believe by a merely aestheticist conception of interpretation in the sense of its complete liberation from any bond, that is, as complete identification of interpretation and transformation (as one finds for example in Deleuze or Derrida), the interpretative character is here tightly anchored to an *experience* of truth. What transforms is truth, and interpretation is not the creative act hovering over the nothingness of nonsense, but rather the transformative rearticulation of meaning (*senso*). The cited definition in fact presupposes that 1) *there is truth*, 2) one *has experience* of truth, 3) such experience is *of an interpretative kind*, and 4) hermeneutics is *a theory* not of truth but *of the experience of truth*. If one wants to speak of nihilism, this does not consist so much in some metaphysical thesis perhaps expressed in the claim that "truth does not exist," but rather in the experience one has thereof.[4] Nihilistic is the way in which such an experience presents itself to "hermeneutic consciousness." The sense of the encounter between nihilism and hermeneutics should be grasped, I argue, on this ground of the experience of truth—perhaps the only way in which one can speak of truth. Without the mediation of experience, such a nexus is doomed to being the statement of the mere idealistic consummation of the world, which subtracts its very effectiveness, that is, its *sense*, from interpretation. In the following pages I attempt an explanation of such a definition of hermeneutics as "the philosophical theory of the interpretative character of every experience of truth" through some central guiding concepts in Vattimo's thought—concepts that implicitly affect the definition and can therefore help to cast some light on it.

The Experience of Truth: Transformation and Event

Hermeneutics is a theory not of truth but of the *experience* of truth. All concepts of truth that it can offer can be understood only if one keeps in mind such a specification. The truth of which hermeneutics speaks is not the object of knowledge but rather the form of an experience. It is not the *telos* of a specific and methodical activity but rather that in which we are constantly immerged and that escapes our ability to mastery. The first connotation of truth understood in this way, that is, from out of the experience one has thereof, is that it transforms.

The vindication of the truth of the humanities (*scienze umane*) is based on such transformative character. That there is a truth of the humanities is attested by the fact that they produce effects, they have their own *Wirkung*, and therefore their own reality (*Wirklichkeit*). The interpretative dimension of the experience of truth consists in this possibility of letting oneself be transformed in the encounter with it, that is, of truly having *an experience*. An experience that is truly such is the one that is true experience, that is, the one "that effectively modifies the one who has it."[5]

As already remarked, Vattimo finds this idea of the transformative character of the experience of truth in Gadamer, who in *Truth and Method* proposes a theory of hermeneutic experience that is at the same time a theory of the hermeneutic character of experience. The dialogical relation enacted in the encounter with a text becomes the model of experience in general. Experience is dialogue, alternation of questions and answers. Questions arise as consequence of an interruption of sense, exactly as when in a text something does not give itself to clear understanding and demands interpretation. This experience is the experience of a shock [*urto*]: "In fact we have experiences when we are shocked by things that do not accord with our expectations. . . . A question presses itself on us; we can no longer avoid it and persist in our accustomed opinion."[6] In this impossibility to avoid the self-imposition of truth from out of the question that it asks, Gadamer sees the objective dimension of the humanities, that is, their escaping the subjectivism in which the unilateral methodical conception belonging to natural sciences would like to exile them. Methodical is the moment of verification, and not the moment in which truth announces itself. The latter is "extra-methodical" precisely because it escapes all subjective mastery and domination. It is not we who guide the unfolding of the game of experience; it is experience that leads us; our task is that of corresponding to such continuous opening of truth, to its character of *event*. The extra-methodical dimension of the truth that Gadamer defends is for Vattimo expressed precisely by such Heideggerian concept.[7] Vattimo emphasizes the expropriating character thereof, which indicates a happening that is not in the subject's mastery. Truth "transforms us" precisely because it takes us away from "our accustomed opinion," from certainty and obviousness. It is opening because it consists in a continuous questioning of our horizons and prejudices.

What emerges powerfully from such hermeneutic conception (of the experience) of truth is its nonconforming character—truth does not conform, it changes. The method by which one ascertains a *new* formulation of truth, that is, by which one ascertains the truth-character of a statement, has the function of "making one find the right way,"[8] of reconstructing a sense after the fact that truth has forced us to deviate—that is, after it has produced a "disjuncture" in our convictions. If hermeneutics raises its protests against the traditional conception of truth as *adaequatio* (conformity) (a conception that is not denied but rather considered as secondary and derivative, as Vattimo remarks following Heidegger), this is because such an idea of truth, although legitimate, represents the conformist moment thereof, and is prone to exposure to ideologization when not even dogmatism. The motivations for this nonconforming but rather disruptive and uncanny conception of the experience of truth are not only ethical. Ultimately there are also strictly gnoseological reasons: truth gives itself first of all as the experience of an interruption.[9] This is true for artistic as well as for scientific experience because it is true for experience in general.[10] Truth can only manifest itself in negative form. Even in scientific experience, the moment when truth shows itself is not the moment of the alleged confirmation of a theory, which after all is always a nonfalsification (a nonnegation); rather, it is the moment of falsification, when the truth is *other* than what one thought. In some passages Vattimo explicitly relates this experience to the ontological difference, that is, to the idea that Being (truth) never completely coincides with any of its historical realizations.[11] Truth (like reality for Heidegger) is the realm of the possible, of the "not yet."

Against Hegel's beautiful ethicity, against the risk of classicism, which he thinks can be detected in Gadamer's aesthetic proposal, Vattimo thinks the experience of truth as a shock similar to the one produced by the encounter with avant-garde art.[12] As we have already remarked, the need for historical continuity ends up prevailing in Gadamer over the experience of interruption that is registered in the encounter with the work of art. Such experience is perhaps better perceived precisely by that which Gadamer criticizes, namely, the punctuality of the aesthetic consciousness. "What takes place in the work of art is a particular instance of the ungrounding of historicity, which is announced as a suspension of the hermeneutic continuity of the subject with itself and with history. Aesthetic consciousness, as an abstract series of discrete instants in time, is the mode by which the subject lives the leap into the *Ab-grund* of its own mortality" (EM 125).

The Being of Truth: Opening as Dwelling

The experience of truth is true experience because it modifies and changes the one who has it. It modifies and changes such an individual in view not of greater conformity but rather of further liberation. It is therefore not possible to describe it in the fundamentally Apollinian terms in which the metaphysical tradition has always described it, that is, as an experience of luminosity, incontrovertible evidence, as harmony, integration, and fulfillment (see BI 107 ff). It is not the case of the bright morning in which, according to Nietzsche's image, the pandemonium of all free spirits rises[13] (the Hegelian intonation of the image cannot be missed; the true, according to Hegel, is the feast of thought, "the Bacchanalian revel in which no member is not drunk").[14] It is rather the crepuscular experience of finitude, limit, and mortality. This does not mean closure; on the contrary, the way in which the hermeneutic notion of truth is usually thought of is "opening" precisely because it is first and foremost an experience that discloses rather than concludes a possibility.

"Opening" means the condition of possibility of all being-true (*esser-vero*)—one can sum up in this way Heidegger's reply to Husserl's exigency to find the conditions of truth of logical formations within a prepredicative terrain. These conditions are made by Heidegger to coincide with Dasein's very existence, which is opening because through its own self-giving it opens a world, that is, it renders beings accessible in the form of pre-apophantic meanings orienting Dasein's behaviors, that is, giving *sense* to Dasein's acting. Truth as opening is being-in-the-world, the *Da* of Dasein, what Heidegger also expresses as "dwelling." There is truth because of the simple fact that Dasein is.

For Vattimo, this way of dwelling in the truth (*essere nella verità*) is similar to the competence of a librarian who knows how to move in his own library. "Whereas the idea of truth as correspondence conceives of knowledge of the true as the possession of an 'object' by way of an adequate representation, the truth of dwelling is by contrast the competence of the librarian who does not possess entirely, in a single act of transparent comprehension, all of the contents of all the books amongst which he lives, nor even the first principles upon which the contents depend. One cannot compare such knowledge-possession through the command of first principles to the competence of librarianship, which knows where to look because it knows how the volumes are classified and is also acquainted with the 'subject catalogue'" (BI 82–83). The "truth" of the librarian is the truth of the one who "knows" the library in such a way as to be able to orient oneself within it, to know how to find a book even when one does not know exactly what the book is about. The librarian knows what to do; he does not possess the whole field of knowledge, but knows the context within which to move so as eventually to gain knowledge. His behavior is guided by that pre-understanding that in *Being and Time*, section 31 Heidegger defines as "*können*," that is, to know how to do, be capable of facing something, be able to. To the extent that this competence is true, it enables one to do things, and it constitutes a "power/ability" (*potere*). In the end, it is the competence of *phronesis*, a pragmatic competence guiding action when a defined method is not available. That spiritual sciences (*scienze dello spirito*) have been dragged into the wave of natural sciences, to the method of which they should conform, constitutes a deep misrecognition of the fact that it is rather the latter that have drawn the sense of their own methodological effectiveness from a realm that is non-naturalistic and not focused on mere observation. Francis Bacon, one of the fathers of modern experimental science, expressed the sense of the scientific method in this manner: "The rule of religion, that a man should show his faith by his works, holds good in natural philosophy too. Science also must be known by works. It is by the witness of works, rather than by logic or even observation, that truth is revealed and established."[15]

The hermeneutic concept of truth is inspired by such a pragmatic effectiveness, which coincides with its transformative power. With good reason can such concept be considered "more originary" than the merely theoretical concept of *adaequatio*. This is something that Vattimo claims even in front of Gadamer's apparent shyness on this point—moving within truth, dwelling in the truth means possessing this kind of orientating knowledge, which could be defined as a "know how" rather than a "know what."

The transcendental character of such a positive definition of the truth as opening gives account also of its negative, as it were "nihilist," definition, that is, of the opening as interruption of a given sense, as rupture of a horizon. Truth opens new possibilities showing that the ones that have already been consolidated and realized can be modified. What one means by "opening" is not a horizon that hovers over and circumscribes experience in a structural and atemporal manner; rather, it is the being open of experience. The transcendental meaning of the notion of truth as opening can be defended only if one considers it, in a Kantian manner, as the form of experience and nothing else. Truth is truth of experience, in the subjective and objective sense of the genitive "of"—it is that which opens experience by rendering its sclerotizations fluid, and it is experience itself insofar as open. The more one experiences truth, the more is one's own experience open, not secured in its own dogmatisms, available to the encounter with the other. As Gadamer writes, "The hermeneutical consciousness culminates not in methodological sureness of itself, but in the same readiness for experience that distinguishes the experienced man from the man captivated by dogma."[16] Experienced human beings are those who, from out of experience and the suffering that experience brings with itself—Aeschylus' *pathei mathos* [learning through suffering]—become aware of their own finitude, and understand the limits within which they can project and a future is open to them; that is, they understand that all of their expectations and projects are limited.[17] This sense of the limit does not translate at all into a closure; it leads to a greater opening toward experience. The experience of truth produces an opening toward new experience. The experienced individual is a human being free for experience—free for truth.[18]

The Interpretative Character of Experience: *Verwindung* as Emancipation

The encounter with truth has the feature of an interruption, the resolution of which implies a transformation. This moment of resolution is the properly interpretative one; the ungrounding effect of truth implies the interruption and becoming opaque of a previously constituted, given, and taken-for-granted sense. The experience of truth is not the moment of the disclosedness or transparent luminosity of sense; rather, it is the moment of its darkening, the moment when the legibility of the text becomes obfuscated, produces a void, undergoes an interruption. The interpretative work inserts itself in this void; like a process of cicatrization that, while it heals a wound, precisely thereby exposes it, interpretation re-creates a connection while it simultaneously brings to evidence the disconnection of which it itself is trace. It is an overcoming of negativity that, as Ernst Jünger writes in *Über die Linie*, can "cover with a new skin like a scar."[19]

Interpretation deals with corrupted, disconnected meanings; at the same time as it recomposes them, it posits itself as trace of the corruption, which is in turn the mark of a distance, of the fact that for us the text is not something immediate but has a provenance. Hermeneutics is a theory of the interpretative character of experience, that is, of the fact that experience is, or demands, a continuous act of "adjustment" that is also an act of distortion, a *Verwindung*. This occurs constantly, at every moment; it is perhaps the meaning of experience, of its ability to be always different and yet have a recognizable meaning, of its ability to confront deep interruptions of its own sense, incomprehensible contingencies, and yet be able to heal, overcome, and recompose them.[20]

The concept of *Verwindung* is another key concept in Vattimo's philosophy. Borrowed from Heidegger, it designates the movement of resolution of metaphysics, its twisting and precisely therefore emancipating acceptance. *Verwinden* means "overcoming" (in the sense in which one overcomes a sickness, recovers from it), but also "distorting, twisting." For its explanation Vattimo refers in particular to two texts by Heidegger, *Identity and Difference* and "Overcoming Metaphysics."[21] Here we wish however to consider another text in which the term *verwinden* appears and displays in a more explicit manner its emancipatory and temporal meaning: "The Anaximander Fragment."[22]

According to Heidegger, the Anaximander fragment speaks of the coming to presence of beings in the form of *adikia*, that is, as disconnected, disjoined, and therefore "unjust" beings. Heidegger in facts translates *adikia* with the term *Unfuge* (disjunction, disconnection), and *dike* with *Fuge* (junction, connection). This condition of disconnection is not the essence of present beings; they must, as the usual translation has it, "pay for" their injustice. The matter would here be that of the *revengeful* conception of time that, in *Il soggetto e la maschera*, Vattimo calls "oedipal" or "ecstatic-functional" (SM 268). Nietzsche describes it thus through the words of madness: "Things are ordered morally according to justice and punishment. . . . Can there be redemption if there is eternal justice? . . . This, this is what is eternal in the punishment called existence, that existence must eternally become deed and guilt again."[23] When understood in light of these words by madness, Anaximander's saying appears as a spring moment in which "in this early fragment of thinking the pessimism—not to say the nihilism—of the Greek experience of Being come to the fore."[24]

Heidegger does not accept such a nihilistic (in the Nietzschean sense of passive nihilism) vision of time; here it is not a matter of revenge but of *donation*. To assert themselves as *present*, because they cannot persist in a condition of complete disjunction, beings must necessarily (the initial *kata to kreon* in Anaximander's fragment is translated thus) "come to an agreement" with their past and future, they must "give . . . jointure" (*didonai . . . diken*). The *dike* that is thus reestablished is a new harmony; it is the reconstitution of a temporal continuity, that is, of a sense that otherwise would be interrupted, fragmented. "What belongs to that which is present is the jointure of its while, which it articulates in its approach and withdrawal. . . . It does not incline toward the disjunction of sheer persistence. The jointure belongs to whatever lingers awhile, which in turns belongs to the jointure."[25]

The term *verwinden* appears at this point. In its very persisting, the present-being "*verwindet den Un-Fug*." As Heidegger writes, "Whatever lingers awhile in presence comes to presence insofar as it lingers; all the while emerging and passing away, and the jointure of the transition from approach to withdrawal, continue. This lingering endurance of the transition is enjoined continuance of what is present. The enjoined continuance does not at all insist upon sheer persistence. It does not fall into disjunction; it surmounts disorder [*verwindet den Un-Fug*]."[26] *Verwindung* is the modality through which, in the present, the break of its very own coming to presence is healed. "What is present comes to presence when it surmounts [*verwindet*] the dis- of disorder, the *a*- of *adikia*."[27] The negative aspect (the *a* in *a-dikia*) of the present insofar as generated by an interruption—one could say, by a trauma—is therefore "unjust," is distorted and thereby overcome in the present itself. *Verwindung* is the modality by which such a wound is healed, in the form of a distortion of temporality.

In the present—in actuality—there is an emancipatory and resolutory power; such is the *Verwindung* of temporality that it enacts; even better, it is *Verwindung* as temporality: "The presencing of what is present *is* such a surmounting [*Anwesen des Anwesendes* ist *solches*

Verwinden]."[28] The present is already in itself resolution, to the point that, paraphrasing Bergson's expression that "time is either invention or is nothing,"[29] one could say that the present is either emancipation or is nothing.

The way in which Heidegger thinks he can render the *didonai diken* from out of *adikia*, the possibility of donating a connection from out of the disconnection, a sense from out of nonsense, is the verb *verwinden*. It confers the character of continuous distortion to temporality; that is, it turns time into something essentially *out of joint* [in English in the text].[30] It is precisely in these terms—according to such neither linear nor continuous but rather discontinuous, distorted, and yet consequent modality—that interpretative work unfolds according to Vattimo:[31] interpretation is the possibility of sense from out of nonsense. The interpretative character of the experience of truth consists in the fact that its nihilistic aspect is not the pure and simple affirmation of nonsense; rather, it is the spur to the production of sense, that is, to its reconfiguration and transformation. Precisely in this consists the hermeneutic superiority of the overman—the individual capable of dwelling in sense beyond nonsense—that is, as Vattimo writes, "his or her ability to constitute signifying unities there where the old man could see and experience only horrid contingencies" (SM 274).[32]

The Eternal Return of the Same: The Experiment of Nihilism

The idea that truth has a transformative power is, as we have said, a peculiar aspect of the hermeneutic conception of the truth, and of the humanities in general. This idea is opposite to the way in which truth is conceived in the realm of logic, that is, as some feature of an assertion that, because it does not imply any predicative variation in the asserted content, turns out to be redundant and therefore superfluous: "it is true that *p*" equals "*p*."

It is not surprising that redundantist, deflationist, and minimalist theories of truth can be considered as heirs of the nihilist discovery of the uselessness of the truth.[33] The hermeneutic conception of the truth instead tries to retrieve an experiential dimension—which can easily be considered as secondary from a logical perspective because "merely subjective"—in which truth is a transformative operator. It is therefore not correct to claim, as is usually done, that truth constitutes the bridge between thought and reality, concept and object, essence and existence in the form of some correspondence. Truth is rather—and this is, I think, the most innovative thesis that can be claimed out of the preceding remarks—the transformative operator of experience, that which enables its modification, its change. This aspect has not escaped Frege, as he writes: "It is . . . worth noticing that the sentence 'I smell the scent of violets' has just the same content as the sentence 'It is true that I smell the scent of violets.' So it seems, then, that nothing is added to the thought by my ascribing to it the property of truth. And yet is it not a great result when the scientist after much hesitations and laborious researches can finally say 'My conjecture is true'? The *Bedeutung* [meaning] of the word 'true' seems to be altogether *sui generis*."[34]

Precisely to mark also graphically the peculiarity of the predicate "is true," Frege assigns to it a mark entirely peculiar in its idiography, the so-called vertical stroke. It means the "success" of the investigator's efforts; it registers, in the succession of hypotheses, the flashing up of their truth. The vertical stroke truly changes something in the tautological order of logical sequences: it says what will never be able to emerge from the simple content, that is, from the horizontal, which not by coincidence is a symbol of logical immanence; it says what transcends the content, that is, its truth and the experience thereof one makes—the "success of the researcher." Tarski's theorem has expressed such verticality of language as a move from language to metalanguage, but in the end it has remained within *logos*, which through the word "true" limits itself from within. The verticality of truth on the contrary marks a scansion that does not belong to the logical order, a power capable of transforming and producing experience. This "subjective" and even temporal aspect in the experience of truth, to which Frege devotes a small vertical stroke, is the whole content of the hermeneutic conception of truth.

"Truth" is not the eternal predicate of a world in itself, of a third realm detached and autonomous with respect to our experience; it is rather that which connects this world to our experience. What remains "immutable" and of which one says "it is true"—the essence, the concept, thought—is ultimately only a temporal dimension of experience, the experience of the past. The past is the fact, that which can no longer be changed. The extreme expression of such intangible factuality is Nietzsche's doctrine of the eternal return of the same.

In conclusion, I wish to consider such a Nietzschean concept. Vattimo's interpretation of it, I think, seems to express the radically experiential character of truth in an incisive manner. The eternal return of the identical affirms the intangibility and nonmodifiability of what has already been. To extirpate the feeling of revenge toward the past (the "already been," the fact), the eternal return extends such unchangeable factuality also to the present and future—to the whole time.[35] Everything has already been. From this perspective, extreme nihilism[36] coincides with extreme positivism; its summarizing formula could be the motto, which at the same time expresses elementary wisdom and a gnoselogical dogma, that *"quel che è fatto, è fatto."*[37] The eternal return of the identical is the affirmation of the absolute impossibility to transcend facts. It expresses the tautological structure of the logical world, which atemporally repeats itself in the most complete immutability.

Vattimo's interpretation, focused on the presentation of the eternal return that Nietzsche offers in *Thus Spoke Zarathustra* and in particular in the section titled "On the Vision and the Riddle," emphasizes instead the peculiar ambiguity in such Nietzsche's doctrine—that is, its character at the same time theoretical and experiential, which is represented in the narrative by the juxtaposition of two scenes: the one with the gateway on which "Moment" is inscribed, and under which the two paths coming from the past and the future meet, and the other with the shepherd's biting the snake's head. The relation between these two moments, Vattimo writes, "cannot be explained otherwise than through the characteristic theoretical-practical ambiguity in the idea of the eternal return. The initial vision is still a metaphysical-essential vision, the theoretical moment of the idea, which is indeed complete in itself yet it acquires its meaning only when the practical decision that it demands intervenes. One cannot explain the relation between the two moments in other manners, because the second moment does not add anything (like the predicate of existence to Kant's famous tallers) to the concept delineated in the first. The entire content of such a concept would nevertheless remain at a purely hypothetical level were the second moment not there" (SM 198–199).[38]

The relation between the first and the second scene is understood on the model of the relation between essence and existence, theoretical and experiential level, hypothesis and truth; "the second moment of the vision is not added to the first as a subsequent stage; rather, it somehow concerns the 'truth' of the entire first moment" (SM 199). Such truth is something lived, is a particular experience of transformation, the outcome of which is the transformation of the subject—the one who *is subjected to* the eternal return—into an overman. The scene of the snake represents the passage from passive to active nihilism.[39] The moment when the "truth" of the eternal return is affirmed—that is, the idea that truth is something intangible and nonmodifiable: this is the essence of nihilism even in its Platonic root—is the moment when one experiences the transformative power of truth;

it is not the moment when one *transcends* the experiential level in the form of some semantic ascent, but rather that in which experience itself is transformed.

From this perspective, as Vattimo writes, the doctrine of the eternal return of the same is not—at least not necessarily—a metaphysical doctrine. It is simply a hypothesis and therefore "the proposal for an experiment" (SM 203). The doctrine of the eternal return is the test bench not for this or that metaphysical hypothesis, but rather for truth *as such*, for its transformative power even regardless of its content; that is, turning its content into something entirely indifferent, the least affected by the fact of being recognized as true or not. The shepherd's bite is acceptance of the truth (the "Yes" transforming his existence), gesture that *liberates* its own ability to create, change, and transform.

The fundamental character [*fondamentalità*] of truth in comparison to interpretation makes sense only when one vindicates its unfounding, that is, its experiential character. Theoretically, truth is that to which one should conform; experimentally, truth is that which dis-conforms, transforms, and distorts itself (or, in Vattimo's language, weakens its interrupting power) in interpretation. As "philosophical theory of the hermeneutic character of every experience of truth," hermeneutics is properly *not* a *theory*. This is perhaps the ultimate counterblow, the point on which are discharged all the domino effects of the nihilistic conception of truth Vattimo defends. If truth has a transformative, and in such sense nihilistic, power, this means that it can never be made an object of theory, as if truth concerned "a world in itself," of which it would be an attribute of intangibility and unmodifiability. Rather, if one had to put it in such terms, truth would be precisely that which connects the intangible world to our world, that which constitutes *the* world of our experience.[40] One could then say that in general, for Vattimo as well as for Nietzsche, all theories are simply the proposal of an experiment, that is, a proposal showing the insufficient and nonautonomous character of theory, the autonomy of which would on the contrary imply the reduction of the subject to "pure contemplating eye," immoveable correlate of immoveable objects, and noninvolved in the contemplated scene. The nihilistic vocation of hermeneutics consists in its systematic and progressive self-denial as simple theory, in the sense that it cannot be thought independently of its application and praxis;[41] it cannot be theory of dialogue without also being dialogue; and it cannot be thought of as theory of experience if it *is* not also experience—experience of truth.

Translated by Silvia Benso

Notes

1. See "Hermeneutics and Nihilism," EM 113–129.
2. *Beyond Interpretation* gathers in a single volume the "Five Italian Lectures" Vattimo gave at the University of Bologna in 1994 and, as Appendices, two previously published articles, "La verità dell'ermeneutica," in *Filosofia '88* (Rome-Bari: Laterza, 1989), and "Ricostruzione della razionalità," in *Filosofia '91* (Rome-Bari: Laterza, 1992). As Vattimo narrated the story once, the title of the volume is a remedial choice because the original title should have been *Consequences of Interpretation*, echoing Richard Rorty's *Consequences of Pragmatism*. Such a title, however, had already been used in 1990 by J. E. Young, *Writing and Rewriting the Holocaust: Narrative and the Consequences of Interpretation*. The meaning of the "beyond" must be understood as "that which comes after," as an effect or, precisely, a consequence.
3. "Ermeneutica nuova koiné," EI 38–48. See the English translation by Peter Carravetta, "Hermeneutics as Koine," in *Theory, Culture & Society* 5 (1988): 399–408.
4. Analogously for Vattimo the "death of God" is not the affirmation of God's inexistence but rather the recording of a typical experience of modernity. See "The God Who Is Dead," AC 11–24.
5. See Gianni Vattimo, "Introduzione" in Hans-Georg Gadamer, *Verità e metodo*, trans. Gianni Vattimo (Milan: Bompiani, 1986), VIII. See also Gianni Vattimo, "Gadamer and the Problem of Ontology," in *Gadamer's Century: Essays in Honor of Hans-Georg Gadamer*, ed. J. Malpas, U. Arnswald, and J. Kertscher (Cambridge: MIT Press, 2002), 301–302.
6. Hans-Georg Gadamer, *Truth and Method*, 2nd revised ed., trans. Joel Weinsheimer and Donald Marshall (New York: Crossroads Publishing, 1989), 360.
7. "We have already mentioned that, in clarifying the extra-methodical experience of truth taking place in art, what is modified and deepened albeit without an explicit thematization is the very concept of truth; this [occurs] in a dimension which we think we can characterize through the term 'event' precisely for the indubitable Heideggerian imprint on this entire theme"; see Vattimo, "Introduzione a *Verità e metodo*," XII.
8. Vattimo describes the way in which Gadamer understands the experience of truth of the work of art as "something certainly other than the provisional getting lost in a dream world; [it is] rather an

actual readjustment of one's whole way of being in the world"; ibid., IX.
9. See "The Truth of Hermeneutics," BI 76. In a passage in this text Vattimo seems to want to scale down precisely that moment of interruption of truth (symbolized in the encounter with the work of art) that seems to me to be the most significant in terms of a determination of the hermeneutic experience of truth. This occurs because Vattimo mistakes it for the moment of certainty, for the *eureka* of the scientist, in which a given content is "imposed." The *eureka* is however a positive experience, which *confirms* hypotheses and convictions, and which is therefore completely different from what Gadamer means when he speaks of "shock," of a negative experience that insinuates an uncertainty and breaks our convictions down.
10. Vattimo, "Gadamer and the Problem of Ontology," 301–302.
11. See for example, Vattimo, "The Nihilistic Vocation of Hermeneutics," in BI 13.
12. On this, see the chapters contained in Gianni Vattimo, *Poesia e ontologia* (Milan: Mursia, 1967). English version edited by Santiago Zabala and translated by Luca D'Isanto, *Art's Claim to Truth* (New York: Columbia University Press, forthcoming).
13. Nietzsche describes in this manner the advent of nihilism (that is, the end of the true world) in the famous section of *Twilight of the Idols* titled "How the 'True World' Finally Became a Fable."
14. G.W.F. Hegel, *Phenomenology of Spirit*, trans. A. V. Miller (Oxford: Oxford University Press, 1977), 27.
15. F. Bacon, "Thoughts and Conclusions," in Benjamin Farrington, *The Philosophy of Francis Bacon* (Chicago: University of Chicago Press, 1966), 93.
16. Gadamer, *Truth and Method*, 355.
17. Vattimo interprets *pathei mathos* precisely in this manner; the experience of suffering does not denounce a metaphysical mistake one needs to expiate; rather, it attests one's own finitude, "the discovery of the alterity from which we never escape" (NE 76).
18. This is clearly a Heideggerian thesis. See Martin Heidegger, "On the Essence of Truth," in *Pathmarks*, ed. William McNeill (Cambridge: Cambridge University Press, 1998). Heidegger argues for such a thesis through reference to Aristotle's definition of apophantic discourse as discourse susceptible of being true or false; the possibility of the alternative alludes precisely to the fact that truth is a possibility, that is, it presupposes freedom. See Martin Heidegger,

Fundamental Concepts of Metaphysics: World, Finitude, Solitude, trans. William McNeill and Nicholas Walker (Bloomington: Indiana University Press, 2001), 339–342.
19. Ernst Jünger and Martin Heidegger, *Oltre la linea*, trans. Franco Volpi (Milan: Adelphi, 1989), 50.
20. "The organic process constantly presupposes INTERPRETATION," Nietzsche maintains in a fragment (148) written in fall 1886. See Friedrich Nietzsche, *Nachgelassene Fragmente 1885–1887*, ed. Giorgio Colli and Mazzino Montinari (Berlin: de Gruyter, 1999), 139.
21. Martin Heidegger, *Identity and Difference*, trans. Joan Stambaugh (New York: Harper & Row, 1969) and "Overcoming Metaphysics," in *The End of Philosophy*, trans. Joan Stambaugh (Chicago: University of Chicago Press, 1973). On Vattimo's notion of *Verwindung*, see Gianni Vattimo, "Nihilism and the Post-modern in Philosophy," in EM 164–181; "Metaphysics, Violence, Secularization," in *Recoding Metaphysics: The New Italian Philosophy*, ed. Giovanna Borradori (Evanston: Northwestern University Press, 1988), and "Ontology of Actuality," in *Contemporary Italian Philosophy: Crossing the Borders of Ethics, Politics, and Religion*, ed. Silvia Benso and Brian Schroeder (Albany: State University of New York Press, 2007). In the last two chapters the meaning of Heidegger's *Verwindung* is paralleled to the concept of "secularization."
22. Martin Heidegger, "The Anaximander Fragment," in *Early Greek Thinking*, trans. David F. Krell and Frank A. Capuzzi (New York: Harper & Row, 1975), 13–58.
23. Friedrich Nietzsche, *Thus Spoke Zarathustra*, in *The Portable Nietzsche*, ed. and trans. Walter Kaufmann (New York: Viking Penguin, 1976), "On Redemption," 252. On the basis of this passage, Vattimo contests the idea that the theories of the later Nietzsche, and especially that of the eternal return, may be considered as an attempt at retrieving Greek thought. Vattimo devotes some considerations to Anaximander's fragment, and positively takes up its expiatory meaning, in NE 76–77.
24. Heidegger, "The Anaximander Fragment," 42. It should be noted that precisely the translation of Anaximander's fragment by the young Nietzsche appears at the beginning of Heidegger's text.
25. Ibid., 43.
26. Ibid., 43–44.
27. Ibid., 50.
28. Ibid., 49.
29. Henri Bergson, *L'évolution créatrice*, in *Oeuvres* (Paris: Press Universitaire de France, 1963), 784.

30. See Jacques Derrida, *Specters of Marx*, trans. Peggy Kamuf (New York: Routledge, 1994), 27.
31. "Everything that gives itself as Being is becoming, that is, interpretative production," AS 41.
32. From here comes the ethical meaning of hermeneutics; an interpretation is preferable to another "not on the basis of proofs and foundations, but on the basis of the fact that it actually 'makes sense'; that is, it enables to connect multiple aspects of existence into an articulated unity, and enables one to speak with (the) others about it" (EI 33).
33. On the connection between nihilism and deflationism and minimalist theories of truth, see Franca D'Agostini, *Disavventure della verità* (Turin: Einaudi, 2002) and Pascal Engel, *La vérité. Reflexions sur quelques truismes* (Paris: Hatier, 1998).
34. Gottlob Frege, "Thought," in *The Frege Reader*, ed. Michael Beaney (Oxford: Blackwell, 1977), 328.
35. "That time does not run backwards, that is his wrath; 'that which was' is the name of the stone it cannot move. And so he moves stones out of wrath and displeasure, and he wreaks revenge on whatever does not feel wraths and displeasure as he does. Thus the will, the liberator, took to hurting; and on all who can suffer he wreaks revenge for his inability to backwards" (Nietzsche, *Thus Spoke Zarathustra*, 252).
36. "Let us think this thought in its most terrible form: existence as it is, without meaning or aim, yet recurring inevitably without any finale of nothingness: '*the eternal recurrence.*' This is the most extreme form of nihilism: the nothing (the 'meaningless'), eternally!" Friedrich Nietzsche, *The Will to Power*, trans. Walter Kaufmann and R. J. Hollingdale (New York: Vintage, 1967), 35–36.
37. The author is playing with the double meaning of the word *fatto*, which in Italian is both a noun (fact or deed) and the past participle of the verb "to do" (done). *Quel che è fatto è fatto* can thus mean that "what is done is done," "a fact is a fact," "what is done is fact," and "a fact is what is done." [Translator's note]
38. The predicate "true" thus assumes a statute similar to Kant's categories of modality; on this I take the liberty to refer to Gaetano Chiurazzi, *Modalità ed esistenza. Dalla critica della ragion pura alla critica della ragion ermeneutica* (Turin: Trauben, 2001).
39. The transformative dimension is announced ever since the *incipit* of *Zarathustra*: "The book of the eternal return begins with the speech 'On the Three Metamorphoses,' which describes and prescribes the way of the subject's renewal" (SM 213).

40. More than a semantic ascent, truth would then rather imply some "semantic descent" from theory—or language—to experience, Baldwin speaks in these terms of Frege's theory of truth, but links it to Davidson's semantic theory. See Thomas Baldwin, "Three Puzzles in Frege's Theory of Truth," in *Frege: Sense and Reference One Hundred Years Later*, ed. John Biro and Petr Kotakto (Dordrecht: Kluwer, 1995), 1–14. It is peculiar that the move from language to metalanguage contemplated in Tarski's biconditional insofar as decitational process is understood as a semantic descent and not an ascent; could one dare infer that metalanguage is experience?

41. The idea of the relation between theory and experience is a central because germinal theme in Vattimo's thought, for its first essay is devoted to the concept of *praxis* in Aristotle. See Gianni Vattimo, *Il concetto di fare in Aristotele* (Turin: Giappichelli, 1961). It is first of all in the encounter with Nietzsche that such a question becomes decisive for him. Nietzsche is the anti-theoretical philosopher par excellence. Everything that in him appears as theory is therefore constantly brought back by Vattimo to an experiential and even practical dimension. Nietzsche's narrative style attests the effort to keep conceptualization and metaphysical description at a distance, emphasizing the appurtenance to a moving history, as is the case especially for *Zarathustra*. This is a story that can only be interpreted, that is, it demands "a practical choice modifying the life of the one who makes it and the world in which he lives" (SM 193).

2

Vattimo's Theory of Truth

FRANCA D'AGOSTINI

Introduction

In *The End of Modernity*, Gianni Vattimo suggests that truth should be seen in a rhetorical rather than logical perspective. Actually, what we call "truth" is the intersubjective agreement on some topics of common use. When we inquire into truth, we are in fact exploring the nature and extension of our agreement. In *Beyond Interpretation* and in *Vocazione e responsabilità del filosofo*, Vattimo points out that friendship is the foundation of truth. Aristotle's saying "*magis amica veritas*" should then be reversed: friendship has a certain primacy over truth.

In what follows I examine Vattimo's particular version of combined pragmatism and coherentism, which significantly also combines Nietzsche's theory of nihilism and the Christian conception of *pietas*. Vattimo's view could be easily misunderstood. By associating truth and friendship, logic and rhetoric, he may be understood to assert the primacy of the latter over the former terms. Yet, it is not properly so. What I call "Vattimo's theory of truth" is based (via Heidegger) on the assumption of friendship as the context of relevance of truth. That is, there is no (question of) truth if we are not interested in agreement; or even, if there is not a problem of agreement. Consequently, rhetoric (in a particular sense of it) is the correct perspective in the consideration of "truth" as a concept of philosophical analysis. Logical truth is based on constructed domains or worlds; philosophical truth instead regards the (truthful-friendly) ways of constructing these domains or worlds.

Anomalous Coherentism

The fundamental goal of the reflection on nihilism and hermeneutic as developed in *The End of Modernity* is, as Vattimo openly declares, "to open up a non-metaphysical conception of truth" (EM 12). This nonmetaphysical conception is defined as based on "art" and "rhetoric." In other words, our experience of truth is to be qualified as "aesthetic and rhetorical" (EM 12). In this sense, "nonmetaphysical" means "not referring to a given conception of objective reality." When things are so stated, however, two specifications become necessary. First, the aesthetic and rhetorical nature of truth has nothing to do with "*subjective* emotions and feelings" (EM 12). Conversely, truth is to be related to the *historical stipulations* that give form to what we consider as objectivity, and that create a sort of "substantiality" (*sostanzialità* is the Italian term significantly used here by Vattimo; EM 12). Second, the intrinsically *intersubjective* status of truth is not to be confused with "common sense." "The passage to the domain of the true . . . is not a simple passage to 'common sense.' . . . To identify in aesthetic experience the model of the experience of truth means also to accept that it has to do with something more" (EM 13). Aesthetic experience and common sense most frequently conflict; the former is a sort of shock, it implies an idea of knowledge as something that suddenly *hits* our usual views; the latter refers to the reassuring world of everyday truth, which is shared by all human beings, and usually entails the awareness of this sharing.

These preliminary points should be carefully taken into account in order to understand the exact nature of Vattimo's point of view. One can easily see that here Vattimo implicitly accepts a coherentist theory of truth but with some significant differences. First, truth is seen in the perspective of experience—that is (as it is implied by the phenomenological-Heideggerian perspective), what we are going to do is not to give a definition of truth as a property of sentences or propositions, but properly to explain or describe the *experience* of truth.[1] Such an experience is not to be linked to science but to art, that is, to the reception (or comprehension) and the production (or creation) of art. Second, the set of truths "K" (that is the set of knowledges in which we can test the coherence of a single proposition in order to state its truth) is not a fixed set; rather, it has a *historical* nature. This means that it is somehow "substantial" insofar as it is intersubjectively fixed, but at the same time it is also moving and flowing.

Some contemporary versions of coherentism, and the various mixtures of coherentism and pragmatism from time to time proposed in the twentieth century (especially those derived from Charles S. Peirce), have admitted of some sort of dynamic vision.[2] Vattimo's view is to be included within such versions. What is puzzling and, I think, most important in Vattimo's view is, however, something rather unexpected—namely, the inclusion of the concept and practice of *nihilism* in the scenario. In other terms, Vattimo grounds his "historical coherentism" on nihilism, and openly shows how the former is a sort of natural consequence of the latter. One ought to be a historical coherentist insofar as one ought to be a nihilist.

Coherentism *and* Nihilism

The point from which to start is the notion of *complete* (fulfilled) nihilism. "True" nihilism is self-contradictory. This is an obvious idea, which was well known to the ancient Greeks, and which has been repeatedly and variously mentioned by the contemporary critics of nihilism. One cannot assert the nonexistence of truth without implying at the same time that such a claim should be in some sense true. One cannot say that "every proposition is false" without self-contradiction; that is, without either: a) assuming that there is at least *one* true proposition, namely, "every proposition is false," or b) assuming that also this *same* proposition is false. So, simply stated, if "there is no truth" is true, it is false; and if it is false, it is false. The proposition "something is true"—like logicians are accustomed to saying—entails its own truth.

Nietzsche himself is in some sense aware of this fact, given his intense and detailed knowledge of ancient philosophy. In any event, he knows that in principle there are two forms of epistemological nihilism: in denying truth one may admit that the nonexistence of truth is true; or else, one may admit that even this is not true. In other words, one may say "there is no truth, and this is true," or else "there is no truth, and even this is not true." The former corresponds to what Nietzsche calls "incomplete nihilism"; the latter corresponds to "complete nihilism."

In Nietzsche's view, axiological nihilism has some primacy over ontological or epistemological nihilism.[3] An incomplete nihilist should say "there are not values, and this holds as a value or as a rule," while a complete nihilist would say "there is no rule or value, and this is not properly a rule or a value." According to Nietzsche, complete nihilism is to be preferred.[4] It is not the case of substituting old with new values; it is not the case of some destruction aimed at creating a new and better society, nor is it a matter of criticizing the stated truths in order to find some new and "truer" truth. A complete nihilist is someone who does not admit any truth, value, or being; furthermore, he or she is someone who does not consider his or her own nihilism as a truth or a value.

According to Vattimo (not unlike Nietzsche, but with a significant difference, as we will see) nihilism is neither properly a choice nor a point of view. It is not a point of view, because it is instead the property and nature of an entire world. More specifically, as Heidegger holds, the same structure of Western *logos* is in a sense "nihilistically oriented." Consequently, nihilism is not a theoretical choice. We are somehow forced to be nihilist. This is what Vattimo expresses by saying that nihilism "*is a destiny*" (EM 17).

So, we are nihilist, and we cannot avoid being such. In this perspective, one can only choose between being a complete and an incomplete nihilist. Incomplete nihilism is for instance what Vattimo sees as the "aesthetic derive" or "aestheticism" typical of Marcuse or of French poststructuralism, namely, Deleuze's "glorification" of shams and simulacra (EM 25). This attitude consists in assigning to the "fable" exactly the relevance of what was once reality. This is precisely what Nietzsche calls "doing away with values, but not with their *place*." Simply stated, tales take the place of reality, stories replace history, and new values take over the old ones.

Complete nihilism is sometimes marked by Nietzsche with the idea of "anthropological mutation," that is, the *Übermensch*. Man ceases to be man (a subject of attributes and powers), and begins to become something other. Vattimo stresses the nature of "*über*" as "beyond," which means that the anthropological mutation is not to be conceived of as an emphasis on humanity as such, a sort of super-humanity provided with forms of super-knowledge. Rather, human beings should become something that is beyond what was believed to be "human" in history. Vattimo openly relates this intuition to a sort of philosophical evolutionism (VRF 72): concepts and words change, and their changes are recorded (and recordable), exactly as the changes in biological species.

Both Nietzsche and Deleuze hold that this "beyond-human" experience ultimately is a new experience of "fullness" (*pienezza*; see EM 25). That is, it is life at the height of its powers. In Vattimo's view it is not so, simply because of the internal structure of complete nihilism. Complete nihilism cannot be a new "more authentic" way of thought or life: "authenticity itself has set," is one with the "death of God." Thus nihilism will not turn into some glory of life, finally free to express itself. Instead, it will rather turn into a new attitude, free from "life," from "nature," as well as from other super-concepts (or "names of being," as Heidegger calls them) that are expected to define the "true" story of being, the "true" truth (so to say).

Is it true that truth has set? More generally, is it true that nihilism, that is, the end of truth and of any other value or principle, is the immanent destiny of our tradition? Is it true that God has died? In which sense could Vattimo's complete nihilism be really coherent, that is, actually complete, despite this apparent self-contradiction? This is the basic question that has always guided Vattimo's reflection about truth.

Nihilism as Method

In *Beyond Interpretation*, which marks an important *mise au point* of Vattimo's philosophy, some clear points are fixed. First of all, the hermeneutical-historical coherentism, which is the "*new koinē*" of our era (BI 1–5), must not present itself as the true, final portrait of some "human experience," finally self-aware of its own historic and linguistic nature. "Hermeneutics is not only a theory of the historicity (horizons) of truth: it is itself a radically historical truth," Vattimo repeats (BI 6). It is the "acknowledgement of a course of events in which we are implicated and that we do not describe objectively, but interpret speculatively" (BI 6–7). This is the principle of complete nihilism assumed in a complete sense. That is, if you assume that there is no truth, but even this is not strictly true, then you are somehow forced to admit that something new has truly happened, but it regards the practical and political impact, the attitude or the ethical spin-offs of your discourse, more than the contents. What has set is not properly "truth," I would argue, but the assertive pretensions about truth. (It should be noticed that Nietzsche himself seems to share this idea. In *Beyond Good and Evil* (§22) he writes: "there are no facts, only interpretations—you may say that this is an interpretation, and I will answer: well, so much the better!")

A second important point is that the primacy of aesthetics and rhetoric should not be seen as a sort of handing over of powers from (natural and exact) sciences to *Geisteswissenschaften*, or from logic to rhetoric, from science (generally speaking) to art (BI 22–23). On the contrary, being aware of nihilism means to lead science itself to acknowledge its own nihilistic nature (so there is a sort of global "unification of sciences" into the nihilist perspective; see BI 26).

A third important point is that the phenomenological-existential perspective, which inspired the previous conception, is abandoned. Now we are not facing the experience of truth, but rather we are dealing with the *construction* of truth. More specifically, we are dealing with the construction of the conditions of truth. One may say that Hegel replaces Heidegger; or rather, if one wants, the "later" Heidegger takes over the "early," especially if one considers the decidedly Hegelian aspects that Heidegger assumes in the second period of his thinking.

These three points should be taken into account in order to understand the complete development of Vattimo's theory of truth. Particularly, while the first point implies that a "methodological turn" is involved, the third point specifies the object, or the "location" of the turn: it does not properly regard truth as the predicate we assign to sentences or statements, but rather truth as the structure that opens the conditions of any further truth, that is, of any further truthful assignation of predicates. (One might ask if this is really what we refer to when we speak of "truth." This is something I consider later.) Finally, the second point clearly suggests that this proposal does not properly regard the *Geisteswissenschaften*, nor postulates some primacy of art or philosophy over (exact and natural) science. It involves instead all kinds of science or knowledge. In this respect, Vattimo adopts a conception of philosophy as a research concerning any kind of being, and whose results involve any kind of human practice. This is something that, in my view, has always marked his difference from Richard Rorty's position. Vattimo basically preserves the traditional meaning of philosophy, while it is exactly this meaning that Rorty aimed to change.

Let us consider the combined action of the three stances. It is fairly evident that this sort of "true" nihilism is prompt to get rid of nihilism. *A sort of precarious negation is included in Vattimo's vision of nihilism.* That "hermeneutics should radically assume its own historicity" means that hermeneutics is an interpretation of history that remains within history and is aware of the "belonging" nature of its own truths. This precarious negation is somehow the rule that should orient the construction of the conditions of truth. One might say that it is the transcendental norm of truth. This norm states that it is in some sense true that there is no (there must not be any particular) truth, and it is absolutely true that any truth is relative. In this way, even the absoluteness of the relative may be put under suspicion, since there might be a situation in which we will be finally in front of a true truth (who may say?).

This has nothing to do, one should take notice, with the obvious facts that there are natural phenomena and that there are tables and chairs. The truth of "this is a table" is evidently a "true" truth if we are in front of a table, in that specific context; but it is not philosophically relevant. What could become relevant is rather the negation of these sorts of trivial statements in cases of doubt, such as when I say "this is a table," and you say "no, it is not." I specifically examine this in the next section.

Truth and Philosophy

In *Vocazione e responsabilità del filosofo*, Vattimo draws the consequences of his historicism in a metaphilosophical perspective. Metaphilosophy, that is, the self-understanding of philosophy, has always been one of the major concerns of Vattimo's thought. One should only recall that the title of the yearly publication edited by Vattimo from 1986 to 1996 was *Filosofia*.

Vattimo outlines the entire course of his own conception of philosophy in *Vocazione e responsabilità del filosofo* by presenting in a simple way his ideas about classic meta-philosophical topics such as the relation between philosophy and science, the relation between philosophy, history and literature, philosophy and logic, and finally philosophy and politics. A specific chapter of this small book is devoted to truth. As Vattimo writes, "in the end, at the bottom of all discussions between hermeneuticians and anti-hermeneuticians there is always the question of truth as adequacy or correspondence" (VRF 101). In fact, in hermeneutics there is "a more complex conception of adequacy," and the aim of these pages is to show what kind of adequacy this is (VRF 101).

Here Vattimo reconsiders the main problem of his version of hermeneutics, that is, as I have suggested, the problem of the need to defend the conception of nihilism as "history of being," but without making of this defense the new assertion of a new absolute truth. "Once I wrote in favor of truth as rhetoric"—he writes quoting *The End of Modernity*—"now I would probably not say exactly the same." And he adds: "I am still sure that truth is neither a problem of political science nor a question of scientific proof: it is a question of *persuasion*" (VRF 71). Yet, he specifies, the persuasion involved in truth is not the one of an individual person who has been led to change his or her mind (more or less fallaciously). Rather, it is a phenomenon that happens "in relation to—and in one with—a collectivity" (VRF 71). The move to a collective subject is what, as we know, allows to eliminate every subjectivist (or also, following Heidegger, "humanist") shadow from the hermeneutical stance. The example chosen by Vattimo is however significant; as he writes, the persuasion involved in truth is not persuasion "in the sense of [saying] 'son, listen to me!' but rather in that of [saying] 'give him a hand!'" (VRF 71).

One can clearly see now what sort of rhetoric Vattimo is here evoking. It is the persuasion of an entire community that is implicated in an action, relative to a problem that is exquisitely political, as it regards solidarity and justice, and the actions geared toward promoting both. This is the proper status of truth, and this is the specific context in which truth is specifically relevant.

It is then clear that what is at stake is always and in each context the proposal of interpreting our common situation according to a certain line, and in virtue of shared premises. [In practice] I try to persuade you by quoting authors that in my opinion you, too, have read and known, authors who in turn did not show that 2+2=4, but who were rather searching for an *interpretation of the shared situation* (VRF 71).

Such are not just any authors. Instead, such authors belong to the history that in some sense supports our same way of being, and they constitute this same history. This is properly the meaning of "the history of being," which is not a unique clear line that we can objectively reconstruct; it is not a progressive and cumulative development. At the same time, however, it is endowed with a certain identifiability, in an interpretative sense. That is, we can, on occasion, devise the direction of its flow, and recognize ourselves in it.

What sort of evidence can have such a referent? If Vattimo follows Rorty in admitting the political relevance of truth, here the divergence could not be clearer. The history of being, he says, has a sort of "providential line," in a totally nonreligious (nor Hegelian) sense: it gives us the instrument of knowing, of exchanging information, of understanding and mutually recognizing our intentions.

Changing the Subject?

Quine famously says that often, when people ask for a new logic, new conception of truth, and so on, in fact, they are changing the subject, that is, they are using the words in a nonstandard way.[5] This is also at the basis of Tugendhat's criticism of Heidegger's theory of truth. Heidegger, Tugendhat claims, is talking about something that is not properly "truth." Probably someone could be tempted to raise the same objection to the theory by Vattimo here exposed. But Vattimo has an answer.

The connections between cultural construction and truth, emancipation and truth, friendship and truth, surely are not "the whole truth." Sure, there is also the basic truth of sentences such as "the cat is on the mat," or "lovely day, today," or of scientific and historical sentences, such as "Napoleon was defeated at Waterloo." In these cases, one might say that there is no question of persuasion, but rather and simply of adequacy: when I say that these sentences are true, I mean that something in the world *makes* them true.⁶ So, one might be tempted to get rid of the word "truth" as referring to the philosophical meaning isolated by Vattimo, and restrict the proper sense of "truth" to the other, definitely simpler, use.

"Sure, one might object that we are talking of different things," writes Vattimo, "that I call 'truth' what others would call 'friendship,'" or courtesy, or a sense of collectivity. But "in fact, it is useful to conserve the same term, and talk of 'truth' also in this field" (VRF 104), since any effort at keeping the two sides distinct actually would simply confirm that the "true truth" is basically cruel and violent, insofar as it is separated from justice and solidarity. This, however, is something that simply is not true. Such an attitude would confirm the wrong idea that truth is substantially blind. Instead, if we consider the word "truth" in the entire range of its philosophical and ordinary implications, we find that by using it we refer to something that is not far from the idea of something effective in the world. The nature of this effectiveness, however, is not reducible to the "effectiveness" of facts (VRF 104).

"It is not true that the one who is searching for the truth is looking for *any sort* of truth," Vattimo writes. "There is an old one-liner in Brecht . . . if one goes in front of a factory, during a strike, and tells the workers that 2+2=4!" (VRF 105), one is surely uttering a universal truth, and probably nobody will take exceptions from it. But in that specific circumstance, the sentence will not be properly true. More specifically, when I am looking for truth I look for something that might be *true* in the same sense of 2+2=4. Yet, there is also something more in saying "true," and this "epistemic surplus," so to say, is linked to the specific situation, even, to the destiny that I am and the history that I express. When talking about truth, we basically talk about "the dynamics of a situation" (VRF 101); this includes also correspondence, but it is not restricted to it.

In this historical-contextual perspective, truth has some structural requisites that are quite easily acknowledgeable, and that the hermeneutical tradition has provided to clarify. First of all is the indeterminacy of the situation, which Gadamer expresses by saying that "being historical means not being able to be completely self-aware." Vattimo interprets this point in the terms that Dilthey called "the reflexivity of belonging (*Zugehörigkheit*)": "there is a situation [let us say, a context], and then there is consciousness of the situation, and then there is consciousness of the consciousness . . ." (VRF 101). This means that our knowledge of being, insofar as we aim at grasping it in its concrete effectiveness (in its space-temporal nature), is doomed to remain unfinished. This is only one aspect, however, of the hermeneutical infinity.

One might say that it is the regressive and iterative aspect of it. Yet, there is something more. Vattimo points out that in the complexity of truth as historically grasped "there is not only the need to remain 'faithful' to the dynamics of the situation" (VRF 101); there is also the fact that "to know all this *helps me to understand something which is not included in all this*" (VRF 101). In this sense, truth is structurally related to some "not only this."

In elementary terms, we can say that when we know that "p" is true, the fact or state of affairs described by p is somehow charged with implications that are not included in the mere description of how things are. This does not mean that p is not made true (as the truthmaker theorists like to say today) by something that is in some sense "the world" or part of the world. When I talk of the truth of a description, surely I am talking of the world; however, the world that is at stake is not only the one described by my words, but something more, for instance the need to consider that specific part of being, the importance of that part for justice, or the emancipation of exploited people, and so on. When I say "'Fa' is true," I am conveying your attention over a fact that is not only Fa (the property F and the object a) but also a complex whole of intentions, origins, destiny, aims, and so on. All this is included in the word "truth": for this reason, any effort to detach what is simply relative to Fa (F and a) is misleading.

"All this brings me far from Rorty, who still recently has maintained the defensibility of the claim 'there is no truth,' and has said that its exact meaning would be 'truth cannot be considered a possible object of research.' I think that this claim—like some other Rorty's claims—corresponds to an effort 'to straighten the legs of dogs.' It is the therapeutic obsession of certain analytic thinking, which wishes to order everything" (VRF 106). Instead, what is interesting in truth, what is still worth trying to research, are its changes of meanings within history. We positively have truth, and it is the development of the concept of truth in history, the story of contradictions and self-contradictions that distinguishes it, relating and opposing truth to other concepts. So it is true that, as Vattimo has written more recently, in our informational and plural society "*la vérité est deshormais concevable seulement comme affaire d'interpretation*" (truth is only conceivable as an interpretative affaire); and there is nobody authorized "*à décider des paradigmes et des vérités qui en découluent* [to decide of paradigms and the ensuing truths]." But this means that something has changed, and the change is philosophically relevant. What we call the *philosophical research* concerning truth concerns exactly this change, insofar as it consists of some "growing" of the concept through times.

Vattimo also gives a specific importance to the concept of freedom, which is the basis of Heidegger's theory of truth as developed in *On the Essence of Truth* (1943). Heidegger's idea is that truth as *adaequatio* is only a marginal aspect of truth, while in fact the "essence" of truth is freedom. Freedom actually is the specific attitude that "opens" the conditions of truth, that is the unconcealing, or rather the unveiling expressed by the Greek term *a-letheia*. Vattimo connects this idea with a twofold scenario. First of all, with the scenario of nihilism. While for Heidegger nihilism ultimately is the opposite of an opening (or an openness), as it rather "closes" thought in formal schemes, parameters, fixed symbols and empty languages, for Vattimo nihilism is instead the cipher of *freedom* from fixed symbols, parameters, and so on. Nihilism is the attitude that opens the conditions of truth. Nihilism is "science that dances with light feet," as Nietzsche says. A nihilistic construction is changeable and ductile, always prompt to self-revision. A nihilistic truth is what is always available to new truths.

The second scenario is defined by the evangelical saying "the truth will set you free" (VRF 103). Vattimo interprets it not (only) in the sense that "if you know the truth, you will be free," but rather in the sense that "if you are free, you will have the truth (or rather: you will *be* truth)." In short, the project of "emancipation through truth" is not to be intended as emancipation through "knowing how things are" (VRF 103). This is clear when one considers the rule of construction (as I called it above) that governs the conditions of truth, namely, the principle of friendship, or if one wants, solidarity. "At this point I cannot manage to see truth as separated from charity. The only emancipation I am able to conceive is an eternal life in charity, which means: spent in listening to others and answering the dialogue with them" (VRF 103). The evangelical tone must not deceive us: the theoretical spin-offs of this attitude are otherwise evident.

Conclusion

Let us summarize the main points. What is (philosophically) important of truth, according to Vattimo's view, is its role in controversial cases. So the (philosophical) starting point is the plurality of truth: "'2+2=4' is true" is philosophically relevant only when—and insofar as—there is someone who says "no, it is not true." But when we speak of different truths, we speak in fact of different systems of constructing the conditions of truth (that is, we speak of something more than different statements, beliefs or experiences). Thus, I say "'2+2=4' is not true" only when—and only if—I am not sure about the classic arithmetical system, when I am persuaded (for some mysterious reason!) that it is not the best system. Thus, to deal with truth (philosophically) means to inquire into the rivalry between controversial systems and, if possible (this is the hermeneutical art of dialogue), construct the conditions of truth as the case may require.

In this sense, Vattimo's view is similar to some contemporary theories of truth, especially those inspired by the coherentism developed by Wittgenstein in the late notes of *On Certainty*. As I like to call it, it is a sort of "anomalous foundationalism," which corresponds to a fairly shared view.

Yet, there also some divergent aspects in Vattimo's theory. The "rules," or "guidelines" for this construction are established first of all by nihilism. Nihilism is the true method of philosophical truth, it is not a decision that involves the contents of truth (for instance, simply asserting the nonexistence of being, or the irrelevance of values); rather, nihilism designates a *practical* attitude toward truth—a way of dealing with (the concept of) truth. At this point, Vattimo's nihilism is connected to the Christian theory of charity (or *pietas*, or *agape*). The regulative principle of the construction is actually friendship (or *pietas*, or charity): which corresponds to the hermeneutical "principle of perfection." All this should be the basis of contemporary *reason*, the principle of which is not (as Gadamer points out) that of having the courage to use one's own reason, but rather that of having the courage to acknowledge the reasons of others.

Freedom (nihilism) and charity (or *pietas*, or solidarity, or friendship) enter the philosophical conception of truth by integrating and not by eliminating the correspondence theory. First, it is simply true that sentences such as "the cat is on the mat" are (contextually) true; it is simply true that "2+2=4" is (extra-contextually) true; but not any truth is involved in truth (that is, in the use of the term "true"). When truth appears, it is because *there is no truth*; that is, because there is *something unclear and controversial*. Second, when we say that something is true, it is because the fact we are referring to implies *something that is not the mere fact*. Third, these different aspects of truth, or different truths (adequacy, freedom, charity) should *be kept together*, because it is exactly their joint effectiveness that we properly call truth. One may say that we use the term "truth," but in fact we mean "truth and something more."

These ideas, even if only outlined in Vattimo's writings, in fact manage to delineate a real theory of truth. It is, I would say, an original mixture of historical coherentism and politically oriented pragmatism combined with—and this is the most amazing aspect, I think—a both nihilistic and anti-deflationary attitude. For such theory implies that—culturally speaking—we are now faced with a sort of disappearance of truth; yet, this is only the symptom of a new conception of truth, which is pushing its way through the impressive amount of alleged truths of our "informational" and "intercultural" life. This new conception of truth does not properly eliminate correspondence; it simply indicates that "there is something more." Amazingly, nihilism shows that the correspondence theory of truth is not wrong; rather, it is "not enough."

Notes

1. I will come back to the divergence concerning *truth bearers*, a divergence that is frequently diagnosed as the basis of the rivalry between theories of truth. In particular, the refusal of truth as a property of statements or assertions (or sentences, and so on) is considered to be the main fault of Heidegger's conception of truth. See particularly Ernst Tugendhat, "Heideggers Idee von Wahrheit," in *Heidegger, Perspektiven zur Deutung seines Werkes*, ed. Otto Pöggeler (Köln-Berlin: Kiepenheuer und Witsch, 1969), 286–297.
2. As a significant example, see Hilary Putnam, *Meaning and the Moral Sciences* (London: Routledge and Kegan Paul, 1978).
3. The primacy of axiological nihilism in Nietzsche's view is a specific result of Müller-Lauter's analysis. See Wolfgang Müller-Lauter, *Nietzsche: His Philosophy of Contradictions and the Contradictions of His Philosophy*, trans. David Parent (Urbana: University of Illinois Press, 1999).
4. Even if this preference—it should be noted—does not *ipso facto* turn Nietzsche into a "nihilist," as Schacht has stressed. See Richard Schacht, *Making Sense of Nietzsche's Reflections Timely and Untimely* (Urbana: University of Illinois Press, 1995).
5. W. V. Quine, *Philosophy of Logic* (Englewood Cliffs, NJ: Prentice-Hall, 1970), 126–127.
6. This is the truthmaker principle, which expresses, as Armstrong says, "what should be saved of the correspondence theory of truth." See D. M. Armstrong, *Truth and Truthmakers* (Cambridge: Cambridge University Press, 2004).

3

Vattimo's Hermeneutics as a Practice of Freedom

DAVID WEBB

For Roy

Gianni Vattimo's interpretation of Heidegger and Nietzsche leads him to propose an ontology that is less dogmatic than traditional metaphysics about the structures that shape our existence. These structures are, in his view, historically variable, but rather than obeying some deep-seated law in their development, they are more open, more fractured, and more responsive to the practice of interpretation. It is the relation between this practice and the structures on which it works that I want to look at in this paper.

Given that Vattimo welcomes what appears to be a decline in the strength of metaphysical principles, and thereby a reduction in their capacity to support violence and authoritarianism, it seems at least plausible that this argument about ontology is driven by an ethical aspiration, which is by no means a criticism; the recognition that ontology and ethics are so closely bound up with one another that to deal with one is already to deal with the other is a feature of several contemporary thinkers, from Jürgen Habermas, to Richard Rorty, to Michel Foucault and Michel Serres, and others. Viewed less charitably, however, to acknowledge an ethical motivation to an ontological discourse could be construed as conceding that the outcome of an inquiry may be evaluated in terms of its ethical implications, accepted or rejected according to whether what follows from it is to our liking or not. One can easily imagine a critic pointing out that we should accept the results of a rational inquiry regardless of our personal preference, or else concede that we are closing the gap between the use of reason and expressions of feeling. However, such an objection trades a limited conception of ontology and ethics that does little to address the question of their relation to one another. As an objection, it has to be addressed, but also problematized. It is fair to say that no single answer to this question suffices for all, as different philosophers tackle and develop the problem in different ways.

Although not always to the fore of the considerations that follow, my aim in this chapter is to examine how this relation occurs in Vattimo's work. Taking up this question from the perspective of Vattimo's understanding of ontology in the wake of the overcoming of metaphysics, I set out a reformulation of Vattimo's thesis in terms of what Heidegger calls the ontic foundation of ontology. Coming back to Vattimo, I then reflect on his suggestion that we need to adopt an ethics of finitude, and that this involves a capacity for attentiveness not just to the material conditions of our lives, but also to the voices of others who speak to us. I ask whether the ontology that emerges from the overcoming of metaphysics in this way is merely a weaker version of the old ontology, and so one more easily shaped or even overridden by the work of interpretation, or whether it is fundamentally changed. To the extent that it changes, the formal structure of ontology will no longer be the point of solid resistance on which the ethical force of hermeneutics works in order to break down the authoritarian tendency within metaphysics and we shall therefore be dealing with a new relation between ethics and ontology.

Vattimo's critique of traditional ontology is well known and so I only repeat it briefly here. A key point of reference is the process of secularization that took hold of European culture in the age of Enlightenment and that led eventually to skepticism regarding the claims of metaphysics to discover the true nature of reality, a truth that would stand over and above the terrestrial world and that would provide the touchstone for true judgment in all matters, from those concerning the essence of human nature to questions of religion, politics, and the natural sciences. This process was thematized most radically and productively by Nietzsche in his analyses of nihilism as the narrowing of the division between reality and appearance, and the closure of the domain where laws and principles of human understanding and action could boast an independent existence of their own. In this sense, at least, Nietzsche can be seen as an Enlightenment thinker exhorting humanity to think for itself, to create, and to emerge from the immaturity of its dependent state; equipped now with a richer understanding of the terrestrial world and more confident in predicting its course, humanity no longer need seek reassurance in patterns of explanation that invoke supernatural powers and transcendent causes. Like Nietzsche, Vattimo regards nihilism as a process that bears the promise of liberation from the necessity imposed by an account of being as universal and unchanging. For Vattimo, this has had an effect that has, at least to some extent, overtaken us all by virtue of the massive intrusion into our lives of the media and the technology of communication. Contrary to the interpretation of the advent of the mass media given by Adorno, Marcuse, and others, in whose view it has closed down dimensions of our existence, Vattimo argues that it has permitted a proliferation of voices able to speak from every point in space—geographical and cultural—with more or less equal force and clarity (TS 6–9). Vattimo's confidence in the ability of individuals and groups to find their voices in this way reflects a democratic tendency in his work that is, I shall suggest, more than just the direction he has chosen to develop his ideas, as though philosophy were the medium in which an extra-philosophical motivation found expression (NE 16–17). Rather, it reflects a specific engagement with the question of the relation between ethics and ontology.

If the true nature of reality is not in some sense pregiven once and for all, a straightforward theory of truth as correspondence is no longer sustainable. As Vattimo reminds us, the thesis that interpretation is intrinsic to truth is the outcome of a broad swathe of early twentieth-century thought, including phenomenology, elements of neo-Kantianism, and of neo-positivism and analytic philosophy (BI 5). However, the act of interpretation needs something to work on, and thus relies on a prior disclosure of some kind. It is Heidegger who developed this idea most clearly and fully in his account of our interpretative activity as the articulation of a "preunderstanding" of Being embedded in our everyday practices and concerns (BI 5). The decisive characteristic of this account is that what is "given" is not first of all an object on which we then overlay an interpretation, but rather a basic and diffuse understanding of Being, and as such is the horizon within which any particular thing may be given at all; before any specific judgment regarding the nature of a thing, we must already have found ourselves within a horizonal structure that allows that thing to show itself to us *as a thing*. A condition of the disclosure of any given thing as this or that, and thereby of the conception of truth as *adequatio intellectus et rei*, is the opening of a dimension in which it can appear at all; although one must also bear in mind that the open dimension cannot literally occur first, as an independent event, but only with and through the disclosure of the thing that nevertheless depends on it. This more original event of opening is what Heidegger calls truth as unconcealment (*aletheia*).

To this phenomenological conception of truth, Vattimo then adds an important historical twist. We must not imagine, he writes, that Heidegger has provided us with a "more adequate" description of truth, as though the previous metaphysical conception were incomplete and inadequate to some deeper reality. With the development of Heidegger's work after *Being and Time*, it becomes increasingly clear that the ontology he proposes is not to be understood as the elaboration of a fixed structure. Our understanding of Being is historical, insofar as it is given with the opening conveyed by outstanding acts of poetic creativity or political constitution; acts that are not themselves the true origin of the opening, but which give concrete form to the history of Being itself. From the point of view of a more traditional metaphysics, the question is what makes Heidegger's critique of the correspondence theory of truth and his account of the history of Being worth taking seriously, if not the fact that they contain some claim to be a "true" description of what is actually the case. For Vattimo the answer is simply that it is a credible response to "the history of Being interpreted as the occurrence of nihilism" (BI 8).

> Hermeneutics, if it wishes to be consistent with its own rejection of metaphysics, cannot but present itself as the most persuasive philosophical interpretation of a situation or "epoch," and thereby, necessarily, of a provenance. . . . its truth may be wholly summed up in the claim to be the most persuasive philosophical interpretation of that course of events of which it feels itself to be the outcome. (BI 10–11)

The ontology that hermeneutics describes is therefore "weak" in the sense that it is not a "real" structure existing independently of the world it grounds and endowed with sufficient authority to dictate a "correct" interpretation of meaning and action. Rather, it consists in the articulation of the history that leads up to the point of interpretation itself. Once this articulation recognizes its own historical situatedness, the truth it proposes can no longer be construed as impervious to further change (unless one were also to regard the moment of interpretation as the end of history). The question—my question here, posed to Vattimo but also with Vattimo—is: What are the consequences of describing this process solely in terms of the historicity of interpretation?

Given the importance of Heidegger for Vattimo, I shall begin by recalling that Heidegger's own elaboration of the radically historical character of ontology led him to propose an epochal history of Being in which the opening within which Being is disclosed can take several forms, and these forms change over time. In this way, there is no final answer to the question of Being, because the history is open-ended, and Being is disclosed according to a form that shifts from one epoch to another. In the present time, Being is disclosed through the frame of technology, which is also to say that the form of disclosure characteristic of technology serves to conceal the ontological difference and thereby the possibility of stepping back from the dominant sense of Being as given. Our response, in Heidegger's view, should involve an attentive recollection of the oblivion of the question of Being that keeps the question open, and with it also the possibility of being responsive to a future epochal shift in the wake of which Being may be given differently. However, there is a kind of passivity in this that does not sit well with Vattimo's concern with interpretation as a creative practice, a concern no doubt derived in part from his proximity to Nietzsche. Being sympathetic to Vattimo's concern, I want to propose a different reading that takes the principle of what, referring to Heidegger, can be called the "ontic foundation of ontology." The reading I set out takes this ontic foundation as the key to understanding both the sense of historical situatedness that characterizes hermeneutics, and the open-endedness of the change in which it is implicated. Moreover, it draws the eye both to the proximity to one another of ethics and ontology, and to the importance of thinking ontologically, precisely in order to engage the transformations underway at this level in late- or postmodernity.

Although it may at first seem surprising that fundamental ontology as Heidegger describes it is to have an ontic foundation, it is in fact an unavoidable implication of his phenomenological method. Since Being is disclosed in and through Dasein, the path toward a thematic understanding of Being must pass through the existential analytic in which the structure of Dasein's disclosive capacity is brought to light, and the existential analytic itself is grounded in Dasein's ontical constitution as a being for which Being is an issue.[1] However, as Heidegger describes it, this determination of the structure in and through which Being is disclosed is not intended merely to neutralize its effect as a lens, all the better to advance to a "true" grasp of Being. "Philosophy is universal phenomenological ontology, and takes its point of departure from the hermeneutic of Dasein, which, as an analytic of *existence*, has made fast the guiding line for all philosophical inquiry at the point where it *arises* and to which it *returns*."[2] The accomplishment of universal phenomenology thereby depends on the success of the existential analytic. But Heidegger is at least equivocal over whether the analytic cannot achieve a definitive formulation. His own ontological interpretation of Dasein is, he observes, inevitably underpinned by a "factical ideal" and the task of philosophy is to unfold both its own presuppositions and that for which they are presuppositions.[3] There are different ways this practice of interpretation may be understood. It certainly leaves open the possibility of conceiving philosophy as proceeding gradually toward a presuppositionless origin, so that while the inquiry repeatedly returns to the factical situation of existence to begin over again, the changed historical conditions that it meets have no tangible effect on the destination of the inquiry. This is what we might expect if the formal structures elicited by philosophy were for all possible beings, and all possible experience. Embedded in this approach is an assumption of the necessary priority of the deep ontological level of analysis that protects it from being called into question by the shifting seas of experience and history above. But this brings us straight back to the interpretation of Heidegger as providing a more adequate account of an actual structure. Alternatively, we can view the return to the ontic domain as more than an opportunity to hone the existing ontological interpretation to the point where it corresponds to an ontological reality. Each return injects something new into the inquiry, if only because our relation to the historical situation from which the interpretation springs will change by virtue of having passed by way of the ontological reflection. In these terms alone, it is hard to see how this changed relation to our own historical situation could *not* then have an effect on the ontological interpretation that follows.

The reading can be taken further. In the context of the question of Being, the task of interpretation is to bring to light the formal structure through which Being is disclosed. For Heidegger, at least in the period of *Being and Time*, this consists in an account of the transcendence of Dasein, understood as an ontological radicalization of the basic phenomenological structure of intentionality. Dasein transcends beings toward their Being; that is, the transcendence of Dasein opens the ontological difference. As we know, intentionality is a relation, and not one that phenomenological consciousness can choose to enter into or not. Similarly, transcendence in its ontological sense is the essential structure of Dasein, its Being-in-the-world, and as such cannot be understood on the model of the literal passage from one point to another that characterizes its ontic signification.[4] Heidegger goes on to describe the essence of transcendence as freedom, where freedom already comprises that for which it is free (MFL 191). In these structures, outlined here in the briefest possible way, the emphasis lies on the relation itself, and not on the relata as existing first and in relation only afterward. Transcendence, then, as the movement from Dasein to the Being of beings, is not a movement that carries Dasein away from itself and away from beings; rather, it is the possibility of being Dasein and of being alongside things in the world. Dasein is, at every moment, already in relation to Being, and exists *as* this relation; that is, Dasein exists as movement considered ontologically as a relation, and not merely as a thing in movement. Existing *as* movement, means that transcendence can never be accomplished "once and for all," because movement itself cannot reach its destination, only what is in movement. This is to say that, as an ontological dimension characterized by the relation between potentiality and actuality, movement itself is always already in relation to its end. Similarly, only what is in movement can begin moving, not movement itself, and this is one reason why Heidegger describes Dasein as always already "underway" to Being. What is important to see here is that being "underway" does not mean being caught in mid-flight, halfway between a beginning that one has left behind, and a destination that is yet to come. Ontologically, Dasein is the whole stretch from beginning to end; that is, transcendence, as an ontological radicalization of intentionality, and understood as movement in this sense. In the same way, the ontological difference is also characterized by movement treated ontologically in the sense that what has to be disclosed is movement (not the thing in movement) and movement itself does not "move." If one then considers the movement of the hermeneutic circle in this light, one sees that it cannot consist in consecutive phases—a turn away from the ontic to the ontological, followed by a return to the ontic again—as though Heidegger were proposing an ascent from the cave and then a descent back into its depths.[5] Just as the ontological difference is a relation that involves both its parts, so the turn from the ontic to the ontological is perpetually underway.[6] Therefore the existential analytic and the determination of the meaning of being are not to be regarded as alternatives, and their separation as sequential phases of an inquiry is only a matter of presentation. The turn from the ontic foundation to the ontological account is not a shift to a new level of questioning. Rather, philosophical questioning in the sense that Heidegger understands it is a perpetual turning from ontic to ontological, from the existential analytic to the ontological horizon.

Paradoxically, it is because transcendence is always already accomplished, in the sense that movement as such does not begin and end, that philosophy finds itself committed to an endless repetition. In the circularity of its movement we see that the turn of philosophy from the ontic foundation into the ontological difference is already a return to the ontic.

What requires clarification here is the relation of the ontological dimension of the disclosure of Being and the act of interpretation it grounds. My own preference here is for a materialist account that treats formal characteristics as emergent from the movement that they come to describe (and which as such is nonreductive). Approached in this way, the ontological dimension of the question of Being remains embedded in the ontic world of Dasein's existence, its concerns, and its involvements. Rather than simply adopting a stance in which the recollection of the oblivion of Being (a relation to an absence) is matched by a pious openness to an undetermined future, the individual engages the disclosure of Being as it is manifest in these concerns and involvements and thereby has a hand in shaping its future, for the disclosure of Being is no longer so radically prior to its ontic manifestation that it remains beyond influence. Although he does not theorize it in this way, Vattimo himself gives an excellent example of this and what it might entail. Like Heidegger, Vattimo regards technology as a decisive feature of modernity, but his view is decidedly more positive, insofar as technology represents an opportunity for a new liberty of interpretative practice in the space opened up by the disappearance of the strong transcendental structures of traditional metaphysics.

Although Heidegger's thesis on technology as a specific way in which Being is disclosed remains hugely significant for Vattimo, it is also the case that the actual development of technology, new discoveries, their dissemination, and the widespread engagement with them on the part of humanity have all accelerated the dissolution of the strong structures of Being. In a way quite unlike anything Heidegger proposed, for Vattimo it is our engagement with technology that both opens our relation to Being and at the same time initiates a transformation in that relation. From this perspective, and taking hermeneutics in its widest sense as an interpretative practice coextensive with our involvement in the world, hermeneutics is an interpretation of Being that engages with its own history, and in which the material conditions of that history are themselves at once shaping the interpretation and shaped by it. Consistency requires that we do not understand this to mean that what were once regarded as the fixed structures of metaphysics have lost their authority and can now be shaped by the practice of interpretation they once surveyed from on high. Rather, something in our understanding of such structures, and our relation to them, has changed; that is, we need to continue to think about the determining ground of our thought and action, but with a recognition that it is implicated in that which it grounds.

Once the absolute priority of ontology over other forms of discourse is set aside, it can no longer be insulated from changes arising from the world at the ontic level. A situation therefore arises in which ontology is placed in a close relation with ethics, insofar as the practice of interpretation, though historically situated and therefore finite, can itself modify the structural characteristics of the disclosure of Being. This is not because value is given precedence over fact, and not because we are at liberty to invent the world in which we exist. To speak of ethics, here, is simply to highlight the embeddedness of interpretation in our own historical situation. For Vattimo, the practice of interpretation is ethical primarily in the sense that it is a response to the dissolution of metaphysical principles that has consequences in terms of how we understand our existence, including our responsibilities and the means to discharge them; and many of the essays in the collection *Nihilism and Emancipation: Ethics Politics and Law* address this problem.

In a further sense, that interpretation is already engaged with ethics because each new act is itself a response to a situation, and leads to new articulation of the conditions shaping that situation. These two senses are always present together. So when Vattimo writes that in order to respond appropriately to the dissolution of metaphysical principles in modernity (that is, to respond without reasserting some further such principle) we have to "set about constructing an ethics around our finitude" (NE 43), we need to read this in both senses: as a recommendation about how we should approach the task of responding to nihilism in general, and as a proposal about how each act of interpretation should be understood as an engagement in our own historical situation. More precisely, such an ethics, writes Vattimo, is neither a preparation for a leap into the infinite, nor an attitude of resignation before our historical situation. It is, first of all, an attempt to recognize that the provenance of one's own existence is at once insuperably finite *and* pluralistic; "who" I am at any moment is a question that can only be answered by appealing to a variety of roles and references (including those of family life, work, and friendship) that are not finally reducible to a single and more fundamental identity. To exist ethically here cannot be to put into practice basic principles we have derived from reflections on human nature or on reason and the necessary conditions of moral law. In fact one must begin, writes Vattimo, by working to clear away the "dense undergrowth of metaphysical absolutes" that still provide our reflections with a kind of sclerotic structure and consistency.

As a positive recommendation, Vattimo advises that an attentiveness to our provenance does not entail a dwelling on the past. The conditions that shape us as finite beings are every bit as much as those of the present, and our provenance is also found in "the voice of the other, of our human contemporaries" (NE 44–45); if hermeneutics requires an attentiveness to the conditions of our provenance, then it is to others around me that I must listen, just as much as to the promptings of cultural traditions and the words of historical texts from which I derive an interpretation of the dissolution of metaphysical principles. Indeed, having adopted the broad stance of an ethics of finitude on the basis of the philosophical interpretation of our historical situation, it is from others that the impetus will most likely come actually to undertake a particular reflection and to amend or even abandon ideas and principles that have hitherto exerted a claim upon us. In terms of the ontic foundation of ontology and what I have described as the embeddedness of ontological thought in the ontic, this is consistent with the idea that the work of interpretation is immersed in the milieu of the world, is shaped by it, and also contributes to its evolution.

The interpretative practice that Vattimo describes is clearly transformative in a way that the traditional metaphysics he opposes does not allow, but he is not subscribing to a free-for-all in which anyone can invent anything; this is to say, nihilism has not led to a situation where "anything goes." There are constraints, and these are historical in the first instance. However, one has to be careful not to allow the idea of historical conditions to do the work of establishing limits to the possibility of interpretation without really clarifying how such conditions bear on the practice of interpretation itself and in what the limits actually consist. There are many questions one might ask here. For example, what is the relation between the historical conditions of interpretation and its ontological ground? Vattimo's account of nihilism and late modernity traces the weakening of metaphysical principles, but is it enough simply to relax these principles, and what does this really mean? Will one be left working in the absence of ontological principles, or will there be principles as before, but more malleable and easily bent to the needs of, and driving, a particular interpretative practice?

There are precedents for saying that one can work in the absence of ontological principles, or at least with indifference toward them. Richard Rorty made a virtue of the fact that there was no credible way to refer to principles beyond what was given in experience, and what we could freely make of it. To suppose that our interpretative activity is grounded in an ontological structure of some kind is, in his view, either self-reassurance or self-aggrandizement, but pointless and groundless either way. Rather, the condition of finitude characteristic of our interpretative activity derives from the historically, culturally, and linguistically bounded conditions in which it is undertaken. Ultimately, these conditions may be those of democratic politics, which are in Rorty's view prior to philosophy in the sense that they are the conditions of any philosophical discourse that might then seek to rationalize them in their turn.

Rorty's radical disavowal of ontology is rigorous and consistent, but undermines its own emphasis on freedom and reinvention by denying itself a valuable resource. Although it may be true that I can never prove the correctness of any particular ontological hypothesis, it does not follow that such a hypothesis is without purpose. Imagining the underlying structure of experience to have a certain form may be a useful heuristic device that promotes the invention of new ways of thinking and acting. The pragmatist's objection to this would be that if one can invent new ways of thinking, there is no need to call on some further structure to legitimate them. However, my point is that once the ontological structure is understood as embedded in the ontic, it is no longer an inaccessible reality, the appeal to which has no genuine epistemic force. For this reason, I feel uneasy when Vattimo writes, in relation to Rorty, that perhaps "we still require an ontology, if for no other purpose than to demonstrate that ontology is headed toward disintegration" (NE 19). The question is not whether we require an ontology, but what kind of ontology we find to be operative in our historical situation and how we can engage with it, for we can no more escape ontology than escape history.

In short, a weakening of metaphysical principles is equivalent not to a weakening of ontology *tout court*, but to its transformation. In fact, Vattimo does not go as far as Rorty in reducing discourse to the positivity of the actual spoken or written form. There is all the more reason, therefore, to suppose that in spite of its history of lending succor to dogmatism and violence, ontology is not for Vattimo a worthless exercise. Following Heidegger, Vattimo understands that the "truth" we perceive is contingent on an event of opening in which the manner of Being's disclosure is given, and he agrees that the form of this event cannot itself be verified. However, as I have already suggested, Vattimo does not adhere to Heidegger's view that one can therefore do no more than maintain an attitude of openness toward this event. Interpretative activity engages with its own conditions in such a way that it modifies the form of its own practice; partly in response to the historical situation in which it finds itself, and partly as a contribution to reshaping that situation. Recognizing an ontological dimension with which interpretation is engaged in dialogue is important because it provides a means for thought to experiment with its own conditions, and thereby to transform itself, while remaining in touch with its historical situation and the voices of others that together form its provenance and thereby the path of its development.

I now want briefly to outline three areas of concern that highlight the importance of continuing to recognize a place for ontology in this way: relations, locality, and power. These closing remarks can only point in the direction of further questions to address and are not intended to be conclusive.

One of the central ideas in Vattimo's reading of nihilism and modernity is the impetus it gives to the trend toward pluralism. With the disappearance of metaphysical principles, including those of essence and substance, the question of the formation of identity is never far away; whether this be individual identity or the identity of larger groups and communities, not least those that are beginning to encroach on the territory once staked out by the nation state. However, Vattimo is the first to recognize not only that individuals are generally formed by a complex pattern of identities overlaying one another and combining in sometimes singular ways, but also that they are never formed in isolation.[7] One is, therefore, obliged to think about the nature of the relation that obtains between the elements of the pluralism that Vattimo describes. No doubt, it is broadly an interpretive relation, and hermeneutics tells us that interpretation always takes place within horizons. In its Gadamerian form, the dialogue between interpretations consists in a merging of these horizons, but Vattimo is wary of giving too much away in this direction. It is in fact just as likely that interpretation may yield specificity and difference, and so any expectation that experience be characterized by harmony and the steady broadening of horizons risks falling back into "an idealization of the beautiful ethical life" (BI 87). This experience of conflict, and its productive resolution, can of course be theorized in different ways; for example, in terms of aesthetic experience, the problem of incommensurability in scientific reason, or perhaps most obviously via Ricoeur's account of the conflict of interpretations. In each case, however, the problem of ontology remains to be addressed. For Vattimo, the problem is particularly clear. Metaphysics gave us not only a theory of identity, but also a theory of relation between identities. Vattimo has shown us how the form of identity has weakened and evolved through the advance of hermeneutics, but it is less clear what we are to make of the form of relation. Yet without a new and appropriate idea of relation, the advocacy of pluralism will struggle to avoid replicating minor versions of the same configurations of identity it claims have been dispelled in the nihilistic course of modernity. What form such an ontology might take is an open question. In spite of the fact that I regard Heidegger's ontology as fundamentally an ontology of relation, the insistence on the absolute priority of the event of Being to which, in thought, word and deed, we can only respond means that it cannot capture the sense of creativity and openness that Vattimo associates with our situation today. Moreover, Michel Serres has sagely warned against assuming that the problems inherent within an ontology of substance can be solved simply by replacing it with an ontology of relation.[8]

Closely linked with the idea of relation is that of locality. As the universal structures of metaphysics break up and pluralism emerges, the whole spatial sense of communication and interpretation needs to be reconsidered. The local cannot be designated as a region of the universal, but taking relation seriously means that neither are local elements within the plurality entirely self-contained principalities; a different relation between locales, and between the local and the wider context that comprises them, in turn means that one requires a new sense of what constitutes the local itself. In a sense, this brings us back to the problem of identity, this time precisely as a problematic and developmental structure. It is fair to say that phenomenology and hermeneutics have contributed hugely to our understanding of this question via the idea of horizonality. However, if one returns to the basic phenomenological sense of horizonality, it tends to encourage an articulation of difference as an engagement with the absolutely other; that is, with what lies beyond the horizon constitutive of the meaning embedded in my existence.[9] Such an idea would not be helpful to hermeneutics as Vattimo conceives it; yet on the other hand, moving away from the rigorous phenomenological idea of horizon toward something more partial and open leaves the idea diluted into something little more than "context," a term that offers little to the attempt to rethink the questions at stake for Vattimo, and one moreover that lends itself easily to the forms with which Vattimo deliberately breaks. It therefore seems to me that the sense of locality that Vattimo's work encourages us to address cannot be easily resolved by appealing to the idea of horizonality.

The final issue I want to raise here is that of power. With the breakdown of metaphysical principles there occurs what Habermas has called a crisis of legitimacy that leaves no means to adjudicate effectively between competing claims arising from the elements of the emerging pluralism. In this situation there is clearly a danger that a "rogue" agent, at any level from the individual to the state, may initiate conduct that is at least coercive and at worst explicitly violent, and that by doing so it may colonize the spaces that Vattimo sees being freed up in late modernity. In effect, such agents, and the forces that work through them, would begin to roll back the changes that have occurred as a consequence of nihilism, reasserting authoritarian structures akin to those that characterized metaphysics. It might be argued that this should not be too great a concern, since if it is old-fashioned forms of power that we are concerned about, we already have the means to recognize them, and to analyze and resist them, both politically, and through the work of interpretation itself. However, in resisting old forms of power, we have to be careful not to reassert old forms of power ourselves. For example, human rights are problematic in this respect precisely by virtue of their appeal to universal human characteristics. As the idiom of universality is left behind, one therefore needs to forge a new means to give expression to the way in which what one is and what one can be are shaped for better or for worse through local practices, communications, distributions, and disputes. From this we can see that the problems of relations and locality are very much tied up with that of power, and it seems unlikely that one could adequately resolve the latter without dealing with the others first. On his part, Vattimo approaches the question of power in terms of violence and authoritarianism, suggesting that we take our lead from the weakening of metaphysics and resist them wherever they occur. To be sure, this provides a useful clear indication of a direction for ethical thought to explore, without insisting on principles that directly govern our actions (a move that would reproduce the form of thought he has pronounced untenable). As such, it fits well with the vision of hermeneutics as an essentially free and transformative practice.

Authoritarianism can take many forms, however, from mild coercion to physical violence, and one has therefore to consider whether we really know what it is that we are trying to avoid, and when we have succeeded in doing so. The simplest option is to rely on the attestations of those who claim to have suffered malpractice, but there are clear problems with doing this. First of all, it promotes a culture in which victimhood confers a certain authority of its own. Although an old idea, no doubt with roots in a variety of cultural phenomena, it is also one that seems to have gained considerable ground recently. One of the difficulties associated with it is its reliance on, and surreptitious reinforcement of, quite traditional forms of identity. To take the most obvious example, the prohibition of a particular cultural or religious practice may be construed as an attack on the identity of the individual or community in question. Less directly, even if one sets aside the essentialism implicit in such an example and construes the prohibition as a constraint placed on a given practice of interpretation, it still too easily allows for the association of what has been done with a fixed standard that has to be protected. Of course, this has little or nothing to do with what Vattimo intends, for he is concerned much less with the "truths" produced by interpretation, than with the practice of interpretation itself. Yet Vattimo's emphasis on the reduction of violence makes it difficult to see where the practice of interpretation itself is unfairly constrained, as opposed to merely shaped by its relations to others and the demands arising from their existence, because the distinction between coercion and the constraints arising from the relation between diverse localities is not easily drawn. In short, "violence" is a category at once too general and too inflexible.

The impetus in Vattimo's work is toward the freedom continually to reinterpret existence, and insofar as the emphasis shifts to the protection of a given interpretation the originality of his philosophical work is diminished. But the protection of a freedom to reinterpret existence is hard to sustain in separation from the freedom to maintain a given interpretation of existence; as just one example of this, the practice of interpretation associated with a secularized Christianity may easily be characterized as an adherence to Western democratic ideals. In view of the need to avoid any retrenchment to a fixed position, it may seem that the last thing one needs is an ontological thesis, but in fact this suspicion rests on the assumption that ontology necessarily brings with it the kind of principles whose decline Vattimo has justifiably celebrated. In fact, if one were to develop an account of what is happening at the ontological level when interpretation transforms the conditions of existence, an account that begins with an understanding of the dynamic processes by which local groupings (cultural, historical, and philosophical, as well as geographical) form, interrelate, and evolve, then it may be possible to approach the question of violence and power in a way that leaves the emphasis firmly on the practice of transformation, and which may even discriminate between greater and lesser offenses without gauging them as forced departures from an identity or fixed norm that has to be defended.

An important consequence of moving toward such an account is that the ethical force driving interpretation is no longer pitted against ontology as a point of resistance, and therefore the relation between ethics and ontology becomes far closer than the historical tendency to align ontology with metaphysics allows. There are possibilities of this kind that one can pursue via the work of philosophers such as Michel Serres, Michel Foucault, Gilles Deleuze, and others, whose engagement with ontology draws on the influence of discourses such as materialism, atomism, and mathematics; and moreover does so precisely as an engagement with the historical conditions that have brought us to the present moment. In this respect, and speaking broadly, their work is entirely consistent with Vattimo's conception of hermeneutics as a radically historical transformative practice of freedom.

Notes

1. Martin Heidegger, *Being and Time*, trans. John Macquarrie and Edward Robinson (Oxford: Blackwell, 1980), §4.
2. Ibid., 62.
3. Ibid., 310.
4. Martin Heidegger, *The Metaphysical Foundations of Logic*, trans. Michael Heim (Bloomington: Indiana University Press, 1984), 135, 166. See also Martin Heidegger, trans. Walter Brogan and Peter Warnek (Bloomington: Indiana University Press, 1995), 44, where Heidegger shows how ontological questioning has to address itself not to the thing in movement, but to movement as such, and thereby to movement as a way of being.
5. The difficulty here is in reflecting the ontological structure, where movement is the relation between all parts, in the inevitably serial form of a practice of interpretation. The two must, as far as possible, be congruent, or else thinking fails to repeat the movement of transcendence, and therefore fails to bring to light the event of ontological difference appropriately.
6. I have explored this idea further in the following papers: David Webb, "Thinking as Mortals: Heidegger and the Finitude of Philosophical Existence," *Philosophy Today* 45 (Fall 2001): 211–224; "Continuity and Difference in Heidegger's *Sophist*," *The Southern Journal of Philosophy* 38, 1 (Spring 2000): 145–169.
7. Vattimo writes: "An ethics of finitude tries to keep faith with the discover that one's own provenance is 'located,' in a way always and insuperably finite, without forgetting the pluralistic implications of this discovery. I go to church with the saints (*santi*), and to the tavern with the 'guys' (*fanti*), as we say in Italian, and I can never delude myself that I am really standing somewhere else, somewhere loftier" (NE 44).
8. Michel Serres, *Genesis*, trans. Geneviève James and James Nielson (Ann Arbor: University of Michigan Press, 1995), 3–4.
9. This is what we find, for example, in Levinas' articulation of alterity on the basis of a phenomenological understanding of intentionality and sense.

4

Weak Thought and the Recovery of Reason

ROBERT T. VALGENTI

In the 1980s Gianni Vattimo introduced the idea that hermeneutics had become a *koine* or general idiom of Western culture.[1] Vattimo's claim is neither theoretical nor descriptive; rather, as much of his work over the past two decades bears out, Vattimo's statement reads more like a diagnosis and prescription. Recovery from this illness requires, above all, an assessment of philosophy's role within the recovery so that it can "redefine itself in a more coherent and rigorous way, rediscovering its original inspiration (namely the Heideggerian meditation on metaphysics and its destiny)."[2] And while this recovery embraces the "irrational" elements of the history of metaphysics interpreted as the occurrence of nihilism, Vattimo somewhat surprisingly declares that "the truth is rather that hermeneutics can defend its theoretical validity only to the precise degree that the interpretative reconstruction of history is a rational activity—in which, that is, one can argue, and not only intuit, *fühlen, einfühlen* etc." (BI 107). I will argue that Gianni Vattimo's philosophical hermeneutics—what he has called "weak thought" and more recently "the ontology of actuality"—not only entails the recovery of its rational justification, but more specifically includes the overlooked and even dismissed inheritance of Kant's critical philosophy.

The Self-Confutation of Hermeneutics

As Vattimo often notes, hermeneutics in its broadest formulation is based on the rather weak and somewhat problematic premise that there are, as Nietzsche claims in *The Will To Power*, no facts, only interpretations. Within this field of thought one finds not only the three pillars of post-Heideggerian hermeneutics—Gadamer, Ricoeur, and Pareyson—but a range of figures including but certainly not limited to Habermas, Apel, Rorty, Taylor, Derrida, and Levinas (BI 1). Yet, despite the quantity of figures engaged in forms of thinking broadly defined as hermeneutic, one of the undeniable consequences of the general diffusion of the hermeneutic paradigm is that the philosophical arguments presented to defend its theoretical validity are often considered "irrationalistic" by critics and supporters alike. Without question, it seems that for a *philosophical* hermeneutics one of the most basic requirements would be a valid and persuasive argument that justifies its centrality and pervasiveness in contemporary thought and that engages and refutes the rationality of other forms of discourse rather than merely dismiss them as "metaphysical," "violent," or "dogmatic."

If one accepts irrationalism as hermeneutics' sole exit strategy from metaphysics, one is left with two rather unsavory options: the first simply replaces traditional, metaphysical rationalism with irrationalism, imposing a new foundation in the name of overturning all rational foundations; the second, which lowers rationalism to the level of an interpretation and thus reduces all possible theoretical paradigms to competing conceptions of reality, dissolves into the impotency of relativism while nonetheless retaining, albeit tacitly, a strong metaphysical notion of the "reality" that rests forever beyond their theoretical grasp. Despite his rather explicit efforts to distance weak thought from these two hermeneutic strategies that retain the logic of metaphysics, Vattimo is nonetheless often accused of irrationalism. In response to such charges, my goal is not only to demonstrate how Vattimo's recovery of rationality is essential to the justification of hermeneutics, but that hermeneutics cannot be *philosophical* unless it presents justifiable reasons for its claim to be, in a weakened and nondogmatic way, *the* philosophy of late modernity.

In her introduction to Vattimo's *Vocazione e resposabilità del filosofo*,[3] Franca D'Agostini provides an instructive outline of the structure of weak thought's hermeneutic self-reflexivity. The first level—that "there are no truths, only interpretations"—can be equated with Nietzsche's incomplete nihilist and is nothing more than a form of relativism immured in the either/or dilemma mentioned above. The second level, equated with Nietzsche's "accomplished nihilist," makes a critical-transcendental assertion that even the aforementioned claim "is only an interpretation." Such an interpretation is valid only within a historical-ethical response to the end of metaphysics as the weakening of Being; but, this is precisely the point where Vattimo's philosophical commitments seem blurred, since this second assertion depends on an interpretation of the history of metaphysics that stands or falls according to the degree to which it can deliver on its promise to have moved beyond dogmatic claims. There has to be some basis for the legitimacy of this reading beyond pragmatic preference and beyond metaphysical speculation. D'Agostini identifies this third level by stating, in relation to the first two theses, that "thinking this self-confuting game is unavoidable" (VRF 15). We now have a new description of the first level, but one that is construed as a historical-linguistic event and carries with it a responsibility more akin to a moral imperative than a descriptive one. Not only are we caught in this game, but we are obliged to recognize this dialectical movement as a response to the sendings and the "patrimony of ideas" that constitute the inherited history of philosophy. If there is a principle of hermeneutics in the weakened sense of a principle that replaces the strong notion of an *arche* with one attenuated both logically and historically, it cannot *not* be interpreted precisely because it is a response to the violence of metaphysical thinking.

Vattimo explains in *Nihilism and Emancipation* that hermeneutics, in order to twist free from the violence of metaphysical thinking, should be reduced neither to "the letting-loose of the conflict of interpretations" nor to "anti-foundationalism." Rather, since both positions are *interpretations*, "then like all interpretations it must strive to articulate, develop, and advance arguments for itself" (NE 94). Hermeneutics entails a philosophy of history "that views hermeneutics as the end of a 'nihilistic' process, in which metaphysical Being, meaning violence, consumes itself" (NE 94). Nonetheless, this interpretation of Being as the history of its weakening retains traces of the rationality it attempts to overcome. Vattimo, referring to Rorty's distinction between a Kantian *lignée* and a Hegelian *lignée* in contemporary thinking, explains that the historical guiding thread of weak thought is markedly Hegelian in character (NE 88). I suggest, however, that the possibility of that guiding thread emerges from a response to Kant's critical philosophy that strives to constitute a hermeneutic principle, and perhaps even to vindicate philosophy in the face of the *koine*.

The False "Siberian Dilemma" of Hermeneutics

If there is a principle for philosophical hermeneutics, it should provide a suitable basis for an interpretation of the history of metaphysics while not itself falling back into those forms of thinking that this interpretation brings into question. Critics of Vattimo's weak thought grant it, at best, the sort of rhetorical force that might be convincing in a social realm where truths are often fuzzy and human experience neither can nor should be reduced to quantifiable data. At worst, weak thought betrays the rigor of philosophy by basing its claims on preferences that, in the estimation of Paolo Flores D'Arcais, are wholly metaphysical and could only be "commanded by a political purpose,"[4] even if it is an anti-authoritarian one. D'Arcais calls the unavoidable theoretical contradictions inherent in Vattimo's position a "Siberian dilemma,"[5] which in hermeneutic terms states that "either there exists a criterion by which to choose one interpretation over another, one that avoids anarchic confusion but supplies a criterion that is (metaphysical) truth and not interpretation, or this criterion does not exist, and consequently everything is really interpretation (including this affirmation), but unavoidably (in its turn a truth, above all!), there is anarchic confusion."[6] This criticism, in its most basic form, is the critique waged against any form of relativism that takes itself to be definitive, and therefore, something other than relative. By D'Arcais' account, Vattimo does offer "proof" that hermeneutics is *the* philosophy of late modernity: as he quotes from *Beyond Interpretation*, the proof amounts to "'a history . . . perhaps also in the sense of 'fable' or myth, in that it presents itself as an interpretation (whose claim to validity is such as will even present itself as a competing interpretation that belies it),' the hermeneutic-nihilistic interpretation of modernity."[7] In the end, D'Arcais suggests that the only way to make rational sense of a purely narrative and rhetorical proof would be through a total renunciation of Being.

What D'Arcais presents as a refutation of Vattimo's position is, however, a false dilemma, one that erroneously presumes a clash between two absolute claims, neither of which Vattimo asserts. In fact, the irresolvable dilemma of hermeneutics can be formulated in the manner presented by D'Arcais only if one has already presupposed a certain knowledge of Being, that is, if one has definitively rejected any knowledge of Being or even affirmed Being as something knowable through merely ontic criteria—in either case, a level of certitude that is the mark of metaphysical thinking rather than a response to it. In this way, the problem that confronts and gives rise to philosophical hermeneutics in the first place is never even recognized as a problem at all. The philosophical "rigor" of weak thought, if one wants to call it that, is precisely its reluctance to accept any foundation or criterion as absolute and unquestionable. This does not mean, however, that weak thought rejects all foundations; rather, it points to a situation where foundations are inherited from a tradition but never accepted as truly foundational, since the taking up and appropriation of those historical foundations not only transforms them, but illustrates that foundations, as historical, are transformable.

By insisting that one renounce Being, D'Arcais has unwittingly and erroneously transformed the hermeneutic dilemma into a hermeneutic antinomy: both claims—the "sure criterion" and the "anarchic confusion"—are set forth as logically possible but mutually exclusive theories that, in D'Arcais' estimation, would aim to adequately correspond to "the way things are." But the dilemma only makes sense as a dilemma if one presupposes, in either case, the logic of truth as correspondence—the logic that hermeneutics seeks to (re-)interpret rather than overcome or affirm definitively. Yet, even if Vattimo is innocent in the face of D'Arcais' charge that weak thought is merely a political choice—which would reduce it to an ideology—and even if Vattimo neither explicitly invokes a criterion for interpretation nor proclaims that the perpetual conflict of interpretations is the best we can do, one can still argue that Vattimo has yet to formulate an adequate justification for the position of philosophical hermeneutics. Vattimo's defense of hermeneutics requires that we accept a rationale that not only moves us dialectically between the two poles of the supposed "Siberian dilemma," but also critically undermines the metaphysical logic required to accept it as a dilemma in the first place. Thus, while D'Arcais encourages the complete renunciation of Being, Vattimo affords us the possibility, less skeptical and ultimately critical, of still *thinking* Being, however weakened, according to a hermeneutic principle. One might even say that, as a response to the inheritance of metaphysics, one chooses a principle from out of the possibility of an "archic" confusion.

The Reconstruction of Rationality

Only by clarifying what Vattimo has in mind when he invokes the term "rationality" can one determine how and why this rationality develops along distinctly Hegelian and Kantian lines. Vattimo's clearest and most emphatic argument for the reconstruction of a hermeneutic rationality can be found in the second appendix to *Beyond Interpretation*. In this short essay, titled "The Reconstruction of Rationality," Vattimo contends that despite the charge of "irrationalism" often leveled against hermeneutics—historically from the camps of historicist rationalism and neo-positivist scientism, and more recently (and generally) from those who maintain that hermeneutics rejects argumentation for a more narrative way of philosophizing—it can and must develop its own rationality so it not only rebuts the accusations of irrationalism, but also reconsiders the inseparable link between hermeneutics and modernity.

Vattimo's case for hermeneutic rationality takes the existence, and the persistent dangers, of a thoroughgoing hermeneutic *koine* to their source in the two most pervasive forms of post-Heideggerian thinking—Derridian deconstruction and Gadamerian hermeneutic ontology. Taking his cue from Richard Rorty's distinction between hermeneutics and epistemology, Vattimo argues that the general charge of irrationalism points to hermeneutics' inability to offer justifications that explain why its nonargumentative aestheticism is preferable to other ways of thinking. No matter whether one follows Derrida's grammatological turn away from rational argumentation or Gadamer's critique of aesthetic consciousness, Vattimo's warning is that either form of hermeneutics represents a betrayal of its own premises and a fall back into metaphysical thinking. Yet, if one follows Vattimo's recommendation to think the relation between the phenomenologico-analytic critique of aesthetic consciousness and the historico-reconstructive understanding of the development of an interpretative philosophy of existence, and thereby radicalize the basic premises of *Truth and Method,* one can "recognize that hermeneutics as theory can only be coherently legitimized by demonstrating that it is in its turn nothing more than a correct hermeneutic interpretation of a message from the past, or in any case from 'somewhere else' to which, in some degree, it itself always already belongs—since this belonging is the very condition for the possibility of receiving messages" (BI 105). Specifically, a hermeneutic rationality will offer an interpretation of the history of philosophy itself that relies neither on a strong, unchanging foundation, nor on a merely aesthetic choice that could be reduced to taste or mere preference. In more positive terms, hermeneutics can avoid metaphysical dogmatism—whether in the sense of an absolute or unchanging truth, or as a form of radical skepticism that accepts the sheer multiplicity of conceptual schemes—only by accepting and interpreting (which is always a challenging and a gathering) the inheritance sent to it as the end of metaphysics and the occurrence of nihilism.

Vattimo states explicitly that the key to this positive, hermeneutic argumentation is "ontology" in the Heideggerian sense that belongs to the "destiny of Being." On the one hand, hermeneutics must let go of the idea that it, as a theory, can correspond to Being in the sense of how things "really are" for us historically and right now. Hermeneutics is only an interpretation that serves not as a phenomenological access to the things themselves, but as "a response to a message, or as the interpretative articulation of its own belonging to a tra-dition [*tra-dizione*], *Über-lieferung*" (BI 108). And yet, on the other hand, this interpretative articulation is not merely one conceptual scheme among others—existing concurrently or arranged in a historical process—none of which, in the end, bear any ontological weight, because thinking in this way would preserve a metaphysical conception of Being as something beyond our interpretations of it. Rather, interpretation is ontological precisely because it is a moment within this destiny and also an author of this destiny through its "reconstruction of the destiny-tradition from which it arises" (BI 108). The validity of hermeneutics therefore relies on a logic that flows from the basic acceptance of the principle that there are no facts, only interpretations. Furthermore, the soundness of this premise can only be argued through a series of interpretations because to verify it in a manner familiar to the positive sciences—one that requires facts—would already require a rejection of the premise one is attempting to verify.

The rationality of hermeneutics therefore "consists in the fact that, essentially involved in a process (into which we are always-already 'thrown') we always-already know, at least to a certain extent, where we are going and how we must go there" (BI 109). There is something of Meno's paradox here, but rather than recollect a lost *arche* that can serve as the touchstone for our reason, we must rather guide our thinking according to the principle handed down to us—even if this is a tacit affirmation of its premise. What safeguards this process is the particular claim made by the principle, one that demands that we interpret it as a response to the weakening of factuality. Based on this principle, there is no truth outside of this process, and rationality "is simply the guiding thread that can be comprehended by listening attentively to the messages of the *Schickung*" (BI 109). Hermeneutics, as both a "consequence" and a "confutation" of the modernity that produces it, must argue persuasively why its principle—the response to the history of Being interpreted as the occurrence of nihilism—is not merely something we accept without any other options, but actively choose through its interpretation. That one can confute the most basic principle of hermeneutics is tacit "proof" not only of the validity of the rationality of hermeneutics, but of the soundness of its initial principle.

If hermeneutics takes this principle of interpretation—in both senses of the genitive—as a "foundation," or something like a foundation, it must accept that principle formation, and likewise principle destruction through critical interpretation, will be the primary task of the thinker who realizes that for hermeneutics "there is no attempt here to rediscover authenticity, to affirm a right exclusive to the name or brand, or to correspond as faithfully as possible to the original intention of the author. It is simply a matter of not laying aside a history of ideas that looks as though it could be more fruitful than it is at present" (BI 2). One could add that hermeneutics becomes specifically "philosophical" when it is no longer concerned with interpretation in its technical application or as a means of verification, but takes up the issue of interpretation as an authentic point of departure for the theoretical problems surrounding the examination of its own principles and foundations. In this way, Vattimo's understanding of tradition, and the role it plays in the justification of hermeneutics, is much more positive than those variations that would reject the argumentative claims of historicism and scientism outright; in fact, as I hope to show, Vattimo's reconstruction of hermeneutics' rationality entails not only the development and transformation of the threads of historicism that develop in the wake of Hegel, but more importantly and less recognizably, the threads of scientism that emerge from the shadow of Kant.

Hermeneutics and Dialectic

Even in its earliest formulations Vattimo's weak thought betrays its Hegelian origins by engaging the problem of radical historicism. Negatively, Vattimo responds to the crisis of historicism by illustrating how a radically historicized understanding can nonetheless avoid being reduced to the history it inherits (a history that grants it "objective" understanding). Positively, Vattimo preserves and develops a dialectical movement of thinking that invigorates and perpetuates the hermeneutic circle of interpretation so that a transcendental foundation of whatever sort is not made absolute and necessary. Both of these movements argue for an understanding of hermeneutics that demonstrates how "the freedom of interpretation is anything but arbitrary and brings with it risk and responsibility" (BI 2). Nowhere is this more evident than in Vattimo's writings from the late 1970s and early 1980s—most notably the essays collected in *The Adventure of Difference* and in his contribution to *Il pensiero debole*.[8]

In the first chapter of *The Adventure of Difference* Vattimo argues that dialectical reason provides a much more suitable response to the problem of the "historical malady" set forth in Nietzsche's second *Un-*

timely Meditation than does the infinite horizon of interpretation set forth by Gadamer's understanding of hermeneutic ontology.[9] The historical malady illustrates Nietzsche's claim that excessive historiographical awareness and an obsession with the science of things past leads to an inability to create new history.[10] What Nietzsche proposes is an equal balance between the unhistorical forces of life and historiographical awareness, a "dialectic" of the nonhistorical element (unconscious) and its rational articulation that also be read as a vision of history as "a dialectic between 'life' and 'form,'" such that any definition of a horizon is possible both as an act of forgetting and at the same time as an act of interior rational articulation; every historical configuration amounts to forgetting inasmuch as it leaves outside its own sphere all 'the rest' of history, and moreover forgets that it is itself surrounded by darkness" (AD 15). Nietzsche ultimately takes his critique beyond the *Untimely Meditations*, constructing in his later works an actual response to the dichotomy between finitude and totalization where one is capable of living the unity of doing and knowing, and "going beyond the historical malady and historical 'consciousness' solely *in so far as one establishes the possibility of a history that is not malady*, a history that does not have as its motor the gulf between *in sich* and *für sich*" (AD 33). In contrast, the response of Gadamerian hermeneutic ontology to this malady fails precisely because, as if one were to accept the anarchic confusion as corresponding to reality, it could not move beyond the distinction between the finitude of existence and the infinity of interpretations, the distinction between doing and knowing—it forgets to treat the split between doing and knowing *as a problem* (AD 30–31). In this regard, Vattimo contends that Sartre's thinking in *Search for a Method* marks a much more fruitful development of Nietzsche's insights than Gadamer's precisely because it can conceive of a future that is not a malady, or in the terms of hermeneutic ontology, it does not understand the infinity of interpretations and the finitude of man to be the only (and thus absolute) response to a Hegelian notion of totalization and the end of history. Sartre responds directly to the problem of "overcoming metaphysics" with a theory or conceptual scheme that takes itself as a universal paradigm or even accepts its weakening into a general *koine* of contemporary society.

Vattimo's positive response to the limits of historicism is closely tied to his understanding of the concept of "difference" and its development in the later work of Heidegger. In the essay "Dialettica, differenza, pensiero debole," Vattimo outlines the shape of a positive response to historicism by placing his own thinking in relation to dialectic and difference, two major themes of post-Kantian thought, in a way that is best described through Heidegger's concept of *Verwindung*—the deviation-distortion, and the recovering/resuming/reentering of the history of metaphysics. In order to begin such a discourse without the imposition of metaphysical biases, Vattimo contends that we must begin—in the manner discussed above—with a hermeneutic principle or "foundation" that is a response to a historical sending.

Vattimo claims that Sartre's *Critique of Dialectical Reason* is a Kantian critique in the sense that it sets out to clarify the conditions for the possibility of constituting the point of view of the totality (and not of ideology). While it is an effective foil to the presumed universality of Gadamer's hermeneutic ontology, the problem is that Sartre's resolution to the problem—that totality is achieved only in the conscience of the group in fusion, the revolutionary group in action where the individual and group form one—is not definitive, and in the end, becomes a new form of domination that is open to the same revolutionary action that brought the former one down. Vattimo then turns to other thinkers of dialectic—Benjamin, Adorno, Bloch—who in reality are thinkers of the dissolution of dialectic and argues that the dialectical approach to the problem of alienation, as it cannot control its dissolutive tendency, fails to criticize adequately its ideas of totality and reappropriation and thus falls back into metaphysical thinking (PD 17–18).

Vattimo introduces the philosophy of difference (that in its most radical form is Heidegger) into this climate of dissolution. The thinking of difference can be understood as the inheritance and radicalization of the dissolutive tendency of dialectic, such that reappropriation is no longer associated with simple presence; rather, "the weakening of (the notion of) Being, the explicit self-giving of its temporal essence (even and above all: ephemeralness, birth-death, faded trans-mission, the accumulation of past relics) profoundly influences the way of conceiving thought and Dasein that is its 'subject'" (PD 20). Both Being and subject are weakened and transformed, but neither is lost nor absolutized. This new ontology is not just a philosophy of difference, but also remembers dialectic, and as such is *verwunden*—that is, thinks the truth of Being intended as *Überlieferung* and *Ge-schick*. In this sense, it is synonymous with *An-denken*, the other and more common term through which Heidegger, in his later works, designates thought after metaphysics as the thinking that never makes Being present but remembers it as already "gone" (PD 22). The reconstruction of dialectic, now radicalized and differentiated in a new constellation of terms—*Verwindung, An-denken, pietas*—illustrates how "the transcendental, that which makes possible every experience in the world, is transience" (PD 23).

In *Verwindung*, Vattimo avoids the collapse of knowing and doing, theory and practice, into an unproblematic, philosophical unity: "Both the content—the traits of metaphysical being re-thought and unfounded—and also the form of thought as *Verwindung*—a legitimization that does not call itself to the structure of being and not even to a logical law of history, but to a 'taking action,' however in some sense still historicized—are ways in which weak thought assumes and follows the heredity of dialectic united with difference" (PD 23). One could argue, nonetheless, that these more Hegelian elements in Vattimo's thinking favor the theoretical content of philosophical hermeneutics—its metaphysical inheritance, the history of philosophy, and so on—over the form of its thinking, and in particular, its ability to provide a foundation for its theoretical validity. The truth of hermeneutics, if we proceed no further than the positive joining of dialectic and difference, can find justification only in virtue of a *pietas*—only in the name of an irreducible respect for monuments and tradition can one talk at one and the same time of transience and duration in the transmission of an inheritance. In response to the accusations of hermeneutics' traditionalism, Vattimo contends that there is not one *pietas*, but *pietates* that are historically determined and consist in the development of truth on the basis of persuasive actions. Yet, here we once again move dangerously close to the "anarchic confusion" of the conflict of interpretations whose validity is based on rhetorical or political force. Dialectic brings Vattimo to the verge of a remetaphysization of its guiding principle that there are not facts, only interpretations. And while Vattimo's historical awareness ensures that the content of hermeneutics will always be an inherited one, what ensures that this inheritance will be interpreted rather than merely accepted as is?

Hermeneutics and Critique

The lineage of Kantian thought in Vattimo's work does not present itself as distinctly as its Hegelian influences. Nonetheless, if weak thought wants to establish its theoretical validity through argument, it must contend with the possibility that its dialectic movement—the inevitability of interpretation's self-confuting game—could be taken (or even misunderstood) as an absolute, stable structure. Such a relapse into metaphysics is avoided if the condition for the possibility of the movement between the first hermeneutic position (there are no facts, only interpretations) and the second hermeneutic position (even this is an interpretation) is understood as a critical-transcendental moment. Not only would the descriptive (and thus metaphysical) force of the first position be removed, but it would be removed by producing a principle that carries both logical and historical force in the sense of a "transient transcendental" mentioned above. While the dialectical and differing movement of *Verwindung* ensures that the content of philosophical hermeneutics will be an ever-changing historical inheritance, the critical principle maintains, in the only way possible, the nihilistic trajectory of philosophy away from absolute assertions and universal truths. Thus, negatively, one can say that the critical element of Vattimo's thinking, as shown in Vattimo's rather careful critique of science, responds to the accusation that the principle of hermeneutics is nothing more than a descriptive assertion of the way things are. Positively, the critical element of Vattimo's thinking establishes a new sort of "foundation" for hermeneutics, one that could follow the careful justification of principles set forth in Kant's method of deduction.

One of the consistent threads in Vattimo's thinking is his recognition of Heidegger's thesis that the truths of science are "secondary" level truths, always dependent on a prior, ontological opening. This stance forms part of a much broader critique of the history of metaphysics in which Being has been reduced to beings, the effects of which are most noticeable in the rise of techno-science and the effective rationalization of the world in the *Ge-stell*. Given that over-rationalization is, for Heidegger, *the* crisis of modernity, it seems likely that any attempt to "overcome" or think beyond metaphysics would include a rejection, or at least a severe limiting, of the dominance of rationality. But as Vattimo makes clear in his understanding of our relation to this history as a *Verwindung*, there is never a simple overcoming, but a recovery-distortion-acceptance of those rationales that have led to the *Ge-stell*. Kant plays a central role in this history, and as Vattimo often portrays it, philosophy after Kant "reduces the realm of truth to the realm of the experimental verifiability of science" (VRF 55). This somewhat simplistic caricature of Kant's contribution to modern philosophy, while widely accepted in post-Heideggerian thinking, overlooks the radical and undoubtedly anti-foundational contributions of Kant's critical philosophy, and in particular, the *Critique of Pure Reason*. As "thrown" beings, we can never stand outside of the experience of a collective history; thus, the response to the destiny of Being cannot *not* use the rationality of modernity in its critique of its own history. Recovering and accepting the inheritance of Kantian critique thus includes not only the possibility of rational argumentation, but more importantly, the formal circularity of a reason that critiques itself because it can never take leave of itself entirely.

While Kant is, in Vattimo's estimation, complicit in the history of metaphysics and the emergence of the *Ge-stell*, he is not excluded from the possibility of the recovery and reconstruction of the rationality of hermeneutics. In fact, as Vattimo argues in *Beyond Interpretation*, the general *koine* of hermeneutics owes much to the resurgence of interest, on the part of the various human sciences, in the precategorial lifeworld as a means of radically critiquing, and ultimately rejecting, the privilege enjoyed by the positive sciences. But Vattimo also contends that if "hermeneutics is presented in these terms as an up-to-date version—in a sense less idealistic, Kantian or transcendentalist than linguistic and communicative—of the phenomenological problematic of the *Lebenswelt*, it risks betraying its own premises" and will be unable "to differentiate itself from a general and often relativistic philosophy of culture" (BI 20). For Vattimo, the response to the "first oppressing flash of *Ereignis*" also includes "an attentiveness to the transformations that science and technology, as determinant factors in modernity, 'bring' to the meaning of Being" (BI 24). Philosophical hermeneutics breaks from the traditional (and ultimately metaphysical) reaction of the human sciences to the ever-threatening reach of the *Ge-stell* and instead initiates a critique of the techno-scientific world that "is aimed, if anything, to aid it in a recognition of its own nihilistic meaning and to take it up as a guiding thread for judgments, choices, and the orientation of individual and collective life" (BI 26). These Kantian elements in Vattimo's thought do not, however, lead us to a Habermasian ethics of communication, which could provide no sufficient "foundation" for hermeneutics (TS 119). Rather they point to the specific way that Kant's critical philosophy responded to the untenable foundations that dogmatism and skepticism constructed for metaphysics.

Critique distinguishes itself from both dogmatism and skepticism in that it does not claim insight into truth or an object so as to assert or deny something, but investigates and justifies the principles that serve as the conditions for the possibility of experience, human freedom, and the meaning of a totality. As such, it rightly serves as a propadeutic or preparation to any possible metaphysics that endeavors to offer up a "theory" or "claim" regarding such experience. Moreover, as Kant notes, critique is also an essential part of metaphysics properly conceived, and so critique always functions as the critical metaphysics of metaphysics, placing the claim of any newly found metaphysics under the same self-reflective scrutiny that has been directed at less circumspective forms of thinking—a metaphysics where no one foundation, but foundations in general, are brought into question.[11]

Reason can never fully divorce itself from the history that includes its errors and its corrections; yet, reason is also unable to return to itself purely theoretically as reason alone. To accept the Kantian inheritance *historically* requires us to place his critical philosophy within the history of Being, a history that illustrates how foundations are questioned, how principles are compromised, and how to manage (to recover-accept-distort in the sense of *Verwindung*) the archic confusion. Kant's transcendental deduction, which sought to provide necessary principles where no real principles could be established with absolute certainty, and "whose transcendental foundation already places particular truths . . . on a secondary level" (BI 88), provides us with a model for the sort of rational justification that Vattimo contends is necessary for philosophical hermeneutics. Kant borrows the method of deduction from the legal practices where the use of an inheritance is justified by reconstructing and defending a lineage that grants the possessor the right to make such a claim.[12] In order to provide rational and coherent justification for the employment of certain concepts and ideas at a time when any solid foundation, or the appeal to an absolute, can no longer sustain itself, the truth of a hermeneutic principle must be argued through what I propose to call a *hermeneutic deduction* that seeks to justify the right to a particular possession (in this case, the inheritance of the principle that there are no facts, only interpretations) when the origin of its inheritance—Being—is not and cannot simply be made present. Just as a transcendental deduction in Kant seeks to legitimize the *a priori* conditions for the experience of nature and moral life, a hermeneutic deduction seeks to justify the logico-historical conditions of the onset of nihilism and the weakening of Being that characterize the end of metaphysics. By listening and responding to the destiny of Being—its prior, present, and future interpretations—hermeneutics reconstructs its own rationality from out of the archic confusion of its own past.[13]

This argumentative direction does not emerge from, but rather pushes us toward a moral or ethical imperative for hermeneutics that is voiced specifically as a call—a sending, *Ge-schick*, *Über-lieferung*—and is constructed *a posteriori* from an inheritance that we cannot *not* interpret. That is, if one accepts the principle of hermeneutics in its weakened and distorted form, "it would appear that we really have no choice except to set about constructing an ethics around our finitude" (NE 43). To reject this call is to reject the principle of hermeneutics and the freedom that flows from it. The freedom of interpretation, which as Vattimo contends always entails risk and responsibility, is therefore not a principle that is merely inherited as a call from the past. In the archic confusion of competing principles, it must also be defended and justified through a hermeneutic deduction, the very act of interpretation that stakes its claim on the destiny of Being and its nihilistic outcome.

Notes

1. Gianni Vattimo, "Ermeneutica nuova koiné" in EI 38–48.
2. Vattimo, "Ermeneutica nuova koiné," 42.
3. Franca D'Agostini, "Dialettica, differenza, ermeneutica, nichilismo: Le ragioni forti del pensiero debole," in VRF 11–44.
4. Paolo Flores D'Arcais, "Hermeneutics as the Primacy of Politics," in *Weakening Philosophy: Essays in Honour of Gianni Vattimo*, ed. Santiago Zabala (Montreal: McGill-Queen's University Press, 2007), 250.
5. D'Arcais explains in a note that a "Siberian dilemma" refers to the particular dangers faced by Russian soldiers: "in the event that the ice breaks and you fall into the icy waters, you die if you are not pulled out within four minutes; but, if they do pull you out in time, the freezing air will kill you in two minutes;" see D'Arcais, "Hermeneutics as the Primacy of Politics," 228.
6. Ibid., 261.
7. Ibid., 262.
8. Gianni Vattimo, "Dialettica, differenza, pensiero debole," in PD 12–28.
9. Although I cannot fully discuss the scope of Gadamer's hermeneutic ontology here, Vattimo grants it three major elements, all of which relate to the notion of a "hermeneutic circle": 1) the rejection of "objectivity" as an ideal of historical knowledge; 2) the extension of the hermeneutical model to all knowledge; and 3) the linguistic nature of Being. See AD 18–19.
10. Friedrich Nietzsche, *Untimely Meditations*, Part II, "On the Uses and Disadvantages of History for Life" (1874), trans. R. J. Hollingdale (Cambridge: Cambridge University Press, 1983), 120.
11. In this regard, my understanding of Kant's method is greatly indebted to the work of Pietro Chiodi. In particular, see Chiodi, *La deduzione nell'opera di Kant* (Turin: Taylor Editore, 1961).
12. See Dieter Henrich, "Kant's Notion of a Deduction and the Methodological Background of the First *Critique*," in *Kant's Transcendental Deductions*, ed. Eckhart Förster (Stanford: Stanford University Press, 1989), 29–46.
13. Kant speaks of the critique of metaphysics in a similar way by suggesting that we must try to reconstruct it from the ruins of past

philosophical systems, that is, historically from past attempts. Until that time (a time that will never come, a time of Reason) when we can *learn* philosophy rationally, we can only learn to philosophize, "that is, to exercise the talent of reason, in accordance with its universal principles, on certain actually existing attempts at philosophy, always, however, reserving the right of reason to investigate, to confirm, or to reject these principles in their very sources"; Immanuel Kant, *Critique of Pure Reason*, trans. Norman Kemp Smith (New York: St. Martin's Press, 1965), A838/B866.

5

Beyond Interpretation?

On Some Perplexities Following Upon Vattimo's "Turn" from Hermeneutics

PETER CARRAVETTA

> My hypothesis: The subject as multiplicity.
> —Friedrich Nietzsche, *The Will to Power*

From Postmodern to Premodern?

For more than forty years, Gianni Vattimo stood fast to the notion that ours is the age of nihilism, of the dissolution of all values, metaphysics having turned into a technoscientific "image" of the world.[1] Critical witness to complex social and political climates, a militant critic, in his scholarly publications he dwelt on these issues consistently and imaginatively, as the signature notion of *weak thought* attests. Alongside many of his contemporaries, Vattimo focused his attention on *both*, the tradition (Aristotle) and the ultimate philosophical avant-garde (Heidegger), and eventually theorized what we might term a "positive" or "constructive" understanding of the crisis of the 1968 to 1969 period and the pervasive nihilism it had ushered in various areas of culture. This conviction allows Vattimo to deground—s-*fondare*—traditional metaphysical "strong thought," an umbrella word that subsumes rational, technical, dogmatic, and axiomatic forms of thinking. Vattimo moreover intended, at least through the 1990s, to abandon the obsessive compulsion to forge a "new" or alternative system or general theory of Being, which was a key element of Modern/Modernist thought and culture, and begins to think of reality and meaning as ever *partial*, more delimited, inscribed in a *finite* existence, one that accepts a "weakened" or we might say softer notion of the once almighty Being, and its Enlightenment incarnation in the discursive formations of Reason. Presumably this would therefore bring the *human* being closer to his or her reality, suggesting a more humble notion of the meaning of existence and at the same time free up creative possibilities of language and understanding. In other words, the task of thinking at the "end of metaphysics," which seemed to consist in practically inventing a different notion of what Being is, or more specifically of talking about Being, appeared to be a tall (and to some paralyzing or "impossible") order, but one that in the last analysis entailed a radical re*th*inking of what it has been all along. This position required therefore a constant attention to what and how we interpret the tradition of metaphysics, and the historiography of interpretation itself. Appearing in Italy in 1994, *Beyond Interpretation* explicitly addressed this situation, and later we look at it closely. For the path from foundationless metaphysics to a contemporary ethics,[2] and finally to religion, requires a long detour through hermeneutics,[3] in order to thematize the process that makes the itinerary possible and meaningful in the first place. Vattimo's *Belief* (published in Italy in 1996) signals in fact a new beginning, one that may suggest that the postmodern thinker has gone completely around to the pre-modern, which is not to say that his thought is diachronically pre-modern, but theoretically in some ways it might be. With *After Christianity* (originally published in 2002), Vattimo continues even more determinedly to seek a "secular Christianity," one that, having been "weakened" through the dissolution of Modernity, may no longer seek a "religious ethics [grounded] upon knowledge of natural essences that are taken as norms, [and] observ[e] instead the freedom of dialogic mediation" (AC 90). This allows him to fish out from the Christian canon not only a nonreligious notion of *pietas*, but St. Paul's *kenosis* (AC 91), a making humble (rather than humiliating), a lowering, or weakening in God.

    This is quite a parabola, if not a swerve, for a philosopher who had spent the first thirty years of his professional life theorizing and locating, in Nietzsche's footsteps, the transvaluation of all beliefs and forms of knowledge, the anti-metaphysical nature of postmodernity, the overcoming of the Subject,[4] the revaluation of the *hubris* of the Overman as essentially an interpretive project within the uncertainties of the world, the untenability of the Enlightenment project, and who has systematically avoided the use of a philosophical vocabulary that harks to transcendentalism or existential phenomenology, which he considers shot through with metaphysics. Consider some passages from the earlier *Belief*. After admitting that perhaps his turn to Christianity may have been triggered by aging or some other personal/philosophical trauma (B 21–24), which of course we respect and cannot either question or investigate, Vattimo does a quick review of some major sociocultural events—such as the fall of the Berlin wall, the end of the Cold War, the disenchantment with the idea of disenchantment, the full onslaught of the technological worldview, and that the real world has become a fable: all of them amply analyzed by much postmodern literature—in order to find the possible explanation for the "return" of religion in our end-of-millennium times. Harking to his reading of Heidegger as the generator of a "weak ontology," Vattimo wishes to show that this weakening "can be thought of as the rediscovery [*ritrovamento*] of Christianity and as the outcome of the permanent action of its tradition [*permanente agire della sua eredità*]" (B 35, translation modified). Permanent action of the Christian tradition? Was not the very word-concept "permanent" banned from postmodern thought, and with it, and in antithesis to religious ideologies, other Enlightenment terms such as "universal reason," "absolute spirit," for being too strong, metaphysical? Or was Vattimo emphasizing the term "tradition?" But in this case we run into two diverging problems, first concerning eschatology, and secondly with the idea of *facticity*, as we will see, because there are objective facts in the memory of this particular, and effectively dominant, tradition that cannot be whisked away by saying, as he does in several places, that "there are no facts only interpretations," and then sustain, from 1998 onward, that "the idea [of] the fulfillment of redemption is not in complete discontinuity with our history and with our earthly projects" (B 24, translation modified). More recently, we can feel the *unease*, the *disagio* the Italians would say, in his response to both Sergio Quinzio and René Girard,[5] when he admits that weak ontology is a "risky interpretation,"[6] because of the complicated relation between "Christian heritage, weak ontology, and the ethics of nonviolence."

Perhaps the basis for this "turn" are embedded in his notion of *weak thought*, insofar as on the one hand he critiques dialectics for its potential for totalization, but vindicates its usefulness, on the other difference for its unresolvable aporias, though it was the unmasking strategy par excellence? Or is the answer to be found in his alleged *overcoming* of interpretation? But how could that be, since he has held fast, especially after what we may call a "conversion," to the dictum that "there are no facts, only interpretations?"

The Basic Ideas of Weak Thought

As can be readily seen in the original 1983 text, "Dialectics, Difference, and Weak Thought,"[7] Vattimo spends less time pointing out where philosophy failed, or dissolved, or proved no longer able to respond (at least credibly) to the great questions of all time (in the West, that is), and prefers instead answering the question: What do we do now? Where do we go from here? And how? This allows him to recover and reposition in a new context several philosophical traditions, but especially *dialectics* and *difference*. By accepting that we cannot "escape" metaphysics, that we cannot possibly think outside of it (as it shapes and informs our language, logic, and *forma mentis*), he therefore has no choice but to search *within* the tradition for the possibility of thinking being and things in untried ways,[8] thus exploring lived-time, the tradition, yet again, recalling it, rewriting it, and remembering. Vattimo speaks to the failing of strong thought without forgetting that, *volens nolens*, that is the form of thinking we have inherited, and as such we must accept it: even though through its twentieth-century fragmentation and expoliations, it points to nihilism. All attempts at ignoring this state of affairs have led to hysterical moralizing and reactionary measures in ill-fated pursuits of "what is no longer," "utopian origins," or ever-elusive full "presence."

Vattimo begins by conjoining two separate areas of inquiry that reflect the heritage of the two great currents of thought, which more than any other have tried to identify and make sense of the late modern decline of western thinking—namely, dialectics and difference. He achieves this by bending them to accept the basic hermeneutic tenet that there is of necessity a human, personal, individual component to making a statement or judging anything, which, if we look closely, is actually what *prevents it from being totalizing and final*. This indelible "human" component entails recognizing its *partisanship*, its *limits*, its *chance occurrence* in a given moment in time. However, as there is no *from-to* passage in a chronological or topographic sense, this implies that there is no possible "overcoming" of either dialectics or difference, whereas, Vattimo argues, at most we reckon with a *Verwindung*, a "necessary" *distortion* in readapting these traditions.[9]

It is around Nietzsche that hermeneutics has been waging several battles to legitimate new readings to support appropriations, which the German thinker had smashed with his philosophical hammer. Because "[i]t is Nietzsche who helped bring this awareness to light with his analysis of metaphysical subjectivity in terms of mastery and with his announcement that God is dead" (PD 18). The sense of this assertion is that the strong frameworks of metaphysics—*archai, Gründe*, primary evidences and ultimate destinies—are only forms of self-assurance for epochs in which technology and social organization have not yet rendered us capable of living in a more open horizon (as is progressively even more so in our day and age), in a horizon less "magically" guaranteed. Therefore, just like the idea of God, and the religions it gave rise to, "the ruling concepts of metaphysics turn out to be means of discipline and reassurance that are no longer necessary in the context of our present day disposition of technology" (PD 18). Vattimo's own basic, nonfoundational ideas concerning a weak ontology revolve around four basic tenets, namely: 1) there is no noetic prehension of evidence, and truth is not of a logical order but rather of a linguistic one; 2) verification and hypothesis always occur in a rhetorical-hermeneutic horizon to which we already belong, and is therefore "impure," but wherein relations and appartenance are informed by "*pietas*," basis of a later attempt at an ethics of "deeds" [*beni*] and not of imperatives; 3) truth is an interpretation, a formulation, a saying that something is so; 4) therefore, that it constitutes itself fully aware of being a declination, a fading of Being within the tradition, the transmission of previously uttered messages (PD 24–26).

Beyond Interpretation?

Ten years after *weak thought*, we can say that Vattimo accepts in the end that we cannot "escape" our history and tradition, and that therefore what may have to change is not the premises for a truth, but rather the articulations of an understanding, a tolerance, a willingness to risk the retelling of the tale all over again. And so why not employ some of the tools or ruins or archives, ultimately, "conventions," left around in the cultural (un)conscious? But when this means readapting some of the onto-theological constructs he has critiqued for so long, one must ask why and how this "turn" can be effected. And although there is a limit to how far we can pursue the "why," insofar as there is no Socratic method to overwhelm with a demonstration, and no dialogic possible to persuade when confronted with belief, but at best a negotiation, or a pact, we can surely look into the "how" this turn is legitimated. For the Vattimo of the 1990s speaks of the need for hermeneutics to regain a certain "rationality" even as it must avoid foundationalism (BI 97–98), and more than that, historical reconstruction itself must be "a rational activity" (BI 107). What surprises is that more than in his earlier analyses, the philosopher addresses the "content" of messages and pays less attention to their actual rhetorical formulation, a move that may prove counterproductive if we recall that when dealing with religion the question of textuality and the rhetoric of the messages is of fundamental importance.

In *Beyond Interpretation* Vattimo begins by referring to a short article he wrote in the late 1980s about hermeneutics being the *koine*, or dominant trope, of our times,[10] reiterating that it is still applicable in the 1990s. But *because* of this, Vattimo continues, hermeneutics may have lost its originary philosophical significance (BI 1). The problem he sets up to resolve is to see why and how this took place, and whether there is a resolution or answer to this state of affairs.

Vattimo falls back on one of the most used and unfortunately often abused citations from Nietzsche, namely, that "there are no facts, only interpretations," and with that theoretical prejudice he proposes to reinterpret the hermeneutic tradition as represented by the axis Heidegger-Gadamer. But is it true that there are "no facts"? And are all interpretations equally valid? In order to respond fairly to Vattimo's claims, let us follow his line of reasoning carefully. What is the issue? He writes: "Whereas, up to a certain point in the history of European culture, the word hermeneutics was always accompanied by an adjective—biblical, juridical, literary or even simply general—in contemporary thought it has begun to appear in its own right" (BI 4). A telling example is Gadamer's project, whose hermeneutics as a general philosophy of culture becomes ultimately a metaphysical "finally true" description of the "(permanent) 'interpretative structure' of human existence" (BI 6). For Vattimo, who had begun to distance himself from Gadamer many years before,[11] hermeneutics had fallen back into metaphysics and perhaps betrayed its original project, at any rate it would no longer be postmodern or at least post-metaphysical.

No doubt other philosophers have called attention to the fact that Gadamer's thought had become "olympic" with its claim to be a "universal" theory, and we need not get into that here. Vattimo's "revisionism" intends to challenge this by recalling Heidegger's idea that *Geworfenheit* demonstrates "the historicity and finitude of pre-understanding" (BI 6). In other words: "hermeneutics is not only a theory of the historicity (horizons) of truth: it is itself a radically historical truth" (BI 6). Because of this, it cannot be thought "metaphysically as a description of one objective structure of existence among others, but only as the response to a sending, to what Heidegger calls *Ge-Schick*" (BI 6).

Vattimo's argument then shifts to Nietzsche's announcement that "God is dead," which should be taken to mean not that God "'objectively . . . does not exist' or that reality is such that he is excluded from it" (BI 6) but, rather, that "God is no longer necessary" (BI 7). We recall that Nietzsche's argument was that the God of metaphysics was necessary so that humanity could organize itself in an orderly, secure social life protected from the ravages of nature through hierarchically structured social undertakings as well as from intestine ravages of a religiously sanctioned morality. But as times have changed, this reassurance could be considered as achieved insofar as we live in a world that, being scientifically and technologically structured, spares us the terror in which primitive human beings lived. In light of this achieved epochal turn, we can understand Nietzsche's revelation, synthesized by Vattimo as follows:

> God seems too extreme, barbaric and excessive a hypothesis. And, moreover, the God that has served as this principle of stability and reassurance is also the one that has always forbidden the lie; so it is to obey him that the faithful have forsworn even that lie which he is himself: it is the faithful that have killed God. . . . (BI 7)

But by "killing" God because he is a lie, the faithful also renege on the value of truth, which, according to Nietzsche, is another name for God: the world become fable has no room for a deeper or higher truth, and that "leaves the field free to the play of interpretations" (BI 7, translation modified). An observation must be made here: Was there no play of interpretation *before* the realization of the death of God? Or phrasing it differently: was the determination of what is true possible only as long as there was a God, that is to say, a *theo*retical *arche, primum mobile, Grund,* or axiom? In other words, having become entirely foundationless, does that mean that we really have no way of establishing from *where* an interpretation derives or is located? Or where it is directed, what *sense* it might have? We should bear in mind as we proceed, that interpretation, insofar as it is embodied in language, requires an *other*, a respondent, an audience, and that as *applicatio* it will impart a meaning, impact on someone, have an effect on this other or others. This problematic picture appears as background to Vattimo's position, as he moves on to his second thesis: "In fact if hermeneutics is not accepted as a comfortable metatheory of the universality of interpretative phenomena, as a sort of view from nowhere of the perennial conflict, or play, of interpretations" (BI 8), then the only plausible alternative left is that of

> Think[ing] the philosophy of interpretation as the final stage in a series of events (theories, vast social and cultural transformations, technologies and scientific "discoveries"), as the conclusion

of a history we feel unable to tell (interpret) except in the terms of nihilism that we find for the first time in Nietzsche. (BI 8)

We must now ask: What happened to the notion that all interpretation is *de facto* perspectival? What happened to that unceasing thrownness of the *Dasein* caught in a web of possibilities of *das Man*, confronted with the dilemma of ascertaining what meaningful facts are in the interplay between presence and absence, articulation and appropriation, *habitus* and memory? Interpretation becomes all the more dramatic, compelling, and risky, precisely *because* of the vanishing of the guarantees afforded by a stable frame of reference—God, universal values, History. And yet interpretation *must* take place insofar as the interpreting being cannot not relate to others, the difficulty remaining as to *what* the other being—him- or herself caught in the same predicament—interprets (about) me and my world, my history.

Vattimo states: "If hermeneutics were only the discovery of the *fact* that there are different perspectives on the 'world,' or on Being, the conception of truth as the objective mirroring of how things are (in this case, of the *fact* that there are multiple perspectives) would be confirmed, whereas it is actually rebutted by the philosophy of interpretation" (BI 8; emphasis in the original). Thus "to accept hermeneutics as an interpretation and not a metaphysical description would, strictly speaking, amount to no more than a matter of taste; indeed not even that, for it would be a case not of choosing but simply of registering a state of mind that remained as wholly inexplicable to oneself as to others" (BI 8). But that is not exactly true, first because there are multiple perspectives by his own definition (that is, there are no facts only interpretations); second, because if reduced to personal choice, interpretation cannot be the *mere* registering of a mood, as choice entails reflection on the descriptions of the world *and* decision to act or utter a statement; and third, because it would imply *confronting* metaphysics (or the fallen or inauthentic or alienated concretions of the lifeworld) insofar as *my* interpretation (assuming with Vattimo's Nietzsche that, once again, there are *only* interpretations) is by default a questioning all other interpretations, all other assumptions (at least within my social-historical horizon). So here is what we have: either the end of hermeneutics itself, having vanished into the impossibility of being anti- or post-metaphysical, or else it is reduced to personal statements, opinions, in short, localized exchanges continually exposed to the risk of being absorbed in chatter. For if hermeneutics confirms the *fact* that indeed there are, and there have long been, "different perspectives" on the world, or on Being, or on God, we might then reasonably add: why is that a bad thing, and who says that hermeneutics "rejects" that? Gadamer presumably, insofar as we are following an argument in which his version of what hermeneutics is is taken to be the Master Code in the field. But even in Gadamer, there is certainly a recognition that there have been different ideas about what hermeneutics was and is.[12] Moreover, the notion of the placing of the interpreting consciousness, or the "situation" of the interpreter in the broader dynamic of the fusing of horizons,[13] addresses precisely the issue of the historicalness not only of the history of hermeneutics *as a discipline*, but of the background facticity of the human *Dasein*, which no interpretation can ignore and which is not limited to Modernity. Nevertheless, given then that hermeneutics wishes to be *more* than a general "metatheory" of the play of interpretations,

> the further step . . . is that of asking whether such a metatheory is not bound to undertake a more radical recognition of its own historicity, its own formal character as interpretation, eliminating the final metaphysical equivocality that stands as a threat to it and which is apt to make of it a purely relativistic philosophy of cultural multiplicity. (BI 9)

Alerting my reader that we are being introduced to a new problematic, to be followed on, which haunts all interpreters and ethicists, namely the *factual* (empirical!) existence of the multiplicity of cultures and the consequent fear of relativism, let us first finish summarizing the argument. Retracing briefly the history of interpretation, Vattimo points out that each theory was always born as the result of specific situations, as a "response to contingent questions" (BI 10). But now our question is: Do we not always respond (to the Gadamerian dialogue, to the Heideggerian sending) on the basis of "contingent questions," or "situations"—whether Nietzschean, Gadamerian or even Sartrean—that is, on the basis of what our present-day worldview is? Is that not the reason why, as we saw above, in the age of the "transparent society," Vattimo is responding to the felt need to oppose strong thought once more and introduce the idea of a weakened being? Why is contingency such a monstrous concept as to be made *a priori* irrelevant or marginal to a reframing of the issue of what interpretation entails?

Another problem arises with Vattimo basing this "beyonding" of hermeneutics on the earlier formulation of hermeneutics as the *koine* of our (then 1980s) era, which he reiterates in the second chapter. Two new and crucial key word-concepts enter the scene: relativism and humanism. Hermeneutics seems to have found the closest manifestation of the "truth" in the aesthetic sphere, which here is taken to include all new paradigm shifts, the work of revolutionary scientists, language games, and all sorts of "redescriptions." It appears that hermeneutics is forever seeking to bring the specialized knowledge of the sciences and their categories within the *Lebenswelt*, the precategorical lifeworld within which new disclosures of truth occur. The danger, according to Vattimo, is that hermeneutics risks being "a general and often *relativistic* philosophy of culture" (BI 20, my emphasis). It risks also being *normative* because it "seems to depend wholly on the fact that in the lifeworld—as the supporting horizon of a culture—belong those argumentative and dialogical features that are in fact specific to Western culture, and perhaps even to the 'transparent' community of modern scientists alone" (BI 20, translation modified). And yet, we read, unlike the Eurologocentric Habermas, Gadamer tends toward a universal theory grounded on the aesthetic and thus "avoids this metaphysical trap," in which presumably Habermas falls, "without falling back into *relativism*, by theorizing the indefinite opening of historical horizons, their unlimited susceptibility to interpretation" (BI 21). But should not this be desirable, after the death of God, on a terrain where we do want things—events, texts, lives—to be predisposed to continued interpretations? Risking normativity can also mean accepting norms for peaceful social coexistence, not necessarily believing in them in some supratemporal or theological manner. And why is relativism such a taboo or harbinger of an unthinkable critical situation?[14] Is it because it harks back to the notion of relation, of intersubjectivity? Is not the determination either explicit or implied in an interpretation *relative to* (or pertaining to) a *Dasein*, a lifeworld, a horizon? Or are we to think of interpretation as aperspectival,[15] as a lyric utterance in a deserted wood, as an evaluation in a nonworld?

Vattimo reiterates that the originary essence of objectification, lodged in Plato's doctrine of ideas, is what grounds modern science and the transformation of the world into "a place where there are no (longer) facts, only interpretations" (BI 26). I insist that Nietzsche's ironic, indeed sarcastic expression does not mean that literally there are no facts, only that without the axiom or the *metron* furnished by a supreme being, the interpretations of the actually happened, existentially lived, and historically transmitted events, situations, phenomena, in the end, facts, have multiplied exponentially. The challenge seems rather that of forging new theories and methods of interpretation on the basis of what humans have constructed, which is all we can possibly know, as Vico taught us, and this includes the creation of the divinity itself. In chapter 3 there appears a term that the Vattimo of the 1970s to 1980s would have shunned:

> Instead of reacting to the dissolution of the principle of reality by attempting to recuperate a sense of identity and belonging that are at once reassuring and punitive, it is a matter of grasping nihilism as a chance of *emancipation*. (BI 40; emphasis added)

Emancipation? Lyotard had considered this one of the three great metanarratives of Modernity, which dissolve and turn practically meaningless in postmodern times, at least in the advanced Western societies. Nevertheless, Vattimo sees its usefulness, which is consistent with what he had laid out in the general premises of weak thought, namely, that a certain aspect of the thought of dialectics could still offer possibilities of development. Ultimately, if we acknowledge that the world is basically informed by the conflict of interpretations, and if we accept that thinking no longer conceives of itself as the recognition and acceptance of objective foundation, having "weakened" precisely because of this endless conflict of positions, then we should conceive of ourselves as the heirs, the "relatives, children, brothers, and friends of those from whom these appeals to co-respond issue [*provengono*]" (BI 40, translation modified) and compel a "new sense of responsibility" (BI 40). And it is from this initial and necessary response, which we suppose is grounded in intersubjectivity (using a language Vattimo carefully avoids), that he jumps to this observation: is it an accident that today people are speaking of the *principle of charity*.[16] Now, Vattimo is fully aware that we may be recovering another metaphysical eternal value to substitute the old one of truth (BI 40). Yet he holds that this is a key authoritative word in the Western nihilistic tradition, and is decisive for philosophy precisely because of "loyalty to its own provenance," and that therefore it "should reappropriate" (BI 40). But not enough is given us as to why this particular theological virtue is to be preferred over the others, and the impact they had on the memory of the collective.

In chapter 4, Vattimo argues that secularization itself is proof that Christianity has developed side by side through Modernity, whereas one can object that secularization has been informed by what amounts to heretical currents, which have challenged the very dogma of Christianity. He writes:

> We are led to the hypothesis that hermeneutics itself, as a philosophy with certain ontological commitments, is the fruit of

secularization as the renewal, pursuit, "application" and interpretation of the substance of the Christian revelation, and preeminently the dogma of the incarnation of God. (BI 52)

This may indeed be radical, but in recent years, indeed for the past two centuries, secularization has been understood and written about as the exact opposite, namely as the discarding, discontinuation, nonapplication, and revision of the contents of the Christian revelation. It is the continuation of that Humanist tradition that places man at the center of the universe and on which the sciences built epistemological castles *not* grounded on the divinity, beyond the necessary show of (political, military) respect. Therefore, is Vattimo not falling into the trap of a dualistic logic where by negating a position one is actually proving that it is valid—which is propositional logic?[17] Is he not putting on the same plane the Enlightenment, radically anti-religious yet metaphysical by virtue of its "faith" in Reason, and Religion, which fought against all evidentiary proofs of the existence of God, and compelled the community not to question belief? Is he unwittingly deploying dialectics, which he had warned is always risking totalization? In his attempt to prove the connection between hermeneutics and Christianity, is he not digging for, and into, an ontotheological foundation and trying to redeem it as the only way we can rethink philosophy at the end of philosophy?

What the philosopher is after, with a wink to Schelling, is to "liberate the positive aspect of mythological, religious and poetic discourses from the obstacles of the rationalistic ideal of truth as objectivity" (BI 46). In order to carry out this task, Vattimo is forced to go back to the beginning of the Western tradition, primarily to shun the Aristotelian tradition of interpretation (so crucial to Christianity) anchored on *substance*, and recover St. Paul, whose theory of interpretation is based on the key *event*, which is the coming of the Christ. As an anti-Aristotelian, Vattimo begins to develop "the plurality of meanings of Being" (BI 47), which can be read in the purview of St. Paul's vision. This reference immediately points to a cluster of other problems of gigantic proportions, which we cannot take up here, among which I recall, first, the relationship between the Greek notion of Being and the Judeo-Christian idea of God;[18] and second, the manifold sense of that "experience" attributed to St. Paul, which even the younger Heidegger considered "special" but which he subsequently abandoned.[19]

As a point of critique, what is not thematized are the notion of *temporality* and of *facticity*, and how these played out in that "history," which, however interpreted—Heidegger used the expressions "authentic" and "inauthentic"—have marked the destiny of the West and have become a heavy, indeed "strong" presence in its collective memory. It is against this fallen, inauthentic if we wish, *Überlieferung* that hermeneutics and the ethics it wishes to establish must struggle. And it must acknowledge that if great minds, city-states, larger than life institutions, indeed entire civilizations have for centuries, that is, *in concreto*, believed in interpreting the Divine Word—which was meant to "liberate us from myths," as Vattimo states—in ultra-metaphysical, dogmatic, when not totalitarian and nondemocratic, ways, then the task of interpretive thought would more likely be found in the direction of a comprehension of the reasons why and how this did happen at all, why it happened in this our world independently of the "Kingdom of God," which by definition is not in our power to know, God remaining mystery, enigma.

Conclusion

Our discussion could continue with an examination of the appendixes to *Beyond Interpretation*, where most of the above is reiterated in a more compact manner, but where we encounter similar arguments, from the idea of freeing hermeneutics of the charge of "irrationalism," to the danger of falling back both upon scientism and the philosophy of the *Lebenswelt*. In the end, sticking to the mantra that all we have is interpretations, which does raise a fundamental difficulty in establishing an ethics of any sort, Vattimo is forced to confront the paradox on the basis of which "it is only the radical awareness of itself as interpretative, and neither descriptive nor objective, that guarantees hermeneutics the possibility of arguing rationally on its own behalf [*di argomentarsi razionalmente*]" (BI 105–106). The statement borders on tautology. Ontology, he says further on, is central to all this because without it "hermeneutics risks appearing as no more than a theory of the multiplicity[20] (irreducible and inexplicable, to be accepted as one accepts life itself, or as an 'ultimate' . . . metaphysical fact)" (BI 107). It is difficult to follow Vattimo after statements of this kind. Is not the manifold a perspective Heidegger theorized as the *Geviert*, which unfortunately in the literature has not been adequately explored and developed? And is not the fact that interpretation (that is, hermeneutics) is "irreducible"—since all we have are interpretations, as he said many times earlier—precisely what Vattimo has been arguing all along, in order to avoid an unwitting yet implied unitary Logos behind all the individual manifestations of being, the interpreting being, that is?

All of this does not square, however, with his often repeated quote from Nietzsche that there are no facts only interpretation. Because although the facts of the history of the church can be subject to different interpretations, it cannot be denied that they took place, that they have *been*. In Heideggerian terms, the *Faktizität* is not only of the *Dasein* as fate (*Schicksal*), but also constitutive of destiny (*Geschick*), which entails a collectivity, one might even hazard the expression "a people." Vattimo places great emphasis on the concept of destiny as "destination" in many of his writings, but a rereading of paragraphs 74–76 of *Being and Time* suggests that the distinction needs further elaboration.[21] "As thrown . . . [*Dasein*] exists factically with Others." It is "lost" in the world of the "they." But this is the bulk of the collective memory, and the interpreting *Dasein* must work with it, against it, "and yet again for it." The predicament, coherently with a hermeneutics, which is *ab initio* tied to its historicality, means that the "resoluteness" attempts to disclose "current factical possibilities of authentic existing, and discloses them in terms of the heritage which that resoluteness, as thrown, takes over." In other words, one comes to one's understanding of his or her own thrownness against the possibilities "that have come down to one, but not necessarily as having thus coming down" (BT 435). Put another way, they may have come down the wrong way, or wearing a particular mask. The authentic *Dasein* effects this in view of one's finitude, "snatching" one from the "endless possibilities which offer themselves as closest to one—those of comfortableness, shirking, and taking things lightly—and brings Dasein into the simplicity of its fate (*Schicksal*)" (BT 435). So far, this reflects the earlier Vattimo's concern with mortality as a constitutive element of the *Dasein* that informs all choices and bespeaks its freedom to choose among a number of possibilities in anticipation of the instance that obliterates all other possibilities.[22] Though fate is something the *Dasein* hands down to itself, it is yet chosen, representing a readiness of the existent: in the clash of events and circumstances, in short, there is chance, or being "fortunate" (Heidegger's term) of encountering futurity, so that this "powerless superior power" amounts to nothing more than what may or may not happen, we might call it an accident in any given Situation. This will be developed later by Sartre. However, "if fateful *Dasein*, as Being-in-the-world, exists essentially in Being-with-Others, its historicizing is a co-historicizing and is determinative for it as *destiny (Geschick)*. This is how we designate the historicizing of the community, of a people . . . Only in communicating and in struggling does the power of destiny become free" (BT 436). Recalling that the term destiny in German is related to both the sense of history as well as to that of vicissitude, it is important to bring the full weight of the series of events, the memories, the lived-experiences of countless beings who, together, in a variously configured co-appartenance, have attempted to interpret, or have been compelled to accept an interpretation, whose narrative[23] has brought light and dark, hope and despair, ecstasies and terror, all as a function of a reified Supreme Being, a Power against which, in Aristotelian fashion, all manifestations of beings have been measured and legitimated. There have been conflicting interpretations of these messages over time, and the events they spawned, but they did happen, they do echo *through* time, not through eternity. The facticity of the collective must be accounted for, because death here is not the individual last possibility for the single *Dasein*, for the *moi*, but that of the not-me, the others in the ontological phrase: Being-with-*Others*. I believe that Vattimo is speaking more in terms of fate, which we may translate as pertaining to the "personal" dimension of Being-there, and less of destiny, which may best reflect the conflicted history of Christianity. For unfortunately we cannot say that the Crusades were only interpretation and not a fact, that the Inquisition, which held court on the proper behavior of "Christians" vis à vis the institutional church for six centuries, and clearly a harbinger of "state terrorism," was only an interpretation and not a fact, and that genocides have not occurred in the name of the Lord.

Perhaps what is needed is an ethics not based on a revealed religion, but an ethics without God. And there is no need here to rehash the arguments made to that effect by Hobbes, Hume, Kant, Mill, and others.[24] But a rereading of the Nietzschean sentence as having finally liberated us from the twisted logic of the Church, eliminating the onto-theological immutable essences of Foundation, Salvation, Eternity, of God *causa sui*, and investing *homo humanus* once again with the responsibility of working out an ethics grounded on human, not divine, values. And when Heidegger said in the often-cited *Der Spiegel* interview that "only a God can save us," we should recall that it is definitely not "the Christian God."[25]

Hermeneutics as the general theory of interpretation should be concerned with the "fallen beings," especially with how these have invented and venerated their gods, including the one that gave rise to monotheism, because of these we do have records, memories, echoes, monuments, in short, *facts*, and the witnesses to "special" or "epochal" or "monstrous" events, where even these are interpretable on the ground (however illusory, or "inauthentic") of a vision, a position, a desire, and an effective course of action. As an enterprise concerned with "effects," with "historical horizons," hermeneutics ought to "save" the early Heidegger, the one of the 1920s, where his analytic of *Dasein* is still so powerfully illuminating; but it must be corroborated by, and integrated into, a broader theory that includes more refined considerations on the nature of language, of metaphor in particular, and tackles on the problem of collective memory, of what exactly an idea of history is, and how its strategies of power and legitimation have impacted on those who come after. The ethical considerations Vattimo introduces as a sort of ground to hermeneutics are not in and by themselves a bad idea at all, and can easily be accommodated within a secular, post-Enlightenment critical practice, except that there inevitably looms in the background the theoretical legitimizing discourse of a religion, which, even "*after* Christianity," wishes to consider the reincarnation of Christ as *the* event that marks the coincidence of temporality and eternity. One cannot be more metaphysical than that. The grounding of hermeneutics in the singularity and uniqueness (because unrepeatable for all eternity) of this particular faith-event (however distorted and politically motivated it ended up being, as Vattimo's letters to the Pope continue to argue), cannot but raise the suspicion of someone born under a different sun, and which in a global context cannot even foster that needed dialogue among peoples,[26] on the basis of the fact that they may have their own monotheism and polytheism to grapple with.

Notes

1. See, for example, the "Preface" to the Italian translation of Heidegger's *Was heißt Denken?, Che cosa significa pensare*, 2 vols., trans. Ugo Ugazio and Gianni Vattimo (Milan: Surgarco, 1978), 22–23, where we can pick some constants throughout Vattimo's thought, but also, retrospectively, some shifts in his views on religion.
2. Vattimo's explicit thematization of ethics begins in chapter 3 of *Beyond Interpretation*, continues in *Belief* and in *Vocazione e responsabilità del filosofo*, and finds a fuller expression in *After Christianity*.
3. The notion that philosophy *tout court*—whether as acknowledgment of its "end" or as exploration of any possible "task" left to it—has turned increasingly to the problem of interpretation is also present in Vattimo's writings of the 1960s to 1970s, but finds full articulation in his *The Adventure of Difference* (18–19) and in *Al di là del soggetto* (8 et infra). With a broad historiographic sweep, in a 1987 article titled "Hermeneutics as Koine," trans. Peter Carravetta, *Theory, Culture & Society* 5, 2–3 (1988): 399–408, Vattimo claims

that the one overarching philosophical current or mood in our Euroamerican cultural context is hermeneutics, displacing structuralism as the dominant theoretical matrix of the 1960s to 1970s, which had followed in turn on the cultural hegemony of Marxism in the 1950s to 1960s.

4. In the Introduction to my translation of *Al di là del soggetto* (1984), which I prepared for Humanities Press (no date of publication yet established), I tried to demonstrate how Vattimo leaves the door open to newer forms of subjectivity, or at least to alternative forms of conceiving it. However, he never returns to the question of the subject, at least thematically.

5. See on this René Girard and Gianni Vattimo, *Verità o fede debole? Dialogo su cristianesimo e relativismo*, ed. Pierpaolo Antonello (Massa: Transeuropa, 2006).

6. Ibid., 38.

7. For a translation of the original essay, which I did with Thomas Harrison, see *Graduate Faculty Philosophy Journal* 10, 1 (Spring 1985): 99–115. My translation of the entire anthology *Weak Thought*, eds. Gianni Vattimo and Pier Aldo Rovatti (*Il pensiero debole*. Milan: Feltrinelli, 1983), is forthcoming from State University of New York Press.

8. I abstain from using the expression "new ways of thinking" insofar as the notion, artistic expression and ideology of the "new" have been object of critique by Vattimo himself in various studies, beginning with *Poesia e ontologia, The End of Modernity* (90–112), and *The Adventure of Difference* (86–102, 161–162).

9. Arguably one of his most fruitful contributions to a theory of interpretation, and easily exportable or translatable outside of continental philosophy, *Verwindung* entails a twisting distortion, or a making recourse to something or someone else, which is inevitably impure and not exactly alike what it refers to or what it can infer from another set of discourses. This applies to the tradition especially, as in its being handed down everything undergoes growth or sedimentation or rewriting, or a combination of the three, and is therefore never equal to itself (except to rationalists and dogmatists). For a reading of the early Vattimo, and discussion on *Verwindung*, see the chapter "Gianni Vattimo and the End(s) of Modernity" in my *Prefaces to the Diaphora. Rhetorics, Allegory and the Interpretation of Postmodernity* (West Lafayette, IN: Purdue University Press, 1991), 215–235.

10. Gianni Vattimo, "Hermeneutics as Koine."

11. See, for instance, the difference between his Introduction to his translation of *Warheit und Methode* into Italian, Hans-Georg Gadamer, *Verità e metodo*, trans. Gianni Vattimo (Milan: Fabbri, 1972), and the "Postilla" he added when the work appeared in a second edition by Bompiani in 1983.
12. Hans-Georg Gadamer, *Truth and Method* (New York: Seabury Press, 1975), 245–267.
13. See Gadamer, *Truth and Method*, 269, 271.
14. See Enzo Di Nuoscio, "Elogio del relativismo," in *Il bello del relativismo. Quel che resta della filosofia nel XXI secolo*, ed. Elisabetta Ambrosi (Venice: Marsilio, 2005), 105–114.
15. A thinker who had thematized the "aperspectival world" is Jean Gebser, whose *The Ever-Present Origin*, trans. Noel Barstad with Algis Mickunas (Athens: Ohio University Press, 1986) was eerily prescient of some aspects of the postmodern condition. See a partial discussion in my *Prefaces to the Diaphora*, cit., 154–157.
16. The reference is to the work of Donald Davidson.
17. This argument is picked up and developed in *After Christianity* by appealing to Karl Barth, according to whom "the secularization of modern man [is] the paradoxical affirmation that God radically transcends any worldly realization" (AC 36).
18. See on this Umberto Regina, "Noi eredi dei cristiani e dei greci. *Destruktion* e *Faktizität* nel cammino di Heidegger," in *Heidegger Oggi*, ed. Eugenio Mazzarella (Bologna: Il Mulino, 1998), 195–215. For a broader historical view, see Lee Martin McDonald, *The Biblical Canon. Its Origin, Transmission, and Authority* (Peabody, MS: Hendrickson, 2007).
19. See Otto Pöggeler, *Martin Heidegger's Path of Thinking*, trans. Daniel Magurshak and Sigmund Barber (Atlantic Highlands, NJ: Humanities Press, 1987), 9–31; and Felix Duque, "Il Contrattempo. Lo spostamento ermeneutico della religione nella fenomenologia heideggeriana," in *Heidegger oggi*, 165–194. The above cited article by Regina and the one by Duque study Heidegger's 1919–1920 and 1920–1921 university courses; in particular Duque details how, whatever Heidegger may have drawn from St. Paul, after Augustine the Christian religion for him becomes "theology" (187). Pöggeler emphasizes the Patristic appropriation of Greek metaphysics (27).
20. "*Teoria della molteplicità*" could also be rendered as "theory of the manifold," though technically if the latter is meant then the Italian should have been "*teoria del molteplice*."
21. Martin Heidegger, *Being and Time*, trans. John Macquarry (New York: Harper & Row, 1962); hereafter referred to as BT.

22. See the powerfully argued position he takes ten years earlier, in his response article in *Che cosa fanno oggi i filosofi?*, ed. Norberto Bobbio (Milan: Bompiani, 1982), 201: "Heidegger calls death the coffer of nothingness, but we can also call it the casket of being. The important thing is the idea of coffer, of a deposit of treasures. It is mortality that furnishes history with its richness, it is mortality that generates the possibility of constructing a life with a meaning, with a continuity, as a discourse, a passage. The language that allows me to accede to being, that discloses the horizons within which things are given to me, is richly stratified and dense precisely because it bears the mark of the generations that have expressed themselves with it. On the ethical plane, our common mortality is perhaps the only value capable of founding a morality, in the sense of the *pietas*, of the respect for the living and its traces."
23. Here we should open a long paragraph on the interconnectedness of discourse and temporality; cf. *Being and Time*, par. 34 and 68d.
24. Cf. Kai Nielsen, *Ethics without God* (New York: Prometheus Books, 1990); Eugenio Lecaldano, *Un'etica senza Dio* (Bari: Laterza, 2007).
25. See Martin Heidegger, "*Beiträge zur Philosophie (Vom Ereignis)*," in *Gesamtausgabe* 65 (Frankfurt: Klostermann, 1989), 403, cited in Regina, 217. See also Günter Figal, "Forgetfulness of God," in *Companion to Heidegger's Contributions to Philosophy*, ed. Charles Scott, et al. (Bloomington: Indiana University Press, 2001), 198–212.
26. See, for instance, Raimon Panikkar, *L'incontro indispensabile: dialogo delle religioni* (Milan: Jaca Book, 2001).

Part Two

Metaphysics and Religion

6

Metaphysics, Violence, and Alterity in Gianni Vattimo

EDISON HIGUERA AGUIRRE

An important trend of twentieth-century philosophy has identified a link between metaphysical thought and the practice of violence. Some historical facts that occurred in the last century have probably helped to deepen such a connection. The reflections by Theodor W. Adorno, Emmanuel Levinas, and Jacques Derrida may be of great importance in the process of exploring the hidden correlations between metaphysical truth and violent actions. Gianni Vattimo, however, thinks that the merit of such a discovery should be attributed mainly to Nietzsche and Heidegger. As he writes, "the most 'resistant' reasons for the refusal of metaphysics in contemporary philosophy are grounded on the connection, which Nietzsche identified and Heidegger radically theorized, between metaphysics and violence."[1]

Levinas and Adorno: The Rejection of Metaphysics

The atrocious actions carried out by Nazism in the first part of the twentieth century against numerous human beings considered as "inferior categories" help us to understand the risks that may hide behind the word "truth" as it is used in some contexts. Adorno and Levinas, who are qualified witnesses of what happened during the Nazi period, join together in their refusal of metaphysics. According to Adorno, now more than ever we realize that "metaphysics has merged with culture,"[2] and that "since Auschwitz, fearing death means fearing worse than death."[3] Levinas has revealed the necessity of breaking the metaphysical connection between human beings and Being. The traditional "relationship" that has been established between these two terms does not allow any space for thinking the difference between the I and the other. The metaphysical concept of Being does not enable us to live the difference, according to Levinas; rather, it is a source of oppression. "One has to find for man another kinship than that which ties him to Being, one that will perhaps enable us to conceive of this difference between me and the other, this inequality, in a sense absolutely opposed to oppression."[4]

Violence nests in metaphysical thinking and manifests itself in various ways, as "knowledge" organizing everything on the basis of a rational system where everything must be explained as well as through the "brutal conquest of beings through violence." Both ways imply a reduction of multiplicity to unity:

> Knowledge or violence would appear in the midst of the multiplicity as events that realize Being. The common knowledge proceeds toward unity, either toward the apparition in the midst of a multiplicity of beings of a rational system in which these beings would be but objects, and in which they would find their being—or toward the brutal conquest of beings outside of every system by violence. Whether in scientific thought or in the object of science, or in history understood as a manifestation of reason, where violence reveals itself to be reason, philosophy presents itself as a realization of Being, that is, as its liberation by the suppression of multiplicity.[5]

The Violent Essence of Metaphysics

Vattimo echoes the lively charges that contemporary thought brings against the "violent essence of metaphysics."[6] According to the reflections that follow, metaphysics becomes a source of "violence" mainly when it claims to have reached *the* truth. In metaphysical thought, "truth" was identified with immutable principles and axioms, with the certainty of the doubting *ego*, with the *a priori*, with the certainty of science, and so on. When this occurs, that is, when truth becomes the possession of one human being, then it dangerously turns into a source of violence. It is a source of violence because, as I show later, in its face the other is called to be silent and not to speak. If one can clarify the reasons that justify the "logical" connection between metaphysics and violence, then one better understands why, according to Vattimo, "all the categories of metaphysics are violent categories" (AD 5).[7]

According to Vattimo, "starting with the 1935 essay *Introduction to Metaphysics*, the term 'metaphysics' takes up in Heidegger a decisively negative connotation" (IH 61). The reason for Heidegger's attitude is simple. "In its essence metaphysics is nihilism";[8] that is, metaphysics is part of that history of Being that can be recapitulated as the history of forgetfulness. In this sense, metaphysics "becomes a synonym of the forgetfulness of Being" (IH 62).[9] It is a synonym for that long period in the history of philosophy that goes from Plato to Nietzsche and "does not ask about the truth of Being itself."[10] The term "metaphysics" for Heidegger becomes a synonym for "reason" that reflects on the truth of beings while "forgetting Being."[11] Vattimo clarifies the meaning of Heidegger's ontological difference. In Heidegger's vocabulary, "the ontological difference is the relation that joins and disjoins Being and beings."[12] As Vattimo explains, "Being, by virtue of which beings are, can never be confused with beings . . . not even as the maximum of all beings."[13] Heidegger's struggle against traditional metaphysics is justified as a reaction to the oblivion of Being because, in short, traditional metaphysics "does not think the difference between Being and beings"[14] and reduces Being to "quantifiable objectivity and rationalized mechanism."[15]

According to Heidegger's claim, "thinking begins only when we have come to know that reason, glorified for centuries, is the most stiff-necked adversary of thought."[16] In this claim, Heidegger distinguishes and sharply opposes "reason" and "thought." Reason is considered "the most stiff-necked adversary of thought." It seems therefore that there is no possible way of reconciling "reason" and "thought." This premise seems to be important for the unfolding of my argumentation. According to Lorenzo Biagi, the "reason" of the Western metaphysical tradition "aimed mainly at determining a unitary, monolithic, stable, and immutable structure of the 'true' through a process of *demonstrations* of enunciates."[17] It is such metaphysical rationality, "the most stiff-necked adversary of thought," that Heidegger radically opposes. According to Vattimo's interpretation, in Heidegger's reflection metaphysics is a source of violence for two reasons: because metaphysics "in its arrival point brings to modern science and technics," and "because it implies a relation to the foundation that is substantially silencing-quieting; the foundation imposes itself as that in front of which one can no longer ask anything."[18] My essay will focus on the analysis of the relation that Vattimo criticizes both with technics as the arrival point of metaphysics and with "silencing" thought as expression of "the metaphysics of foundation." As it will become clear in the following pages, Vattimo's attitude toward technics is not of the same kind as the relation with "the metaphysics of foundation." Modern technics is considered by Vattimo as the extreme way to bring metaphysics to fulfillment, and needs to be seconded. The same is not true, however, for "silencing-quieting" thought, which limits dialogue and tolerance, and needs to be rejected.

Metaphysics and Peremptoriness of Being

Vattimo's weak thought is connected to a Nietzschean-Heideggerian tradition that considers reason as the source of the violence exercised in the West in the name of truth. Already in *Il soggetto e la maschera*, Vattimo considers Socratic rationality as the model of a force that seeks "the integration of the single into the whole" (SM 60). Socrates favored the coincidence of rationality and happiness (SM 59). Thus, the individuals' desires "are simply replaced with the tyranny of reason" (SM 60). For Nietzsche, then, the entire history of rationalism can be summed up in terms of violence (SM 60). The history of rationalism "is essentially the violence of social integration, of the fixation of roles in which the victory of the Apollinian principle over the Dionysian is stabilized" (SM 60). Socratic rationality comes to mean something very specific. It represents, in Nietzschean language, a system of "imposition." To say it briefly, it is the imposition of the rigidity of the Apollinian principle over the Dionysian. One could say that Socratic rationality represents "the fixation of the mask into a defined and stable social role, the fixation of a canonical system of logical rules for distinguishing the true from the false, and the integration of the individuals into a rationality that escapes their concrete ability for comprehension and control" (SM 60).

From what was said earlier, one can infer that Vattimo finds in Nietzsche's thought the grounds for the struggle against such a "Socratism." We are called to carry out a "rebellion" against this "Socratism" that does not allow individuals to experience their own existence as individuals (SM 60). In sum, the matter is that of a call to a struggle against "the abstract rationality that claims one's adherence to it without letting itself be experienced concretely in individual existence" (SM 60). The entire Western thought—and therefore "modernity"—has been dominated by this Socratic *ratio*. According to Vattimo, it is a real "system of domination" that has presented itself under the name of "metaphysics." Metaphysics, according to Vattimo's interpretation of Heidegger, "conceives true Being as that which objectively occurs before our eyes (those of the mind or the body) and that maintains itself stably in that definiteness" (NE 154). The domination and domain of metaphysics[19] is vast: it extends from Plato's philosophy to Nietzsche, and not even the various philosophies of history that, during modernity, have developed on the basis of "faith in progress" (such as the Enlightenment, Marxism, and positivism) escape such a domain and domination (NE 153). Besides Socrates, the roots of metaphysical thought are to be found in Plato and Aristotle, and perhaps even in Parmenides (NE 154).

Heidegger's severe criticism of metaphysical thought is fundamentally due to the way in which metaphysics conceives of Being, that is, as stability, so that Being is forced to lose its characters of historicity and freedom (NE 154). Heidegger's objection goes as such: If Being is something given in a definite manner once and for all, what happens to human existence that occurs historically? What happens to Dasein as "thrown project?"[20]

It is precisely the peremptoriness of Being that manifests the violent essence of metaphysics. If Being *is*, that is, if Being gives itself in objectivity and immutability, then everyone must be silent in front of such evidence. In this sense, metaphysics is violence because it imposes itself with the authority of the one who possesses all principles of explanation of reality (BI 30–31). In this sense, (the violence of) metaphysics mines the possibility of the opening of a dialogue with the other, for if there is one who possesses *the* truth, what consequently follows is the interruption of the dialogue made of questions and answers; this is, according to Vattimo, "silencing" (NE 147 n, 10).

Metaphysics of Ground and "Truth"

I claimed earlier that metaphysical thought becomes a possible source of violence when it thinks of itself as a depository of *the* truth, thereby turning itself into the cause of the interruption of dialogue among human beings. The unveiling of metaphysics as violent thought is made possible through the same conditions that require the overcoming of modernity and metaphysics (NE 22).

It is not difficult to find the connection between such notion of "metaphysics" as thought of the foundation and the kind of thought that is at the basis of some totalitarian political parties and some religious groups. History works as witness for how they have turned the world into a scenario of material violence in the name of the "truth" of their own ideologies and faith. One can think of the various totalitarian ideologies (for example, the Marxist ideology, presented as "class struggle" and as the establishment of paradise on earth); of the preachers of the "holy war," to which still today various fundamentalist groups appeal; of the medieval institution of the crusades; of the aberrations of the Inquisition, and so on. History has not been empty of those who, speaking "in the name of God," have thereby justified concrete violence against specific human groups, as it happened for example in the concentration camps.[21] In all the examples I mentioned, the agents think they are acting in defense and in the name of *the* "truth"—a truth that today reveals itself as unsustainable and certainly criticizable when we analyze it through the lens of either Vattimo's nihilism or Popper's epistemology. In several cases religious groups have become accomplices in violence by calling their faithful to ("holy") war or by preaching a certain "prudence" "with the tone of the one who resigns to the inevitability of violence in the things of the world, ready, when necessary, to bless the armies, and then to console the mothers and widows and celebrate the memory of the dead."[22] Because of all this, in order that the overcoming of violent metaphysical thought may be achieved one needs nonmetaphysical thinking, that is, a nonfoundational thinking (see NE 11).

Therefore, "in the overcoming of metaphysics, the issue cannot be that of searching for a new notion of Being, but rather and foremost searching for a new way of practicing thinking itself" (IH 98). For this reason, postmodern thinking tries to be post-metaphysical thinking, that is, a thinking that is no (longer) metaphysical in the traditional sense. Thinking is called to a real "turn" capable of overcoming the violence hidden in the metaphysics of foundations; this, however, on condition that such a thinking does not delude itself into believing that it has "overcome" metaphysics *tout court*. As Vattimo writes, "the 'turn' to which thinking is called to overcome metaphysics and its attending violence is increasingly configured in Heidegger's later essays as a 'torsion,' a recovery and twisting prosecution of metaphysics itself."[23] Post-metaphysical thinking is thinking that tries to speak of the historicity of Dasein and no longer of the peremptoriness of first principles or of Being as it is.

Vattimo thinks that Christianity too has historically developed on the ground of metaphysical doctrines, and that therefore it could not escape having an element of violence. He writes that "violence found its way into Christianity when Christianity made an alliance with metaphysics as 'the science of Being as being,' that is, as the knowledge of first principles" (AC 117). According to Vattimo, a link can be found between the notion of metaphysics-violence and the notion of natural law as it is often referred to in the moral discourse of the Roman Catholic Church (AC 114). The notion of a morality that is basically grounded on respect for natural law is repudiated as a child of the violent metaphysical tradition: "the idea that morality has to do with the respect of natural laws belongs to the same tradition" (AC 118). Vattimo seems to suggest that as soon as foundational metaphysics loses the force that sustained it, then also the correlate notions in the moral sphere, mainly the notion of "natural law," become unsustainable.[24]

Can We Exit Metaphysics?

What should be done, then? How can one exit this "vicious circle" of metaphysics and violence? Is there a real way to exit metaphysics? It seems that in our contemporary condition it is not possible not to think metaphysically since metaphysics is "our very essence" and constitutes "our destiny" (IH 79). In "The Overcoming of Metaphysics," Heidegger reminds us that we cannot exit metaphysics because it cannot "be abolished like an opinion. One can by no means leave it behind as a doctrine no longer believed and represented."[25] Metaphysics is "the destiny of Being"[26] because according to Heidegger nihilism is "a history that runs its course along with Being itself."[27] However, metaphysics is simultaneously the history of Being and our own history (IH 80).

If things are like this, the question comes spontaneous: How and when is metaphysics brought to an "ending"? Heidegger's answer is this: "Metaphysics comes to an ending in Nietzsche insofar as he self-presents himself as the first true nihilist; and the deepest essence of metaphysics is precisely nihilism: 'The essence of nihilism is the history in which there is nothing to Being itself'" (IH 83).[28] From the previous claim one can derive a real equation between metaphysics and nihilism, so that, still with Heidegger, one could claim that *"Metaphysics as metaphysics is nihilism proper."*[29]

The fact that metaphysics was not successful in thinking Being "would lie in Being's own essence . . . because [Being] withdraws,"[30] because the truth of Being "conceals itself in such harboring";[31] thus, it never gives itself in its completeness. "According to this, metaphysics itself would not be merely a neglect of a question still to be pondered concerning Being."[32] In metaphysics, it is Being itself that gives itself by withdrawing itself. If it is true, however, as it was said, that in its essence metaphysics "is nihilism,"[33] nevertheless metaphysics is the only way in which "Being itself comes to presence."[34] Therefore, we cannot abandon metaphysics as if it were a piece of garment we no longer wear (EI 33). Vattimo concludes that metaphysics remains in us as the trace of an illness. In other words, it becomes evident that a true "overcoming" (*Überwindung*) of metaphysics is not possible. Therefore, because metaphysics cannot be actually "overcome," Vattimo suggests that the only path to be trodden in our contemporary condition is the acceptance both of metaphysics and of the *Ge-stell* as a *chance* for Dasein (see EM 173).

The First Flashing Up of the Event of Being

The *Ge-stell* is a term from Heidegger's vocabulary that is used to sum up, according to Vattimo, the meaning of technics for Dasein within the context of the contemporary world (AS 66). The only text "in which Heidegger claims that the *Ge-Stell* can be looked at as a first flashing up of the event of Being" (VRF 55) is found in *Identity and Difference*.[35] As system of total organization, the *Ge-stell* "represents the most advanced development of metaphysics" (EM 40), that is, it is "completed metaphysics" (EI 66). One should recall, however, that unlike *Identity and Difference*, Heidegger's text to which Vattimo refers, in which Heidegger refers to the *Ge-stell* as to "a first flashing up of the *Ereignis*," there is a page in *An Introduction to Metaphysics* in which Heidegger lets us know his deep uneasiness toward the "dreary technological frenzy" and the "unrestricted organization of the average man," where even time becomes "simultaneity" and "time as history" has vanished.[36]

How can one explain the relation between metaphysics and technics if, according to Heidegger, "the essence of technology is nothing technological"?[37] For Vattimo, technics and metaphysics are "but different moments of a same process" (EM 40).[38] It is precisely in technics that metaphysics "hands itself down" to us[39] and comes to its completion. "*Technics* is precisely the phenomenon that, at the level of the human way of being in the world, expresses the unfolding of metaphysics and its coming to completion" (IH 89).[40] It is, in a sense, our "destiny."[41] If we want therefore to overcome and exit it, we must paradoxically start with metaphysics itself and with its completed form, namely, technics (see IH 91). What has just been said reveals the presence of an indissoluble link between technics and existence insofar as technics constitutes "the main 'novelty' which human existence must confront in our time."[42]

One of the facts that "the hidden essence of technics" shows us is the use it makes of nature as a mere standing-reserve.[43] The world of *Ge-stell* is the world of the mutual "pro-vocation" between human beings and technics (AD 169; see also AS 67). This abnormal relation between human beings and technics becomes a real "trans-propriation":

"The reciprocal provocation in which Being and man are related in the im-position that characterizes the technical world is the event of the reciprocal trans-propriation of man and Being" (AD 170). In this reciprocal provocation, which ends up being a transpropriation, human beings and the Being of beings shed their traditional attributes of "subject" and "object" since they reciprocally reach each other in their essence. As Heidegger says, "the event of appropriation (*Er-eignis*) is that realm, vibrating within itself, through which man and Being reach each other in their nature, achieve their active nature by losing those qualities with which metaphysics has endowed them."[44] Technics thus discloses itself as the end of metaphysics in the sense that it makes "Being as foundation" disappear (AD 171) and renews the very bases of Dasein.

In the technical world where everything can be manipulated, human beings, too, become manipulable. Humans are thus turned into "objects" of analysis and manipulation, "but this is not merely a sign of some demoniacal character in technology, it is also and inseparably the shining of *Ereignis*, as the crisis and dissolution of the metaphysical determinants of man and Being" (AD 174). This "fall" of human beings into the "manipulability" belonging to objects does not signify a negative aspect of technics that should be demonized. The extreme loss of the metaphysical features of "subject" and "object" as a consequence of the *Ge-stell* must be considered as the opening space for the *Ereignis* of Being (AS 68). This is the step that should be taken "to begin to listen to the call of *Ereignis*" (AD 172). "To listen to the call of the *Ge-Stell* as a 'first flashing up of the *Ereignis*' thus means to allow oneself to live radically the crisis of humanism. This does not mean . . . that one should yield without reserve to the laws of technonology" (EM 46). Thanks to the technical world, "Being as foundation" (AD 171) definitely disappears. It is thus the world of planned production (*Ge-stell*) that let us bring to completion the annihilation of foundational thinking.[45] Paradoxically, *Ge-stell* lets us see the "ontological difference" that has been always forgotten in the metaphysical tradition (AD 171).

"Unfounding" as Destiny of Being

Vattimo claims that "today we are not in a situation of uneasiness because we are nihilists, but rather because we are too little nihilists, because we are not capable of living to its end the experience of the dissolution of Being."[46] He remarks that "philosophy answers its vocation to secularization"[47] only when it definitely gives up knowledge as foundation. That is, the fact "of taking seriously the 'unfoundation' [*sfondamento*] of Being seems to require that, against all returns even in terms of negative theology to metaphysical being, one follows the path of secularization to its end."[48]

According to Vattimo, twentieth-century philosophy has "witnessed the dissolution of every project of 'reappropriation'" (EM 23).[49] It is not difficult to identify in the course of last century thinkers who speak of the epistemological impossibility of accessing absolute certainty. Neither philosophy nor science can claim to possess the truth, because one has become aware that truth is not something that can be grasped once and for all. According to Karl Popper, our entire human knowledge has a conjectural form, and we can never arrive at the truth. "Criticism and critical discussion are our only means of getting nearer to the truth," and never can we grasp "final and certain truths."[50] Popper's critical rationalism "does not believe in 'foundations'"[51]—and in this it coincides, I argue, with Vattimo's weak thought—and therefore it proclaims that "all life is problem solving."[52] According to Dario Antiseri, the true "logic" that enables the growth of philosophical and scientific thinking is "the logic of discord" or the logic "of dissent."[53] This means that, after having elaborated their "theory," the philosopher and the scientist must wait as a counterpart for such theory to be criticized by the opponents and even for it to be confuted. Thus, according to Antiseri all scientific and philosophical theories have a feature of "confutability" and "criticizability," and never of "finality."[54] Antiseri has also advanced a convincing criticism against the notion on which science thinks it rests, namely, "facts." "Facts" cannot be considered as solid and conclusive constructions, because as human descriptions they "have a history" that shows their evolution.[55] Antiseri writes that "the twentieth-century epistemological reflection has dissolved the myth of the *sacredness of facts*." But what exactly are "facts"? Antiseri's answer, which might at first seems disquieting, is that facts are artifacts. "One can somehow claim that *facts*, that is, the foundations of science, *are artifacts that are continuously remade through theoretical demolitions and reconstructions*."[56]

What associates, albeit in their deep differences, the twentieth-century Popperian school and Vattimo's weak thought is, I argue, their fight against all attempts at "conclusive foundation."[57] Vattimo's thought as well as Heidegger's is radically opposed to the idea of truth as conformity of the proposition to the thing. Truth is not something that can be accessed as a given; rather, truth gives itself as historico-linguistic "opening." It is not human beings who own the truth, but perhaps rather the opposite. Vattimo thus emphasizes that "one gets back to truth as opening by taking the unfoundation as destiny" (BI 93–94). The "true" reappropriation that human beings achieve in the time of the end of metaphysics is "a dissolution" (EM 28), that is, the decision to bring about the "leap into the *Abgrund* of Dasein's mortal constitution" (AS 73).

The acceptance of "Being's vocation for the reduction and dissolution of strong characteristics" (BI 94) can turn into "a possible guiding thread for interpretations, choices, and even moral options, far beyond the pure and simple affirmation of the plurality of paradigms" (BI 94). This is the way in which one can fully live nihilism, namely, going through "a fictionalized experience of reality which is also our only possibility for freedom" (EM 29); that is, going through an experience of the "finitude that is constitutive of existence" (AD 5). As Santiago Zabala puts it, thanks so the conquering of their own finitude, contemporary human beings have "learned to live without anxiety in the relative world of half-truths."[58] If, after the series of "dissolutions" that nihilism produced, one still wishes to look for a foundation, then one should be aware that, according to Vattimo, "the sole *foundation*" is rightly "this dissolution" (NE 40). It is obvious that the new foundation is going to be "however *sui generis* and *verwunden*" (NE 40). It is the only one, however, that allows us not to be left with the pretensions to "cogency" and "peremptoriness" of Being and truth. Postmodern human beings, who are aware of the dissolution of all kinds of foundation/founding, feel very compelled to assume nihilism as their only chance: "The accomplished nihilist has understood that nihilism is his or her sole opportunity" (EM 19).[59]

The only viable way to carry forth such a task is, according to Vattimo, the way of "weakness" and "secularization" (see NE 30). To make the way of weakness and secularization one's own also means to accept that one cannot speak of Being and truth as of things that can be grasped once and forever. Thought will not therefore be able to appeal to some "final order" or general "logic" that can be used at all times and places. The aid for thought becomes rather a justification that, because it does not wish to proceed according to traditional logic, should be rather called "rhetoric."[60] Vattimo's postmodern thinking claims for itself a "hermeneutic foundation,"[61] that is, a "'hermeneutic' persuasiveness."[62] What is, however, this hermeneutic foundation of which Vattimo speaks? Vattimo's answer relates Dasein and historicity: "Beings give themselves to Dasein within the horizon of a project, which is not the transcendental constitution of Kantian reason but rather the historical-finite thrownness that unfolds between birth and death, within the limits of an epoch, a language, and a society" (AS 64). Were one to present the so-called hermeneutic foundation with the demand for rigor, then Vattimo's answer would be that "if it is possible [to demand] from philosophical discourse any rigor, then for Heidegger it is the rigor proper to the hermeneutic discourse."[63]

Truth and Weakening of Being

Given that neither Being nor truth ever give themselves in their fullness, what is the "truth" of Vattimo's nihilistic hermeneutics? According to Vattimo, in the world of nihilism in action, Being can *only* give itself in the form of "impoverishment" (EM 161). It is the "poverty of the inapparent and the marginal, or of contamination lived as the only possible *Ausweg* from the dreams of metaphysics, no matter how they may be disguised" (EM 161). The impoverishment of Being is an acceptance of "contamination" as something that belongs to it. It is therefore possible to speak of an "interminable weakening of Being" (BI 13), or a vocation of Being for weakening (BI 14). Vattimo thinks that the vocation of Being for weakening is the only way for the westernization of the world.[64] It seems important to underline that weakening is not an extrinsic element to Being, but rather "Being is the very principle of weakening."[65] The dilution and weakening of Being are the only ways for the conclusive elimination of the pretensions of "absolute truth and validity" (see NE 57). The only claim to "conclusiveness" ["*ultimità*"] that Being can advocate for itself in our current condition is "the conclusiveness of the minimum, understood both as mortal and as punctual, as it were as light and ephemeral."[66] In this sense, the tendency of Being toward weakening is the "truth" of nihilism.

> This, above all, is the "nihilistic" meaning of hermeneutics. If we do not think that the transition from the metaphysics of presence to the ontology of provenance is an error, but the event of Being itself, the indication of a "destiny," then the tendency to weakening . . . that this course manifests is the truth of Nietzsche's nihilism, the very meaning of the death of God, of the dissolution of truth as incontrovertible and "objective" clearness . . . (BI 14)

Some important consequences, first of all at the epistemological level, derive from what has been previously said. A thought that recognizes its own cognitive limits, namely its historicity and finitude, knows that it does not possess *the* truth. Therefore, the tendency of Being to dissolution and weakening must be retained as our only criterion for truth. The truth is that we cannot possess *the* truth in the same way in which we possess a thing, since one should say that truth is not a thing. In this new epistemological horizon, truth is built thanks to argumentation and discussion, that is, in the name of the very criterion of weakness. "A philosophy of secularized and weakened universality does argue, debate, 'disturb,' precisely because its criteria are those of weakening and secularization" (NE 33). According to Vattimo, in current philosophy and culture there is a strong "secularizing tendency."[67] Secularization should not be understood as an extrinsic feature of post-metaphysical or post-foundational thought. Conversely, post-metaphysical and post-foundational thinking belongs to secularization in the double sense of the genitive in the expression "thought of secularization"—in the subjective sense of the genitive, post-metaphysical thinking "belongs to secularization"; in the objective sense of the genitive, it is "a thought that has secularization as its theme."[68] Secularization is what enables us "to think in post-metaphysical terms"[69] and not on the ground of the logic of foundation.

Not every author has received positively Vattimo's identification of metaphysics and violence. Nevertheless, one must recognize that not few "truths" that have been reached through a "metaphysical" way are at the foundation of many acts of violence perpetrated by people and institutions of very various kinds, and history can tell us an innumerable number of cases. As examples one can refer to the excess of the Inquisition, which to ensure unity and repress heresy allowed torture and death penalty; the brutalities carried out by Nazism, which to promote the "truth" of the Party carried out "a program of elimination, even physical, of political opponents and people belonging to categories considered to be inferior, such a Jews, Jehovah's witnesses, Slavians, homosexuals, handicapped and mentally retarded individuals,"[70] and so on. One could continue with other examples, but this is not my goal. What I would like to emphasize is this: "behind" all acts of personal or institutional violence is almost certainly hidden a "truth" that one tries to protect *at all costs*. One should furthermore underline that the expression *at all costs* is full of meaning. It literally means that people's and groups' truth must be preserved "dogmatically" even if one has to step over or kill other people at the same time. In a sociopolitical context, every external manifestation of violence should therefore be questioned on the ground of an absolute truth that one seeks to defend *at all costs* in the sense I just described. The Italian philosopher Dario Antiseri thinks that the so-called totalizing metaphysics are incompatible with the Christian faith because they have always tried to build "'earthly absolutes' that are configured as negations of the 'divine Absolute.'"[71]

When Gianni Vattimo speaks, therefore, of the "violence" of metaphysics understood as the defense, *at all costs,* of *the* peremptory truth of a person, group, or institution, it might be that he is quite correct.

Metaphysics and Silencing

Insofar as it thinks it can arrive at the possession of the first principles or the immutable truths, metaphysics is violent thought.[72] According to Vattimo, nihilism has no relation with violence (see BI 29). One could claim that, thanks to its unfounding action, nihilism can eliminate the source that nourishes and sustains metaphysical violence (BI 29).

In our concrete world, metaphysical violence manifests itself as interruption of questioning, according to Vattimo. The authority that speaks in the name of first principles thinks it can silence the other in the name of "truth." Vattimo's ethics of finitude advances the exclusion of such authoritarian attitude. "This is the overall significance of this ethics of finitude: the exclusion of violence that thinks itself legitimate and the exclusion of all violence coinciding with the interruption of questioning, with the authoritarian silencing of the other in the name of first principles" (NE 46). Even when it recognizes its own weakness and finitude, Vattimo's ethics of finitude refuses violence precisely by appealing to the precept of charity (see B 44).

Nihilistic Hermeneutics and Alterity

A "nihilistic hermeneutic," like Vattimo's, which speaks out of its own contingency, wishes to keep open the space for dialogue and tolerance of the other. In Heideggerian language, one could say that by considering as starting point the recognition of Dasein's constitutive mortality, one coherently arrives at a state of opening toward the other and the respect for "differences." Even more clearly: Dasein's innermost possibility, that is, the possibility not to be Dasein any longer, makes us acknowledge ourselves as humans among humans; it makes us recognize that we are the possessors not of *the* truth, but of relative truths, and it makes us free for dialogue and respect for alterity. When understood in this manner, a "nihilistic hermeneutic" leaves room for the other's freedom. As Vattimo says, it is fundamental "to let the other be." It is not the case then of a hermeneutic that tries to concentrate everyone around "one" truth where other persons lose their individuality. Vattimo's nihilistic hermeneutic is a "situating hermeneutic" that respects the other's identity. "Thought as 'situating hermeneutic' means exactly, first of all, *to let the other be*. The appeal is something that transcends the answers that are given time after time, and only this guarantees that history continues as history, that our existence as 'mortals' . . . may truly be a project. In this way, hermeneutic thinking is the only one that can truly satisfy the need for 'alterity' moving metaphysics itself" (IH 133–134).

In this new situation, "the real enemy of liberty is the person who thinks she can and should preach final and definitive truth" (NE 56). Vattimo thinks that when confronted with the increasingly complex diversification in our Western society, the attitude that can help is that of "a 'tourist' in the history park" (NE 56). In this metaphor is a clear allusion to Nietzsche's thought. It is not simply a matter of thinking about the adequacy of the metaphor; it is also a matter of thinking about the use of Nietzsche's "proposal" as an answer to the situation in the epoch of completed nihilism; and this seems to me to be important.

Vattimo's appeal to let the other be is a way of talking about "differences." The theme of differences is recurrent in Vattimo's thought, who has tried, in various situations, to give a philosophical "justification" for them. According to him, accepting differences enables human beings to have a peaceful coexistence and opens a space for the sharing of different life styles and ethics without resort to violence and exclusion. "The variety of lifestyles and the diversity of ethical codes will be able to coexist without bloody clashes only if they are considered, precisely, styles, not reciprocally exclusive but compatible, like the artistic styles within an art collection" (NE 58). When the other is let be other, the bases are cast so that "truth" may emerge from a dialogical consensus and not from the imposition of authority. "Here one might proceed in different ways. For example, one might ask how we can rationally argue once we forgo the claim of grasping an ultimate foundation that would be valid for all, above and beyond any cultural differences. To this one might answer: the universal validity of an assertion can be construed by building consensus in dialogue, though without claiming any right in the name of an absolute truth. Dialogical consensus may be reached by acknowledging that we share a heritage of cultural, historical, and technological-scientific acquisitions" (AC 5).

Conclusion

In conclusion, I can recapitulate what I have said in this manner: First, Vattimo's nihilism does not wish to have any relation with the metaphysics of foundation because as expression of the omni-comprehensive *ratio*, the latter claims to possess the truth, and thereby it favors violence against individuals and groups. Second, despite the fact that in Heidegger's line of thinking technics represents the extreme manifestation of metaphysics, Vattimo does not consider it as something to exorcise. Rather, it is the key that Being itself gives to us, in the time of the end of metaphysics, for the elimination of the notion of Being as foundation. And third, the acceptance of the weakening of Being and the correlative historicity of human beings open us to respect for alterity and differences.

TRANSLATED BY SILVIA BENSO

Notes

1. Gianni Vattimo, "Ritorno alla (questione della) metafisica," in *Theoria* 6 (1986): 71.
2. Theodor W. Adorno, *Negative Dialectics*, trans. E. B. Ashton (New York and London: Routledge, 1990), 367.
3. Adorno, *Negative Dialectics*, 371.
4. Emmanuel Levinas, *Otherwise than Being or Beyond Essence*, trans. Alphonso Lingis (The Hague: Nijhoff, 1981), 177.
5. Emmanuel Levinas, *Totality and Infinity*, trans. Alphonso Lingis (Pittsburgh: Duquesne University Press, 1969), 302.
6. Gianni Vattimo, "Metaphysics, Violence, Secularization," in *Recoding Metaphysics: The New Italian Philosophy*, ed. Giovanna Borradori (Evanston: Northwestern University Press, 1988), 48.
7. One should notice, however, that not few thinkers have looked with diffidence on Vattimo's categorization of metaphysics. Among others, one could see Enrico Berti, "Credere di credere: L'interpretazione del Cristianesimo di Gianni Vattimo," in *Studia Patavina* 44, 2 (1997): 61–67; Angelo Bertuletti, "Fede cristiana e ontologia debole," in *Studia Patavina* 44, 2 (1997): 118–119; Gian Luigi Brena, "Un confronto tra pensiero debole e metafisica classica," in *Studia Patavina* 44, 2 (1997): 77–83; Antonino Poppi, "Una duplice infondatezza dell'"etica debole,'" in *Studia Patavina* 44, 2 (1997): 91–99; Carmelo Vigna, "Metafisica ed ermeneutica," in *Hermeneutica*, nuova serie (1997): 23–43.
8. Martin Heidegger, "The Word of Nietzsche: 'God is Dead,'" in *The Question Concerning Technology and Other Essays*, trans. W. Lovitt (New York: Harper & Row, 1977), 110.

9. See also Gianni Vattimo, *Essere, storia e linguaggio in Heidegger* (Genoa: Marietti, 1989), 25.
10. Martin Heidegger, "Letter on Humanism," in *Pathmarks*, ed. William McNeill (Cambridge: Cambridge University Press, 1998), 246.
11. Heidegger, "The Word of Nietzsche: 'God is Dead,'" 109. See Martin Heidegger, *Being and Time*, trans. Joan Stambaugh (Albany: State University of New York Press, 1996), 1; and Heidegger, "Letter on Humanism," 245–246.
12. Gianni Vattimo, *Poesia e ontologia* (Milan: Mursia, 1985), 9. English version edited by Santiago Zabala and translated by Luca D'Isanto, *Art's Claim to Truth* (New York: Columbia University Press, forthcoming).
13. Vattimo, *Poesia e ontologia*, 10.
14. Heidegger, "Letter on Humanism," 246. It is precisely "in the forgetfulness of the ontological difference" that the "origin of violence" should be sought. See Gianni Vattimo, "Il fondamento secolarizzato," in *Il problema del fondamento e la filosofia italiana del Novecento*, ed. Pietro Ciaravolo (Rome: Centro per la filosofia italiana, 1992), 57.
15. Gianni Vattimo and René Girard, *Verità o fede debole? Dialogo su cristianesimo e relativismo* (Massa: Transeuropa, 2006), 66.
16. Heidegger, "The Word of Nietzsche: 'God is Dead,'" 112.
17. Lorenzo Biagi, "Il pensiero debole e l'etica della '*pietas*,'" in *Rivista di Teologia Morale* 85 (1990): 45.
18. Vattimo, "Il fondamento secolarizzato," 56.
19. The Italian *dominio* implies both domination and domain [Trans. Note].
20. Heidegger writes: "*The 'essence' of Dasein lies in its existence.* The characteristics to be found in this being are thus not objectively present 'attributes' of an objectively present being which has such and such an 'outward appearance,' but rather possible ways for it to be, and only this"; see Heidegger, *Being and Time*, 40. See also Heidegger, "Letter on Humanism," 247–248.
21. See Gianni Vattimo, *Filosofia al presente. Conversazioni con Francesco Barone, Remo Bodei, Italo Mancini, Vittorio Mathieu, Mario Perniola, Pier Aldo Rovatti, Emanuele Severino, Carlo Sini* (Milan: Garzanti, 1990), 72–73.
22. Gianni Vattimo, "Dio, Allah, Buddha, Yahvé aiutaci tu," [http://lgxserver.uniba.it/lei/ rassegna/0111 07.htm].
23. Gianni Vattimo, "Ontology of Actuality," in *Contemporary Italian Philosophy: Crossing the Borders of Ethics, Politics, and Religion*, ed. Silvia Benso and Brian Schroeder (Albany: State University of New York Press, 2007), 94.

24. It seems to me that one could interpret in this direction Gianni Vattimo, *La vita dell'altro. Bioetica senza metafisica* (Lungro di Cosenza: Marco Editore, 2006).
25. Martin Heidegger, "Overcoming Metaphysics," in *The End of Philosophy*, ed. Joan Stambaugh (New York: Harper & Row, 1973), 85.
26. Gianni Vattimo, "Introduzione," in Martin Heidegger, *Saggi e discorsi*, trans. Gianni Vattimo (Milan: Mursia, 1976), XI.
27. Heidegger, "The Word of Nietzsche: 'God is Dead,'" 110.
28. Martin Heidegger, "Nihilism and the History of Being," in *Nietzsche*, vol. 4, trans. Frank Capuzzi (New York: Harper & Row, 1982), 201.
29. Ibid., 205.
30. Heidegger, "The Word of Nietzsche: 'God is Dead,'" 110.
31. Ibid.
32. Ibid.
33. Ibid.
34. Ibid.
35. Martin Heidegger, *Identity and Difference*, trans. Joan Stambaugh (New York: Harper & Row, 1969), 38.
36. Martin Heidegger, *An Introduction to Metaphysics*, trans. Ralph Manheim (New Haven: Yale University Press, 1959), 37–38.
37. Martin Heidegger, "The Question Concerning Technology," in *The Question Concerning Technology*, 4.
38. See Paolo Volonté, "Crisi della ragione e pensiero debole. Uno sguardo sulla filosofia italiana di oggi," in *Vita e Pensiero* 70 (1987): 230.
39. Vattimo, "Ritorno alla (questione della) metafisica," 68.
40. See also Vattimo, "Ontology of Actuality," 94.
41. See Martin Heidegger, "The Question Concerning Technology," 28.
42. Gianni Vattimo, *Tecnica ed esistenza. Una mappa filosofica del Novecento*, ed. Luca Bagetto (Turin: Paravia Scriptorium, 1997), 9.
43. See Heidegger, "The Question Concerning Technology," 17.
44. Martin Heidegger, *Identity and Difference*, trans. Joan Stambaugh (New York: HarperCollins, 1969), 37. See Vattimo, "Introduzione," in Heidegger, *Saggi e discorsi*, xviii; AD 173–174; AS 68.
45. See Claudio Berto, "Il problema del nichilismo in alcuni attuali interpreti italiani di Nietzsche," in *Friedrich Nietzsche o la verità come problema*, ed. Giorgio Penzo (Bologna: Patron, 1984), 91.
46. Vattimo, *Filosofia al presente*, 26.
47. Vattimo, "Il fondamento secolarizzato," 78.
48. Ibid.
49. See Dario Antiseri, *Le ragioni del pensiero debole* (Rome: Borla, 1993), 37.

50. Karl Popper, *The World of Parmenides. Essays on the Presocratic Enlightenment* (New York: Routledge, 1998), 23.
51. Ibid., 152.
52. Karl Popper, *All Life Is Problem Solving* (New York: Routledge, 1999), 100.
53. Giovanni Reale and Dario Antiseri, *Quale ragione?* (Milan: Raffaello Cortina, 2001), 147.
54. Ibid., 148–149.
55. Ibid., 56.
56. bid., 56.
57. See Franca D'Agostini, *Analitici e Continentali. Guida alla filosofia degli ultimi trenta anni*, with Preface by Gianni Vattimo (Milan: Raffaello Cortina, 1997), 196.
58. Santiago Zabala, "A Religion Without Theists or Atheists," in FR 12.
59. See Gianni Vattimo, *Le mezze verità* (Turin: La Stampa, 1988), xii.
60. See Franca D'Agostini, *Logica del nichilismo. Dialettica, differenza, ricorsività* (Rome-Bari: Laterza, 2000).
61. Gianni Vattimo, "Dialettica, differenza, pensiero debole," in PD 13; see AS 62. Armido Rizzi, "Le sfide del pensiero debole," in *Rassegna di teologia* 27 (1986): 5; Biagi, "Il pensiero debole e l'etica della '*pietas*,'" 49.
62. Vattimo, "La secolarizzazione della filosofia," 602; EI 33.
63. Vattimo, *Essere, storia e linguaggio in Heidegger*, 231.
64. D'Agostini thinks that "the logical and metalogical importance of the notion of 'weakening'" is, fundamentally, "the novel element introduced by the hypothesis of 'weak thinking' with respect to the two great themes in contemporary logic, namely, dialectic and difference". (D'Agostini, *Logica del nichilismo*, 352–353).
65. Vattimo and Girard, *Verità o fede debole?*, 70.
66. Vattimo, "Ritorno alla (questione della) metafisica," 75.
67. Vattimo, "Introduzione," in *Filosofia '86*, ed. Gianni Vattimo (Rome-Bari: Laterza, 1987), V.
68. Vattimo, "Il fondamento secolarizzato," 58.
69. Ibid., 60.
70. *Nazionalsocialismo* [http://it.wikipedia.org/wiki/Nazismo].
71. Dario Antiseri, *Ragioni della razionalità. I. Proposte teoretiche* (Soveria Mannelli: Rubbettino Editore, 2004), 373.
72. See Vattimo, "Metaphysics, Violence, Secularization," 45–62; Luca D'Isanto, "Gianni Vattimo's Hermeneutics and the Trace of Divinity," in *Modern Theology* 10 (1994): 361–364.

7

Thinking the Origin, Awaiting Salvation

CLAUDIO CIANCIO

The Origin in Heidegger and Vattimo

Vattimo's thought certainly weakens the origin, yet it does not forget it.[1] In "The Trace of the Trace," Vattimo writes that "the philosophy that poses the problem of overcoming metaphysics is the same as that which discovers the positivity in religious experience. Yet this discovery signifies precisely the awareness of provenance. Can or must such an awareness come down to a return to its own origin?" (R 90). The answer is the opposite of what one might expect, because it is sought through resorting to the religious tradition. Vattimo in fact answers the question:

> This would be so, if the theological element revealed here as origin did not itself wholly renounce the metaphysical superiority of the origin; if, that is, the theology in question were not a Trinitarian theology. . . . The Trinitarian God is not one who calls us to return to the foundation in the metaphysical sense of the word, but, in the New Testament expression, calls us rather to read the signs of the times. In short, Nietzsche's "radical" saying . . . holds, albeit in different terms, as much for philosophy as for the religion it rediscovers: the more one knows of the origin, the less significant it becomes. (R 90)

If its relevance must be drastically reduced, the origin ought not be excluded because it is constitutive of human finitude and of the event-like [*eventuale*][2] character of Being. In this sense, one should recognize not only the Trinitarian but also the paternal aspect of God in Schleiermacher's sense of the feeling of dependency, of a provenance that is not at human disposal, of a "kernel that, in my view, cannot be an object of reduction or demythification" (B 78). Can one then properly speak of an insignificance of the origin? Could it rather be the case of a transformation of its meaning? And could this transformation be defined in a different manner than as defined by Vattimo, that is, in the sense of an origin that remains determinant (thereby not insignificant) not because it oppresses and reduces to itself, but rather because it offers possibilities of a genuine future, that is, of creativity and novelty?

A certain oscillation between these two reinterpretations of the origin is perhaps inevitable. The oscillation is symptomatic of the difficulty in thinking a figure of the origin that escapes the lien [*ipoteca*] of the metaphysical tradition. It is meaningful to note how an analogous difficulty is found in Levinas who, guided by the Jewish emphasis on the primacy of the future, makes the idea of origin withdraw out of fear of its totalizing effects. In Levinas' thinking, creation plays a fundamental part, yet one that remains, literally, elusive. Levinas underscores the paradoxical character of creation as the idea of an infinite that admits to a being outside itself; that is, the idea of an exceptional dependence, a dependence from which independence arises.[3] This idea is employed to represent the break in the totality: "that there could be a more than being or an above being is expressed in the idea of creation which, in God, exceeds a being eternally satisfied with itself."[4] The meaning of creation lies precisely in its making explicit such movement of rupture in the totality, of overcoming a "being eternally satisfied with itself." Yet it also contains something different, because what is affirmed in it is simultaneously "the kinship of beings among themselves" and "their radical heterogeneity."[5] The kinship of beings, founded on their common origin in creation, can well be understood as a condition of their relation, which is a relation among heterogeneous beings, among others. Out of fear of falling back into the totality, however, Levinas prohibits himself any other word regarding this relation. Therefore the origin is, as I said earlier, gazed elusively; it is a preliminary negative condition, and the story (and thereby also thinking) can start only from the second letter of the alphabet, the letter *beth*, according to a widespread Jewish exegesis of *bereshit* in *Genesis*.

Vattimo refers not to Levinas but to Heidegger. This may seem surprising especially with respect to the question of the origin, given that

Heidegger's thought is oriented toward the origin and precisely for this reason is harshly rejected by Levinas. The reference to Heidegger becomes fruitful in Vattimo only because he translates into Christian language the thought of the origin that Heidegger had explicitly unfolded in anti-Christian terms. How does this translation occur? Moreover, is it a legitimate operation? That is, how can one go around the evident anti-Christian sentiment of the later Heidegger? Resuming the theme of *Andenken*, Vattimo remarks that precisely the reference to the tradition shows that "Being is neither objective nor stable. Being manifests itself as an event with respect to which we are always engaged as interpreters somehow 'on the way'" (AC 22). Certainly the nonobjectifiability and historicity of Being can be seen as a Christian legacy; likewise, a Christian undertone (but merely an undertone) is in the references to a saving God and a new beginning. Yet, as is well known, the differences are quite relevant.

First of all, Heidegger's historical-ontological model has a circular character, whereas Vattimo's—closer to Christianity—is rectilinear. In the "other beginning," Heidegger thinks a return to the beginning that occurs once the development generated by it is completed. It is a circular model because the end coincides with the beginning; the end of the unfolding of the first beginning is the greatest distance from it because in that end the oblivion of the beginning is consumed. Precisely in this way one returns to the beginning, insofar as beginning of the oblivion. To return to the beginning means awareness of the beginning, which therefore becomes a new beginning. We cannot say anything regarding what will be generated by the new beginning. Heidegger in fact emphasizes the preparatory character of such thinking. "The preparatory thinking in question does not wish and is not able to predict the future. It only attempts to say something to the present which was already said a long time ago precisely at the beginning of philosophy and for that beginning, but has not been explicitly thought."[6] One may assume that from the new beginning comes something simultaneously identical to and different from the first cycle; that is, there comes an aware repetition, according to the model of authentic future contained in *Being and Time*—a future that brings back to what one already is precisely by assuming what makes creative action possible. This is probably the only sense in which one can talk of such a beginning as the beginning of "immeasurable possibilities for our history."[7]

This remains in any event a cyclical structure of which there is no trace in Vattimo. Correspondingly different are the conceptions of the divine. Heidegger's last god, "the totally other against gods who have been, especially over against the Christian God,"[8] is under the sign of the refusal;[9] it is the fulfilled manifestation of the essence of the divine as pure withdrawing, as a need for being that cannot be satisfied and that as such therefore discloses the radical finitude of Being.[10] For Vattimo, instead, the radical finitude of Being is manifested by a divine that does not withdraw but rather incarnates itself, and in this sense lowers itself. This movement is opposite to the one indicated by Heidegger, who in a passage from *Contributions* asks precisely whether to speak of a last god means to lower, debase, and even blaspheme such a god.[11] Heidegger answers that this is not likely, because "the last god has to be so named because . . . [it] elevates to the highest degree the sense of the uniqueness of the divine being."[12] In Vattimo there is a god who gives himself and not a god who withdraws and elevates himself; it is a god who donates himself not in refusal but in the renunciation of his own mastery and omnipotence.

Vattimo's is an ontology of weakening that directs one toward *pietas* and charity; it can indicate in that direction precisely because of its provenance from an origin that contains at least the germ of the principle of charity. Heidegger's ontology, on the other hand, is of the most radical and unintentional contingency. Its beginning is not the eternal,[13] the weakening of which one may then think of; it is a real but contingent [*eventuale*] beginning. What is the figure of this beginning, which is a beginning that gives itself its own foundation[14] not as eternal necessity but rather as absolute contingency that is neither prejudged nor constituted by any intentionality? This figure can only be that of "destinality" [*destinalità*], the destinality of a history that can only unfold and retrieve the beginning, albeit in a nonidentical manner. The beginning does not empty itself of its power; on the contrary, it "preserves within itself the highest reign."[15] This beginning is the more determinant the more absent any intention is in the historical movement that originates from it. On the contrary, in Vattimo the historical process seems to be oriented toward a goal of liberation, which he strictly connects to the origin, and, first of all, to divine paternity and creation.

> My entire argument concerning the overcoming of metaphysics—which has led me no longer to speak of Being as the eternal structure—leads me to think of Being as event, as something begun by an initiative that is not mine. The historicity of my existence is provenance, and emancipation—salvation or redemption—consists also in recognizing the event-like character of Being. (B 78; translation modified)

Furthermore, the redemptive orientation refers to the Christian theme of the Incarnation.

It is only in so far as it rediscovers its own provenance in the New Testament that this post-metaphysical thinking can take the form of a thinking of the event-like character of Being that is not simply reducible to a bare acceptance of the existent or to pure historical and cultural relativism. If you will: it is the fact of the Incarnation that confers on history the sense of a redemptive revelation, as opposed to a confused accumulation of happenings that unsettle the pure structural quality of true Being. (R 92)

The emancipatory interpretation of the themes of the end of metaphysics and the event-like character of Being that Vattimo proposes gives them an ethical connotation that does not seem to find adequate justification in an origin understood as an emergence void of intentionality and as the beginning of a destinal path. Therefore the claim that "Heidegger's philosophy can (be understood) as a sort of philosophical transcription, more or less conscious, of the Judeo-Christian revelation"[16] seems to me to be difficult.

Vattimo can refer to Heidegger because he thinks the origin in a twofold manner: on the one hand, as absolute ground with respect to which one can only demand a liberating distancing; on the other hand, as Trinity and Incarnation, and in this sense as condition of possibility of the path of liberation that history displays. That is, history is not simply liberation from the violence of the beginning and the sacred; in it, there is also the unfolding of the intention of salvation that is contained in the origin and, more widely, in the religious tradition.

The Origin as Freedom and Promise of Future

An origin that is pregnant with the future, and with a future endowed with a superior value, can only be an origin that is neither immoveable necessity and perfection, which simply forces and brings back to itself all historical movements, nor beginning destined to a mere progressive emptying out, nor destinal event. If the origin is not and does not remain an inexhaustible fullness, if it is only the *terminus a quo* [term from which] that progressively weakens itself, then should one not think of a process of consummation, of an entropy rather than of a future that opens new possibilities? In this manner, however, does not the ontological weakening become also projectual and creative weakness? And does it not also become a reduction of the energy that the moral action demands in the fight against evil? This point requires special attention because I have the impression that here, too, weak thought oscillates. The project of liberation through weakening has as its condition, on the one hand, the fight against evil, understood mainly as violence, and on the other hand, a reductive interpretation of reality and the relevance of evil. Now, one cannot provide proofs regarding the existence and relevance of evil as well as regarding the existence and nature of God; one can only put forth ethico-existential instances and, at the philosophical level, deepen and explain the bearings and consequences of the various options. The emphasis on evil, which characterizes the tragic thought that Vattimo contests (see B 83–84), presupposes the conviction that the origin is fullness, benediction, and promise, which are, however, denied in history; one can actually only think of such an origin because one presupposes an unacceptable and meaningless presence of evil and renders it the target of a radical and uncompromising resistance; evil is something that would have no meaning if it did not refer to an originary positivity and a possibility of salvation. Between evil and God there is a closed circle, which one cannot access except by leaping into it. Otherwise, one must welcome the invitation not "to exaggerate the enormous power of evil in the world" (B 89), even though I find that it is difficult to attribute such an ultimately naturalistic view of evil (one can avoid exaggerating the relevance of evil only if one recognizes it as a natural dimension) to Christianity, that is, to the least naturalistic of all religions. I find it difficult to interpret the redemption from sins operated by Christ as the unveiling of its nothingness, as its ironical dissolution (B 88–89). I find it equally difficult to interpret the Pauline passage on the victory over death in the sense that this victory "would be that of taking it too seriously."[17] I do not think that there can be Christianity if, in a complete denaturalization of history, one expunges from it the wait for the kingdom of God, for another world, for an *eschaton* that subtracts the world from the infinite circle and redeems all the positive potentialities that have been expressed historically. To return to the fundamental question: How is it possible to think of the reduction of evil as liberation from violence, if it is true that such liberation is not an unavoidable process at least as for its times and modes, and therefore the fight against the evil of violence seems necessary? The way to overcome violence is certainly that of giving it up. Even when it is true that what one must do is "to reduce violence rather than recognize it,"[18] how can one reduce it if one does not oppose violence through the harsh resistance that consists in undergoing it without returning it?

I think that, from out of the experience of evil and the will to liberation, a different conception of the origin is inevitable. It is a conception of the origin as positivity and fullness, yet completely opposite to the metaphysical conception of the absolute that is presupposed in the representation of the origin as simple *terminus a quo*. The latter origin does not promise or make possible any future; one can only liberate oneself from it and its oppression. The negation of the negative, however, does not produce a positive; the negation of the negation of freedom does not produce freedom in its positive sense. Here lies the reason for the failure of all revolutionary projects, which claim to find the contents and the necessary energy for their realization in the future alone. In this way, however, they are void of inspiration, support, and the tranquil strength that is born out of the wait for fulfillment based on promise, and they end up replacing creativity with destructive action. What arises from the negation of the origin, from provenance from nothingness is a work of nothingness. Revolutions become the parodic reversal of the exodus of Abraham and of that of the Jewish people from Egypt, which are events of liberation and openings of the future that are made possible by the fullness of the divine promise. When the origin is thought of as necessary and necessitating objectivity, then a future can be opened only through a weakening of the origin, by acting in such a way that violence becomes progressively less violent up to its own dissolution. Yet, I wish to repeat, the negation of the negative does not produce the positive unless, as in Hegel, the result coincides with the beginning. The positivity that the Hegelian form of return to the origin enables is unacceptable, though, because even positing the future as origin means closing it.

It seems difficult that, from out of the simple negation of the negativity of the violence of the origin or from its weakening, there can emerge a society guided by the principle of charity, whose realization requires energy, commitment, and ability to take suffering upon oneself. The case is different when the originary [*l'originario*] is infinite freedom and creativity, and therefore inexhaustible source, which is *terminus a quo* but also *ad quem* [toward which], in the sense of being the term toward which (through its historical manifestations) a return is always necessary in order to attain creative energy, draw inspiration, and open the future. Only the ontology of freedom, that is, the ontology that posits freedom as originary principle, enables thinking an origin that has neither the oppressiveness of metaphysical necessity nor the binding character of the destiny that cannot be overcome, nor is simply the initial term in a progressive loss of relevance and meaning. Only the ontology of freedom enables the thought of an origin capable of liberating creativity and innovation, and of opening the future.

Thinking the originary as originary freedom has two other important consequences. The first is that history loses all features of destinality, and thus it cannot be read as univocal process. We are still too accustomed to reading history (and the history of philosophy) as a unitary and univocal unfolding (regardless of the possible meaning of such unfolding). It is not difficult, however, to read history as a confrontation or contest of alternative possibilities, the unfolding of which cannot be interpreted as coherent thread, the outcome of which does not correspond to a stringent logic, and in which the prevailing of any of the possibilities could be nonconclusive and the alternatives could present themselves again. The nondestinal character of history does not mean that at every moment anything is possible, but rather that at every moment various alternatives present themselves and their outcomes are unforeseeable. As for the history of philosophy in particular, one should free oneself from the Heideggerian reading, whose claim of reducing the entire history of philosophy to ontic metaphysics can be supported only on the basis of acts of power and simplification. This occurs, for example, with respect to Heidegger's reading of the Neoplatonic tradition, which cannot be reduced to metaphysics because in Neoplatonism the ontological difference is not overlooked.

The second consequence is that, if it cannot be thought of as fullness that must simply unfold or empty itself out, the originary cannot even be considered as indeterminacy that leaves room for any possibility. Originary freedom can be recognized insofar as it has manifested itself, and in its manifestation has expressed an intention endowed with a normative bearing even if, precisely as norm of and for freedom, it gives itself to a multiplicity of interpretations and to the possibility of being contradicted; therefore, it offers itself to the possibility of ontological increase or decrease.

The origin that can be thought of from out of the experience of freedom can be defined as originary creative intention, which, by becoming normative, becomes vocation. Since it does not result into an emptying itself out but rather is an inexhaustible source of potentialities and realizing power, it also becomes promise—all terms that are loaded with the future. The (Christian) religious experience is such an experience of the origin, which can become violent and oppressive (and denies the future) only when it is objectified in a metaphysical structure or is secularized [*mondanizzata*] in a binding historical *primum*, as an origin demanding only a folding upon itself and thereby denying the future.

To think the origin means therefore to interpret and retrieve the originary intention (which is the source of inexhaustible creativity) on the basis of its own manifestations but also obscurations by reconfirming it and correcting the deviations thereof. To think the origin means to respond creatively to its appeal. It means to wait for the future because the origin is creative vocation. This is what in the Biblical revelation is defined as duty to multiply the generations and make the earth hospitable (see *Genesis* 1:28) and then, when the task fails, is defined as promise of a variously configured redemption. Such an origin, which makes the future possible, is not that which should be weakened but rather that from which one should draw; this is so not in the sense of a return to the identical, not even in the Heideggerian form of another beginning. Another beginning is not necessary if the distancing from the first beginning has not been merely oblivion and has not produced merely impoverishment—oblivion and impoverishment that would require precisely a return to the origin. Even when one grants that creative intention, vocation, and promise may imply fulfillment (the idea of fulfillment is the idea of the safeguard of that which has been realized in response to the vocation: it is the content of the promise), such a fulfillment will not be a mere return to the origin. Both the need for a progressive distancing from the origin and that for a mere return to it transform the origin into a totalizing principle.

For this reason, I think I should take some distance from some passages in Luigi Pareyson's later meditations on the theme of eschatology (such meditations have been left to us in the form of fragments and incomplete elaborations). In them, on the basis of the originary understood as unconditioned freedom, Pareyson thinks the history of the eternal, which would have a cyclical character.[19] The difference between protology and eschatology would be such only for humans, and not for God. "Human history has added nothing to God's eternal history, which is victory over evil both at the beginning and at the end of times," Pareyson writes. *Apocatastasis* is novelty for human beings, whereas "for God it is re-establishment, riveting, restoration, return, repetition (if one can say so of something that remains eternal, and is divided only from the human perspective)."[20] This can be said because history is an eternal history, which as history implies different moments, and as eternal encompasses all of them in an immutable manner. Because of the first feature one can say that "to the extent that human beings change (they cooperate freely), eternity changes too."[21] Because of the second, one must say that "eternity before and after the end of history is identical: God does not change."[22] There are nevertheless passages where immutability seems to slip into the identity of beginning and end, as when Pareyson writes that "*apocatastasis* reaches (identifies itself with) divine self-origination."[23] I am afraid that in Pareyson the principle of identity (at least as a philosophical legacy from Plotinus and the Neoplatonic tradition to which he refers) ends up prevailing, mistaking the eternity of the moments of divine history for the identity of the first and the last of such moments. This empties human history and the intertwined divine history of all meaning. Such a conception runs the risk of considering historical vicissitudes as ontologically irrelevant because what is relevant has already been decided once and for all. If the origin is not the Moloch that swallows everything and from which one should only liberate oneself, if it is rather source, impulse, inspiration, support, and promise, then the future is open and history is not indifferent. The originary is indeed such power of the future precisely because it cannot be destroyed nor reduced. The end, however, does not coincide with the beginning. If, because of such power, we can hope that the ontological richness that history expresses will not go lost, nevertheless its what, how, and how much have not been decided *a priori* (even when it is the case of eternal history). In particular, the reality of evil and the fight against it are absolutely decisive, ontologically decisive.

The Origin as Unity and Alterity

The relation between philosophy and religion, too, is declined in the way of thinking the origin, as it is clear in Vattimo's thought. Religion is first of all experience of the origin, no matter how the origin is conceived. The fundamental alternative is that between an experience of the origin (religion) of which philosophy can take possession, and a religion that philosophy can access but not possess (philosophy cannot intellectualize it); that is, a religion to which philosophy must rather continuously return. In the first case, the origin remains simply a provenance void of consequences, or better, whose consequences are appropriated by philosophy in such a way that it no longer needs reference to the origin. One can avoid that philosophy swallows up religion in various ways only if religion is understood as experience of that which cannot be overcome [*inoltrepassabile*], experience of that from which we come and in which we always and already are. If on the contrary it is understood mainly as knowledge, then it cannot withstand philosophy. This happened in most philosophical positions, from Enlightenment critiques to idealistic *Aufhebung* to contemporary philosophies of finitude, whether of a Heideggerian or hermeneutic kind. Vattimo's philosophy is perhaps included in them because it considers weak thought as the secularized assumption of the religious myth, the authentic meaning of which it would exhaust.

How can philosophy relate to religion as to its source without thereby being dominated by it, and therefore without renouncing its own critical freedom? It can do so only if the religious experience is itself already an experience of freedom; that is, if the originary is itself essentially freedom. Philosophy inserts itself precisely in this space of freedom, which implies both the practical dimension of choice (so that the origin can be welcomed or refused) and the dimension of critical distance.

A conception of religion that forgets such a dimension of freedom falls into oppressiveness by the objectified originary and truth. Vindicating the primacy of religion amounts to vindicating the primacy of the origin. It is however important to avoid that the vindication of the origin implies a return to its oppressive forms; that is, to the origin as necessary and absolute foundation or even as principle that through its objectification in historical forms dominates the future, deprives it of all freedom, and makes everything that happens beyond itself appear as impoverishment or betrayal. The ontology of weakening constitutes the simple overturn of the ontologies founded on such figures of the origin (I disregard here the oscillation on the role of the origin that I have mentioned earlier). In such ontologies, the origin brings everything back to itself; in the ontology of weakening, everything is progressively liberated from its dependence on the origin. In the first case, the future is denied in favor of the past; in the second, the past is denied in favor of the future. In the first case, history is distance from the origin that assumes a negative connotation; in the second, it is the same but with a positive connotation. This symmetry reveals how there is convergence between the two conceptions of the origin; in both, the origin assumes an oppressive and violent character. The two conceptions are not truly alternative to each other. Only a conception of the origin as freedom constitutes an alternative.

The risk of falling back into an oppressive form of the origin is present also in this latter conception. I am thinking, to resume Vattimo's discourse, of the theme of God's paternity, which is acknowledged positively as expression of the feeling of dependence yet with the addition that "if the God that philosophy rediscovers is only God the Father, little headway is made beyond the metaphysical thinking of foundation—indeed, it may be that one takes a step or two backwards" (R 92). Vattimo is correct in demanding that God the Father be overcome in favor of a Trinitarian God whose life is love. This distinction between the simple, unique, and absolute God and the Trinitarian God is important and can be made productive so as to depurate even the conception of the origin as absolute freedom from any residue of violent sacredness and oppressiveness. The originary is oppressive not only as absolute and necessary ground, but also insofar as in it there prevails the moment of unity without liberation and unfolding of alterity. Only if the unity is originarily articulated, only if the originary unity implies alterity does it become possible to think of what is generated by the origin as of something that is nonreducible to rigid unity, free in the relation, and an actual ontological increment over the originary unity.

One could aptly retrieve here a great thought by Schelling who, precisely on the idea of an origin that is simultaneously absolute unity and originary articulation, founds a conception of the history of Being the outcome of which is an ontological increment. In his 1809 *Philosophical Investigations*, in clear opposition to Hegelian dialectics, Schelling elaborates a theory of the beginnings (or principles) that implies two opposites and their synthesis, which is spirit, but also, above this triad, a fourth beginning—the originary indifference, which is also called nonground. This fourth and superior beginning (which, one should notice, perfectly corresponds to the demands of Heidegger's ontological difference) enables avoidance of the dualism of the opposite beginnings, and also prevents that duality may be overcome only *a posteriori*, that is, through the third beginning, namely spirit. The two opposed beginnings (ground and intelligence) cannot in fact hold as originary precisely because above them they have the indifference from which they originate. The originary appears as absolutely transcendent unity, which, as such, neither contains within itself nor even less depends on the opposite beginnings. Duality immediately originates (*hervorbricht*) from the originary indifference. This duality, which is not originary and therefore does not destroy the unity, does not dissolve into identity, because in either beginning the originary unity is "in each in the same way, thus, in each the whole."[24] That is, indifference reproduces itself in each of the opposites. Therefore, "*without* indifference, that is, *without* a non-ground, there would be no two-ness of principles."[25] What is interesting in Schelling's thesis is the fact that he can think of alterity within the unity of the origin. Each principle is in fact irreducible because it is the same originary absolute albeit specified in a form. Schelling thinks of the originary indifference as of the principle that, at the end of the process, assumes the form of love. He even considers precisely love as the reason for exiting the originary indifference: "the non-ground divides itself into the two exactly equal beginnings, only so that the two, which could not exist simultaneously or be one in it as the non-ground, become one through love."[26] Love is even above spirit. Although it is in fact true that spirit realizes the unity of the two beginnings, it should also be said that spirit presupposes the other two beginnings and the unity that it realizes is made possible by the originary unity presiding over the whole process. "Above spirit, however, is the initial non-ground that is no longer indifference (neutrality) and yet not the identity of both principles, but rather a general unity that is the same for all and yet gripped by nothing that is free from all and yet a beneficence acting in all, in a word, love, which is all in all."[27]

I do not mean forcefully to impose Schelling's system onto other perspectives. I simply wish to grasp its productive suggestions, which can be welcome also without sharing all of its systematic presuppositions. At this juncture, I find much fecundity in the idea of love as that which corresponds to the originary unity after the occurrence of distinctions and separations. This means that precisely the originary and unerring unity in its absolute transcendence is the condition of an ontological increment, which is the transformation of pure unity into the bond of love. The increment consists in the fact that love "links such things of which each could exist for itself, yet does not and cannot exist without the other."[28] That is, it consists in the fact that in love the originary unity becomes a deeper unity, the unity that realizes itself while preserving the most irreducible difference, the unity that, far from being oppressive originary unity, is rather precisely the condition of charity. In charity, then, the origin is neither lost nor does it remain closed in an immutable and suffocating identity. Charity that does not cross through and preserve the most radical differences is not charity. A new figure of the origin manifests itself in charity: one that, together with the deepest bond of unity, unfolds the inexhaustible richness originating only from a co-originary principle of alterity. Thinking the other in the origin so as not to lose the origin forever—this is one of the most important tasks that Vattimo's philosophy consigns to us, although I have taken it in a different direction than his. The attempt to carry out this task is, however, a testimony of my admiration and gratitude for his thinking.

TRANSLATED BY SILVIA BENSO

Notes

1. This chapter was first published as an essay in Italian as "Pensare l'origine, attendere la salvezza," in *Pensare l'attualità, cambiare il mondo*, ed. Gaetano Chiurazzi (Milan: Mondadori, 2007), 113–126.
2. The Italian terms *eventuale* and *eventualità* derive from *evento*, which has become the standard translation of *Ereignis*, in Heidegger's sense of the word. *Eventuale* and *eventualità* can also mean contingent and contingency, respectively. [Translator's note]

3. Emmanuel Levinas, *Totality and Infinity*, trans. Alphonso Lingis (Pittsburgh: Duquesne University Press, 1969), 104–105.
4. Ibid., 218.
5. Ibid., 293.
6. Martin Heidegger, "The End of Philosophy and the Task of Thinking," in *On Time and Being*, trans. Joan Stambaugh (New York: Harper & Row, 1972), 60–61.
7. Martin Heidegger, *Contributions to Philosophy (From Enowning)*, trans. Parvis Emad and Kenneth Maly (Bloomington: Indiana University Press, 1999), 289.
8. Ibid., 283.
9. Ibid., 285.
10. See Costantino Esposito, "Die Geschichte des letzten Gottes in Heideggers *Beiträge zur Philosophie*," *Heidegger Studies* 11 (1995): 51–52.
11. Heidegger uses the term *Herabsetzung*, by which the theological and philosophical tradition has indicted the kenotic movement of the Christian God. It is difficult, however, to see an explicit reference to this tradition; rather, one can think of an unaware echo, or at the most a parodic intention. In any event, in this passage Heidegger thinks of an elevation, not a lowering.
12. Heidegger, *Contributions*, 286; translation modified.
13. Ibid., 39.
14. Ibid.
15. Ibid., 40.
16. René Girard and Gianni Vattimo, *Verità o fede debole?* (Massa: Transeuropa, 2006), 65.
17. Ibid., 54.
18. Ibid., 27.
19. Luigi Pareyson, *Ontologia della libertà* (Turin: Einaudi, 1995), 303.
20. Ibid., 306–307.
21. Ibid., 309.
22. Ibid., 308.
23. Ibid., 312.
24. Friedrich Wilhelm Joseph Schelling, *Philosophical Investigations into the Essence of Human Freedom*, trans. Jeff Love and Johannes Schmidt (Albany: State University of New York Press, 2006), 70.
25. Ibid., 69.
26. Ibid., 70.
27. Ibid.
28. Ibid.

8

Postmodern Salvation

Gianni Vattimo's Philosophy of Religion

GIOVANNA BORRADORI

To those philosophers and public intellectuals who went through the 1990s convinced that, finally, they had all earned access to a purely secular age the beginning of the millennium must have come as a shock. From the declarations of the masterminds of the terrorist attacks of September 11, 2001, which justified their motives on extremist religious grounds, to the ideological underpinning of the American response to those attacks, which also carried strong religious elements, the world must have seemed to have been reversed overnight. "Was I the same when I got up this morning?" Alice ponders shortly after being thrown into Wonderland. And yet, unlike real people in the real world, even at that moment of complete disorientation she does not lose her composure and unbiased inquisitiveness. "I almost think I can remember feeling a little different," she says. "But if I'm not the same, the next question is 'Who in the world am I?'"

In the months and years after the tragic events that came to be known as 9/11, few American voices could be heard showing as much composure and genuine wish to understand as Alice. The loudest cry on the radical left was Noam Chomsky's, who expressed no interest in investigating the question of religion and violence, limiting his critique to the United States foreign policy.[1] The neoconservative right simply closed ranks behind the staple of the first Bush administration: a shallow polarization of the world between good and evil, respectable and rogue states, friends and enemies. This rhetoric spread panic about security, which gained absolute priority in all arenas. As a result, key theoretical issues with immense political influence lost relevance: among them, the distinction between religion and politics, the concept of secularism, the presumed secularism of liberal institutions, including democracy. Had a sustained public debate occurred on these issues, perhaps a number of reckless political decisions would have looked even more absurd than they already did.

Gianni Vattimo's work on religion is a remarkable European exception. His focus on religion testifies to his formidable philosophical and political intuition, and to his sense of obligation to the historical challenges of his time. The originality of Vattimo's philosophy of religion, which he has been expanding since the mid-1990s, applies as much to his provocative theses as to his conviction that they originate from "elsewhere" than himself. As he wrote in one of his key texts on religion:

> It seems necessary to clarify from the outset that I have resolved to speak and write on faith and religion, because I take the subject matter to be more than a concern of my own renewed personal interest in this theme; the decisive factor is that I sense a renewed interest in religion in the cultural atmosphere around me. However, by seeking to justify and document it I hope to make some progress towards the clarification of this theme. The renewed religious sensibility I "feel" around me, which appears to be imprecise and not definable with any rigor, corresponds well to the topic (to believe in belief) around which my argument revolves. (B 20–21)

What Vattimo calls "cultural climate" is not a *description* of a historical present, populated by facts that may prove or disprove the description. A cultural climate rather consists, for him, in the *interpretation* of those transformative intellectual and social forces that make the present unfold into a unique future. To state the same point from another perspective, Vattimo's "elsewhere" does not draw its validity from the neutral and safe arena of philosophical argument. His "elsewhere" is firmly anchored in an altogether different conception of the relation between philosophy and the world. This conception lies at the core of the great Italian tradition of the *intellettuale organico*, which I will roughly and insufficiently translate as "public intellectual." Launched by Antonio Gramsci and key to his unique brand of Marxism, in Italy the figure of the public intellectual has defined the Catholic leftist lineage as well the secular one. As it has been the case with many intellectuals who played a decisive role in the Resistance against fascism, in parliamentary politics after the war, and in the public sphere, Vattimo's case represents a distinctly Italian synthesis of Marxism and leftist Catholicism.

In this chapter, I discuss some of the main tenets of Vattimo's philosophy of religion, showing how his willingness to take on religion is part and parcel of his political commitment. I claim that it is precisely Vattimo's sense of political responsibility toward the public sphere that gave him a much deeper reading than most other thinkers on the place of religion in contemporary democracy, starting from 1990s. Vattimo's work throws new light on the origin and motives of the violent eruption of religion as an actor in world politics in the new millennium.

Vattimo's proposal for a synergy between the Christian tradition and a progressive political agenda comes to full fruition in the context of his reflection on the European identity, which he developed alongside one of the orienting figures of his generation: Jacques Derrida. Both Vattimo and Derrida have played an active public role in defining the identity and goals of the European Union. From 1999 to 2004 Vattimo was elected to the European Parliament as a member of the group of the Socialist European Party. Derrida studied both the promise of the new continent-wide alliance and its contradictions, by weighing in on pivotal issues such as the European Constitution, and the stature and integration of illegal immigrants in France.[2]

The occasion of the encounter between Vattimo and Derrida on the issue of religion came in the context of a European initiative. Giuseppe Laterza, from Editori Laterza, arguably the most distinguished Italian publisher of the social sciences, offered Vattimo and Derrida to direct a yearly series of books on the state of philosophy in Europe. They both accepted and when it came to decide the topic of the first volume Vattimo from Turin and Derrida from Paris, without having talked to each other, thought that religion was the most urgent issue.

In the second half of this chapter, I juxtapose Vattimo and Derrida's philosophies of religion, both of which took off at a three-day conference on the island of Capri, in the winter of 1994, and I show how Vattimo's discussion of the relation between religion and politics represents the mirror image of Derrida's discussion of the same question.

During that first meeting in Capri, which occasioned an extensive essay entitled "Faith and Knowledge," Derrida developed one of his crucial theses on the topic: that religion is not a primitive term but a specifically Roman and Christian institution. On this basis, he called into question the universality of the Enlightenment project of separating "politics" from "religion," which revolves around the creation of a "secular" and public space for the former, and a "religious" and private space for the latter. Derrida warns contemporary democracies against the illusion of operating in the safety of a secular political space, for the reality is that their mostly unacknowledged Christian heritage tends to regulate and limit the participation of new "others."

By contrast, in "The Trace of the Trace," which records his Capri contribution, Vattimo pursues a similar line of argument but in the reverse direction. For him, secularization is the ultimate message of Christianity. By descending on earth and taking up human pain and mortality, the Christian God inaugurated the interminable process of his own secularization. Salvation, in Vattimo's reading, thus amounts to embracing and implementing the interminable process of the secularization of the sacred that he claims is the violent kernel of the Christian faith. In defending that secularization is essential to Christianity, Vattimo redefines the criteria of the "religiosity" of a religion.

In a nutshell: whereas Derrida unearths the Christian structure underlying democratic secular space, Vattimo makes Christian faith indistinguishable from secular discourse. If Derrida asks his fellow secular thinker to reconsider her faith in democratic politics in light of its religious elements, Vattimo asks his fellow religious believer to reconsider her faith in Christianity in light of its secularizing message.

Religious Traces in Christianity

The subtlety, depth, and originality of Vattimo's theoretical project lie in his philosophical engagement with the cultural atmosphere around him, which emanates in the midst of the human world. This is a world of people with whom Vattimo is in constant contact. They read his books and his columns on the Turin daily *La Stampa*, they hear him lecture in academic and nonacademic settings, and they watch him on television discussing gay rights and female priesthood. It is Vattimo's intensive involvement with the public sphere that has allowed him to re-think the distinction between cultural atmosphere and the historicist notion of "spirit of the time," or *Zeitgeist*.

Classical nineteenth- and early-twentieth-century historicists, from Wilhelm Dilthey to Benedetto Croce, viewed philosophy as the *expression* of its time, a position that inevitably translated it into a normative validation of the status quo and conservative politics. In contrast, Vattimo sees philosophy as uniquely situated to capture the emerging, rather than prevalent or mainstream, sentiments of its time. In line with the early Heidegger of *Being and Time*, Vattimo thematizes the human subject as a being-in-the-world who cares about what happens in it. In line with Gadamer, Vattimo relies on the presupposition that human activity becomes visible only against a "horizon" drawn by our historically determined situation. If a "context" contains the totality of the conditions that theoretically limit our understanding, a "horizon" emerges against a backdrop of prior *involvement* with those conditions. In other words, we exist within a horizon that our interests have opened for us.

Moreover Vattimo combines Gadamer's hermeneutical historicism with the later Heideggerian theory of the present time as the affirmation of an inheritance that is passed on to us by the language we speak, the books that define our formation, the religion of our childhood, our neighbors, and our friends. Heidegger calls this trajectory destiny (*Geschick*) without giving to this notion any of its traditional connotations of predetermination. As humans who are aware of our mortal condition, we have a destiny, but only to the extent that who we are is sent down to us from a past that does not belong to us. The fluidity of this historical movement does not provide stability nor does it presuppose a sharply individuated agent that can own it and control it. We are historical creatures who reconstitute ourselves constantly by producing narratives about who we are.

Unlike the late Heidegger, Vattimo's interest in the notions of destiny and inheritance remains anchored in a commitment to having philosophy act on the present. In the end, I suggest that he develops something close to Foucault's "ontology of actuality."[3] Vattimo's anchor is in the present in the two senses of actuality, a term that both in French (*actualité*) and in Italian (*attualità*) harbors the double meaning of what happens during the present time and what makes news in it. This anchor is the reason why Richard Rorty has defined Vattimo's approach as "common sense Heideggerianism."[4] Such common sense, which is testimony to Vattimo's loyalty to Heidegger's existential analytic, as pursued in *Being and Time*, recognizes the primacy of points of reference, which exceed justification but delimit the horizon in which we exist. Therefore, we are not only always already in connection with a place, at a specific time, under unique circumstances, but we are also, through this connection, in touch with others and their interests, assumptions, fulfilled and unfilled aspirations, and frustrations. This is where Vattimo's commonsense Heideggerianism converges with his progressive politics and his philosophy of religion.

"The Trace of the Trace," the very complex essay that records Vattimo's contribution at Capri, opens with two questions: *Who* speaks of religion today? And *in what language*? In this essay, as in most of Vattimo's other ones, there are many speakers, coming from the present as well as from the past, and many languages, including but not limited to, original theoretical speculation, highly technical philosophical commentary, and political analysis. But here, two speakers and two languages dominate the stage. There is what Vattimo calls "common consciousness" that speaks the language of actuality, in the sense of what makes news and preoccupies the public sphere. And then there is philosophy, which speaks of actuality in terms of ontology of the now, and does so in the many idioms it inherits from the past. Both the social and theoretical registers, and this is one of Vattimo's central claims in the essay, share a "need for foundations," which is behind the return of religion in the public sphere of democratic nations, in philosophy, and in world politics. Vattimo examines the figure of the return from close by asking himself whether it is the essential figure of religion: "In religion something that we had thought irrevocably forgotten is made present again, a dormant trace is reawakened, a wound re-opened, the repressed returns . . . a long convalescence that has once again to come to terms with the indelible trace of its sickness" (R 79).

Vattimo wavers, however, between the ontological path and his commonsense Heideggerianism, which would render the return of religion a contingent feature of "our conditions of existence in modernity (The Christian West, secularized modernity, a *fin-de-siècle* state of anxiety over the impending threat of new and apocalyptic dangers)" (R 79). Vattimo settles on an original solution that combines both alternatives: "If we accept that it is not an external aspect accidental to the religious experience, then the actual forms taken by this return in our highly specific historical conditions will themselves be considered essential" (R 80).

Here is one of the most distinctive "Vattimo moves." On the one hand, Vattimo historicizes, and thus "weakens," the foundational role of ontology; on the other hand, he ontologizes the conditions of experience, so as to dissolve the metaphysical logic of oppositional pairs (necessary versus contingent, ontological versus historical, inside versus outside) in the fluidity of a hermeneutical horizon.

The figure of the "return" features prominently in both social consciousness and the theoretical realm, which share the need to find a stable and secure ground. Vattimo does not deny that this common longing for stability is a response to fear. Indeed, as he describes it, it is a kind of panic that begins after World War II and is "motivated above all by the sense of impending global threats that appear quite new and without precedent in the history of humanity" (R 80). In social consciousness, this panic originates from the threats of war and genetic engineering; from the lack of a comprehensive meaning of life; from the elusiveness of a recipe against the sheer boredom of consumerism. This panic is also the reason for the resistance to modernization that Vattimo sees at the heart of the violent return of religion, and that is usually accompanied by the affirmation of ethnic and tribal identities. In philosophy, the same kind of panic exists, but it follows "the dissolution of metaphysical meta-narratives" (R 82). The breakdown of "the philosophical prohibition of religion," prohibition that had characterized the project of modernity from Kant onward, "coincides with the dissolution of the great systems that accompanied the development of science, technology and modern social organization, but thereby also with the breakdown of all fundamentalism—that is, of what, so it seems, popular consciousness is looking for in its return to religion" (R 81).

Vattimo warns, however, that philosophy cannot afford to fall prey to such panic. If philosophy were indeed to let itself be controlled by fear, it would make itself responsible for multiplying violence rather than reducing it. Two reasons motivate Vattimo's warning. First, religion would have to be philosophically understood as having a foundational essence of its own, providing the guarantee of a safe ground. But this means to validate and promote the kind of religious dogmatism of which philosophical meta-narratives are the parallel. To give in to religion as the ultimate ground of stability, safety, and authenticity, would mean for philosophy to subscribe to the most violent of all possible responses. Second, in its craving for religion, social consciousness (and unreflective metaphysical philosophy) "tends to conduct itself reactively." The notion of reactivity comes to Vattimo from Nietzsche and describes the passivity of any "nostalgic search for an ultimate and unshaken foundation" (R 83).

In the face of this spreading panic, philosophy's responsibility is to see itself as the critical consciousness of social consciousness. Vattimo's suggestion is for philosophy to conceive itself as a kind of immanent critique of society, modeled after the Frankfurt School of Critical Theory. Philosophy's main responsibility would thus be, "without surrendering its own theoretical motivation and indeed while establishing this motivation as the basis for a critical radicalization of popular consciousness" (R 82), to produce an alternative, nonmetaphysical conception of religion.

Besides reducing violence, this methodological posture would facilitate transforming the return to religion into an active and life-affirming force, rather than a reactive and nostalgic one. "It is (only) because metaphysical meta-narratives have been dissolved that philosophy has rediscovered the plausibility of religion and can consequently approach the religious need of common consciousness independently of the framework of Enlightenment critique" (R 84).

Philosophy should take the return of religion as an opportunity to question the (mostly unexamined and hypocritical) dualism that

Enlightenment thought posited between political and religious spheres of competence. "The critical task of thinking in relation to common consciousness consists here, and now, in showing that even for this consciousness the rediscovery of religion is *positively* qualified by the fact of presenting itself in the world of late-modern technoscience, and thus that the relation with this world cannot be conceived only in terms of flight and polemical alternatives" (R 84).

With this observation comes Vattimo's final answer to the two connected questions regarding the significance of today's "return of religion" and the nature of the experience of the "return" *in* religion.

1. The significance of today's "return of religion." The fact that religion "returns" today, in the age of technoscience, is essential and not accidental, or residual, to a nonviolent, nondogmatic, post-metaphysical conception of religion, which is both new and extremely old: as old as religion itself, Vattimo claims. Only the circumstances of this epoch, our epoch, have rendered the return of religion possible, acceptable, indeed, positive. The opportunity opened by the return of religion today will allow philosophy to play a critical role in containing common consciousness's tendency to view religion as an escape. Such escapism, which often makes despair and anger turn to religion, is also, if I may add my own alongside Vattimo's, one of the greatest facilitators in the use of religion as a political, and often violent, ideology.

2. The nature of the experience of the "return" *in* religion. By definition, religion returns to "an originary factuality" (R 81), which does not need to be dogmatically anchored in the sacred text. Such originary factuality may apply, instead, to basic spiritual needs. These needs are not subjective but intrinsic to the human condition. Luigi Pareyson, one of the closest figures to Vattimo since he was a student at the University of Turin, suggested thinking of these originary needs in terms of the need for forgiveness, the enigma of death, the reality of suffering, and the experience of prayer.

A Religion of Nonviolence

The concept of return is explored further in Vattimo's 1996 book, *Credere di Credere,* puzzlingly translated as *Belief.* Written in the first person, it testifies to his conviction that it is impossible to speak meaningfully of religion without assuming the risk of a full engagement with it on a personal level. And yet, what constitutes religious experience is not, for Vattimo, faithful belief, or even the choice that one makes to exit the secular justificatory realm to embrace a superior, higher order. In fact, the opposite is true. For Vattimo, religious faith is a "recovery of an experience that one has somehow already had. None of us in our Western culture—and perhaps not in any culture—begins from zero with the question of religious faith" (B 21). This "recovery" of the familiar, as opposed to the leap in the unfamiliar, is "the re-presentation of the core contents of consciousness we had forgotten" (B 21). The English term "re-presentation" translates only vaguely "*ripresentarsi*," the Italian verb Vattimo uses here, which more closely means to come back or to reemerge. This specification is important because the "core contents of consciousness" are not for Vattimo mental contents, in the sense of "represented" contents, but rather experiences that come back, reemerge tectonically and spontaneously as soon as we weaken our metaphysical commitment to secularism.

Vattimo is careful to distinguish himself from those believing believers (*credenti-credenti*) who are interested in creationism and for whom the idea of return is "the search for the origin, namely, the creature's dependence on God" (B 21). Creationism and belief in the possibility of reappropriating the origin are precisely the kind of foundational metaphysical claims that Vattimo's hermeneutical project rejects wholesale. Vattimo's return is, instead, modeled after Heidegger's interpretation of the metaphysical tradition in terms of a "forgetting of Being."

In Vattimo's interpretation, Heidegger's notion of forgetting is not an exhortation to recollect "the forgotten origin by making it present again." Rather, forgetting the origin suggests that "we have always already forgotten it, and that the recollection of this forgetfulness and this distance constitutes the sole authentic religious experience" (B 22). An irreducible sense of distance, and not appropriation, a distance that prevents the return from reaching its destination, is thus Vattimo's characterization of the religious experience. Exploring that distance is what Vattimo means by secularization: "a relation of provenance from a sacred core from which one has moved away, but which nevertheless remains active even in its 'fallen,' distorted version, reduced to purely worldly terms" (B 21–22). Such relation of provenance is the only metaphysical commitment that Vattimo agrees to in redefining the religiosity of religion. No doubt, this is a staggeringly "weak" claim about what is distinctly and truly "religious" in religion. Vattimo's religiosity, however, does not admit the dogmatic kernel of belief required not only by Christianity, but by the Abrahamic heritage, as Derrida called it "in order to bring together Judaism, the Christianities, and the Islams."[5]

Although I believe that Vattimo's Heideggerian interpretation of the religiosity of religion may apply to the Abrahamic umbrella in its entirety, I can also see how Vattimo's work on religion could lend itself to the charge of offering an apology of Christianity. This reading could stress that the Christian dogma of the Incarnation plays a paramount role in Vattimo's philosophy of religion, even though, as I am about to discuss, he interprets it as the secular dogma par excellence. If the dogma of the Incarnation holds the sole key for the desacralization of religion, Vattimo's take could come close to Kant's doctrine of the "reflective faith," in which Christianity emerges as the only moral religion.

I believe that the risk of misreading Vattimo's philosophy of religion in apologetic terms is real, but only if one misses both the Heideggerianism and the Gadamerianism of his strategy. Vattimo's Heideggerianism requires that the origin, which for Christianity is the New Testament, is not an object to be appropriated but a heritage, a *Geschick*, with which one has to come to terms and interminably negotiate. Conjointly, Vattimo's Gadamerianism requires that religion, if hermeneutically conceived, be part of the horizon that our interests have opened for us. These interests are points of reference beyond justification, which nonetheless do delimit the line of the horizon. According to these hermeneutical constraints, Vattimo's overwhelming focus on Christianity is not apologetic as Christianity belongs to his life-story and heritage.

Vattimo's nihilistic rediscovery of Christianity (see B 34) runs parallel to his interpretation of modernity as the final consummation of a nihilistic trajectory. This means that "Being has a nihilistic vocation and that diminishment, withdrawal and weakening are the traits that Being assigns to itself in the epoch of the end of metaphysics and of the becoming problematic of objectivity" (B 35).

The "nihilistic vocation" of the Western metaphysical tradition serves as the model for Vattimo's rediscovery of religion, which has deep roots in the tradition of critical thought. For Max Weber, for example, capitalism, as the defining paradigm of modernity, arises from a "transformation" of the Christian tradition rather than from its elimination. Unlike Weber, however, Vattimo believes that Christianity by its own movement unfolds into secularization. For Vattimo, "a secularized culture is not one that has simply left the religious elements of its tradition behind, but one that continues to live them as traces, as hidden and distorted models that are nonetheless profoundly present" (TS 40).

This is where Vattimo's philosophy of religion joins his theorization of "weak ontology," where a "strong," namely power-laden overcoming of metaphysics (*Überwindung*) is reformulated in terms of a twisting, distortion, or deformation (*Verwindung*) of the tradition. For Vattimo, such twisting is aimed at weakening all foundational force, which he sees as the most effective strategy to avoid reinstituting a metaphysical edifice. Both secular theoretical reason and religious belief are thus engaged in an ontology of actuality. "Philosophy might do better to think of itself as a critical listening . . . to the call that only becomes audible in the condition of inauthenticity itself" (R 84).

As it is the case with the double register of the ontology of actuality—assumed as what makes news and what is present—critical listening entails the deep political and social engagement with the here and now that Vattimo has cultivated throughout his career. The struggle against the oppression and exclusion of minority groups is not, for Vattimo, a distinctly secular value. Modern European culture, which is Vattimo's own heritage, is still linked "to its own religious past not only by a relation of overcoming and emancipation, but also, and inseparably, by a relation of conservation-distortion-evacuation" (TS 42). Conservation here refers to the notion of provenance that is part of the richness of tradition and culture. Distortion is already implied in the turning of a foundational principle or theory into a trace, namely, a marginal and contingent fragment of a complicated texture. Evacuation is an "emptying out," or *kenosis*, "the abasement of God, which undermines the natural features of divinity" (B 47). From this point of view, the object of revelation is not some kind of "truth" but rather "an ongoing salvation. . . . The history of salvation and the history of interpretation are much more tied to each other than Catholic orthodoxy concedes" (B 48–49).

What is truly incompatible with Vattimo's return to religion is violence, and violence, in his world, is intrinsic to metaphysics, which does not only name a philosophical field but taps into what René Girard called "the sacred." "Metaphysical violence is, generally, all identification between law and nature, which has dominated the traditional teaching of the Church" (AC 114). The blessed use of sexuality, embodied by the institution of heterosexual marriage, and the theory of just war are, for Vattimo, examples of metaphysical violence. The secularization he advocates is a kind of desacralization, which Vattimo reads as the true and deepest message of the Christian dogma of the Incarnation. To have faith does not permit any literalist claims regarding the sacred text or blind reliance on religious authority. To believe in salvation is "to understand the meaning of the evangelical text for me, here, now. In other words, reading the signs of the times with no other provision than the commandment of love, which cannot be secularized" (B 66).

The Christian Roots of Politics versus the Secular Roots of Christianity: Vattimo and Derrida

As I anticipated in the beginning of this chapter, Vattimo's philosophical interest in religion arose at the same time as Derrida's. However, after their initial conversation on the island of Capri, their paths never really intersected again.[6] This fact seems all the more surprising given that, despite the difference of their philosophical orientations, each of their positions on the issue of religion appears to be the mirror image of the other. While Vattimo's desacralization of Christianity renders it almost indistinguishable from secular discourse, Derrida, through his deconstruction of the distinction between theology and politics, renders the secular space of politics, and particularly the supposed secularism of the modern nation-state, almost indistinguishable from Christianity. In conclusion, I briefly recall the main tenets of Derrida's deconstruction of the theologico-political and show its relation to Vattimo's desacralization, or secularization, of Christianity. To discuss in detail their mutual reservations, which are many, would be the subject of another chapter. Here, I limit myself to pointing out how neither one of them believes in the sharp distinction between the secular and the religious domains. This position, which makes them critical of the naïveté of a certain liberal tradition, has allowed both of them to anticipate the most pressing dilemma of our time: the eruption of religion on the geopolitical scene.

Some critics have correctly claimed that in "Derrida's texts of the past few decades, deconstruction became almost coextensive with the deconstruction of an unthought and still-operative theological heritage in Western political thought."[7] I believe, however, that the story is a bit more complicated. Derrida's program of deconstruction of the theologico-political should be schematized into two large categories: one is his critique of the notion of sovereignty as the indivisible core of the theologico-political. The other is Derrida's critique of the Enlightenment and more specifically of Kant. While the deconstruction of sovereignty occurs in terms of the whole "Abrahamic filiation," an expression in which Derrida groups the three religions of the book, the deconstruction of the Enlightenment and of Kant focuses more distinctly on Christianity. In his Capri address, from which "Faith and Knowledge" takes off, Derrida pursues three connected but distinct targets relevant to his juxtaposition with Vattimo:

1. A genealogy of the concept of religion. Based on Emile Benveniste's claim that there is no indo-European correlative for what we call religion, Derrida examines the double Roman and Christian origin of the concept, which demonstrates its inadequacy for use as a primitive term. This introduces "the strange phenomenon of Latinity and of its globalization,"[8] which, for this reason, Derrida renames "globalatinization."
2. A critique of the Enlightenment's separation between the secular space of politics and the religious space of faith. The subtitle of "Faith and Knowledge," which reads, "Two Sources of 'Religion' at the Limits of Reason Alone," subtly distorts the title of Kant's classical treatise, "Religion Within the Limits of Reason Alone." In it, with the concept of "reflective faith," Kant indicated that Christianity is the only "moral" religion. From Voltaire to Kant, from Marx to Hegel, up until Heidegger, Derrida believes that "the fundamentally Christian axiomatics of Kant"[9] remains fundamentally uncontested.
3. A deep link binding religion, the (Latin) concept of community, and violence.

The Christian matrix Derrida retrieves in the concept of religion; the Christian bias that he finds in the philosophical tradition of political philosophy, from Kant onward; and finally, the unearthing of the link between religion, community, and violence all together give Derrida a toolbox with which to attack several key institutions of Western culture, politics, and society. From the nation-state to tolerance, from democracy to the juridical concept of "crimes against humanity," from cosmopolitanism to marriage, Derrida dismantles the integrity of the secular. In order to become really secular, if it were ever possible, all of these concepts and institutions would have to be reinvented.

Conversely, Vattimo believes that secularization is the constitutive trait of Christianity and that salvation ought to be understood as the history of secularization. Loyal to his hermeneutical approach, Vattimo focuses mostly on Christianity, which represents his own heritage.

Vattimo and Derrida are on the same page in claiming that not only Western political discourse and its institutions, but also the philosophical tradition harbors a steady Christian allegiance. However, while Derrida deconstructs the Christian model within the concept of religion, Vattimo hopes to open a space for a nonreligious Christianity, free of dogmatic and metaphysical violence. If Derrida's first commitment is to reveal the theological foundations of politics, Vattimo's is to discover the secular vocation of religion.

Notes

1. Chomsky correctly pointed out how the United States' declaration of war against terrorism flies in the face of the American administrations' financing of all sorts of terrorist groups in the past three decades, from the Contras in Nicaragua to the Mujahedeen in Afghanistan. See Noam Chomsky, *9–11* (New York: Seven Stories Press, 2001); *Power and Terror: Post 9/11 Talks and Interviews* (New York: Seven Stories Press, 2003).
2. Derrida's interest in the European Union is linked to his hope that new forms of sovereignty will arise from the impending ashes of the nineteenth-century model of the nation-state. See Jacques Derrida, *The Other Heading: Reflections on Today's Europe*, trans. Pascale-Anne Brault and Michael Naas (Bloomington: Indiana University Press, 1991). For Derrida's contribution to the debate on illegal immigrants in France, see his essay, "On Cosmopolitanism," in *Cosmopolitanism and Forgiveness*, trans. Mark Dooley and Michael Huges (London and New York: Routledge, 1997).
3. Santiago Zabala had this intuition, too. See his "Introduction: Gianni Vattimo and Weak Philosophy," in *Weakening Philosophy: Essays in Honour of Gianni Vattimo*, ed. Santiago Zabala (Montreal: McGill-Queens University Press, 2007), 21.
4. Richard Rorty, "Heideggerianism and Leftist Politics," in *Weakening Philosophy*, 149.
5. Jacques Derrida, "On Forgiveness," in *Questioning God*, eds. John D. Caputo, Mark Dooley, and Mark J. Scanlon (Bloomington: Indiana University Press, 2001), 28.
6. In 2000, Vattimo participated to a conference in honor of Derrida's philosophy of religion entitled *Judéités. Questions pour Jacques Derrida*, ed. and trans. Bettina Bergo, Joseph Cohen, Raphel Zagury-Orly, and Michael B. Smith (New York: Fordham University Press, 2007). However, and surprisingly, his essay "Historicity and Difference" does not really address any issue that could be relevant here.
7. Michael Naas, "Derrida's Laïcité," *The New Centennial Review* 7,. 2 (2007): 25.
8. Jacques Derrida, "Faith and Knowledge," in R 29. The globalization of Latin and Christian terminology is for Derrida a hyper-imperialist phenomenon, which "imposes itself in a particularly palpable manner within the conceptual apparatus of international law and global political rhetoric" (Ibid.).
9. Ibid., 52.

9

Secularization as a Post-Metaphysical Religious Vocation
Gianni Vattimo's Post-Secular Faith

EDUARDO MENDIETA

Introduction

Whether we accept secularization as being *sui generis* to the West is not as important as whether we recognize that secularization has been central in the constitution of the West itself. Yet, the so-called resurgence of religion in contemporary societies, after centuries of putative secularization, urges us to ask whether secularization is actually unique to the West, a type of *Sonderweg*, that is, a societal process autochthonous to the West, and thus unlikely to take root in other social orders. The fact is that even in the so-called West, secularization itself is not to be taken for granted. While Europe can claim to be secularized, the United States has lived a recrudescence of religious belief. In the United States, in fact, cultural, political, and social identity is intricately woven with religious beliefs and practices. In Latin America, which in the second half of the twentieth century underwent a kind of second reformation that achieved its theological articulation through liberation theology, religion has remained a vital element of public and social life. It may turn out that secularization is a short-lived process, a hiatus, in a long history of religious confessions and practice. Secularization may turn out to be the exception, and not the rule of social evolution.

It is one of the distinct virtues of Gianni Vattimo's work to have sought to go behind the socio-theoretical questioning about the sources, durability, depth, and reach of secularization to its philosophical sources. Vattimo has argued over the last two decades, in numerous publications, that secularization is not just the fate of the West, but the very "essence of Christianity" (B 50). Secularization is the fate of the West. For Vattimo, secularization is not a societal process, one catalyzed by religious wars, the rise of the secular state, the needs of capitalism, and the corrosive effects of the scientific and industrial revolutions. Instead, it is the Judeo-Christian tradition itself that unleashed secularization, as the manifestation of its most central commitments and world outlook. Additionally, the philosophical outlook of the West is rooted in the Judeo-Christian tradition to such an extent that even when it is most anti-Christian that philosophy expresses the religious character of the West. The religious vocation of "Western" philosophy manifests itself in its atheism. Yet it is that very atheism that keeps Western philosophy within the horizon of the Judeo-Christian philosophical outlook. Thus, the religious vocation of "Western" philosophy is expressed in its atheism, an atheism that culminates in nihilisms. For Vattimo, nihilism is the philosophical expression of secularization, but also the actualization of an inner logic, the logic of atheism. Nietzsche's nihilism is the secularization of philosophy. Nihilism, the expression of decadence and the unmasking and demystification of every metaphysical system and postulate, is secularization of the supra-sensual world that awakens us to the fact that all we have are the stories we tell ourselves about how we became who we have become.[1] For Vattimo, however, Nietzsche's nihilism has become hermeneutics as the *koine* of our *Zeitgeist*. All we have are "interpretations," and this itself is an interpretation (BI 1–14). Hermeneutics carries out the work of nihilism by immersing us in our historicality and the *Wirkungsgeschichte* of the religious and nonreligious texts through which we read ourselves into becoming who we become. Thus, in Vattimo's work we encounter a generative series of propositions: secularization is not aleatory to the West; rather, it is its very acme. Nihilism is the philosophical articulation of secularization. Hermeneutics is the most contemporary expression of philosophical nihilism. Without both nihilism and secularization the West cannot become what it is fated to become. Christian atheism (and one could ask with Jean-Luc Nancy whether there is any other kind)[2] produces secularization and thus nihilism. But at the very moment that nihilism triumphs in hermeneutics as the *koine* of our time, religion is allowed to emerge untethered to metaphysical and supra-sensory mystification, that is, religion without fetishes or false idols. Secularization and nihilism are means by which we can become "truly" Christian. Or, in the words of Ernst Bloch, "only an atheist can be a good Christian; only a Christian can be a good atheist."[3] Thus, in Vattimo, like in Bloch, we encounter the following two-step proposition: "secularized philosophy is the philosophy of secularization,"[4] just as secularized Christianity is the Christianization of secularity. If the first step urges us to think through the secularity of contemporary philosophy in terms of how it becomes godless for the sake of its origins, the second step urges us to recognize that secularity, or achieved secularization, remains true to its demystification of all fetishes and gods only if it assumes the form of charity. Secularization, in Vattimo's work, then becomes a form of gratuitous gift and hospitality that epitomize the event of incarnation through divine *kenosis*. Secularity thus is the abasement of god, who withdraws in order to grant human freedom its horizon of efficacy. Consequently, secularity can only remain true to its source, Judeo-Christian love, as the peace of solidaristic and empathic cosmopolitan and ecumenical coexistence. How Vattimo arrived at this momentous insight is the subject of this chapter. First, I discuss Vattimo's appropriation of Nietzsche's alleged atheism. Then, I turn to Heidegger's reading of Nietzsche, in particular the former's reading of the latter's word "God is dead." In the third and final section, I argue that Vattimo's theses about the relationship among metaphysics, hermeneutics, and nihilism, are mirrored and echoed in Jürgen Habermas' linking of postmetaphysical thinking to postsecular reason. The claim is that Vattimo's *credere di credere* [believing to believe] finds an unusual ally in Habermas' *selbstreflexiv aufgeklärtes Verhalten*.

Nietzsche: "God is dead.... And we have killed him"

While Vattimo's work is marked by typical European ecumenism and transnational engagement with a variety of thinkers, two have occupied a unique place in his thinking: Friedrich Nietzsche and Martin Heidegger. In fact, Vattimo confesses without apology that he has based "all of [his] philosophical research" on these philosophers.[5] Thus, for a proper understanding of Vattimo's arguments about secularization, nihilism, and the fate of Christianity, it is indispensable that we turn to his readings of both Nietzsche and Heidegger. Additionally, as it will be shown, not only does Vattimo read Nietzsche through Heidegger, but he also reads Heidegger through Nietzsche, thus turning on its head Heidegger's claim that Nietzsche's thinking is the fulfillment of Western metaphysics by claiming that it is Heidegger who still has not lived out the fate of Western nihilism and secularization by ceasing to wait for the gods. To Heidegger's "only a God can save us," Vattimo responds, "we alone can save ourselves."

Nietzsche's name is indissolubly linked to two expressions: the *Übermensch* and "God is dead." Indeed, Nietzsche's pronouncement that God is dead has been one of the most quoted and also least understood claims. There are two key points of reference for what Nietzsche may have meant by "God is dead." First, we have to analyze the relevant and connected passages in *The Gay Science* and *Thus Spoke Zarathustra*. God's death is announced in the *Gay Science*, in the section titled "New Struggles." There, Nietzsche writes: "After Buddha was dead, his shadow was still shown for centuries in a cave—a tremendous, gruesome shadow. God is dead; but given the way of men, there may still be caves for thousands of year in which his shadow will be shown.—And we—we still have to vanquish his shadow, too."[6] God, notice here, is no longer in the supra-sensory world, in the beyond of the metaphysical world. So long as God was alive, God could be an underwriter of the metaphysical world. Yet, although God is dead, his shadow endures in the caves of those who remain prisoners in their darkness, though the brightness of the metaphysical world no longer blinds them. Nietzsche's reversal of Plato's cave is explicit: it is not that we have to be liberated by the philosopher from the cave and ascend to the luminescence of the metaphysical sun; it is that we remain enthralled by metaphysical shadows long after their source has vanished. A new struggle still awaits us, or at least those who face cheerfully and with joy the struggle against the trace and shadows of false gods.

"God is dead" is the good news that philosophers, the "free spirits," receive "as if a new dawn shone." The news opens up a new horizon, and the hearts of the joyful ones "overflow with gratitude, amazement, premonition, expectation. At long last the horizon appears freed to us again, even if it should not be bright; at long last our ships may venture out again, venture out to face any danger."[7] God's death discloses the open sea.[8] The death of God announces both new struggles, against those who refuse to give up their idolatries and immaturities, but also anticipates the awakening of a new project, the sending into the sea of new challenges and discoveries. God's absence frees us to assume charge of our lives, to live without guarantees or warrants that our commitments may find no more justification than that we allow through our commitment to them. It is our commitment to them that is their warrant. God's death removes the moral and metaphysical banisters that we used as supports for our refusal to venture beyond the values that cripple our moral responsibility. God can no longer be either our alibi or our witness. Such loneliness can be terrifying, but for Nietzsche it is liberating.

Yet, the most telling passage in Nietzsche's announcements of God's death is found in *The Gay Science*, in the section titled "The madman,"[9] framed as a parable: "Have you not heard of that madman who lit a lantern in the bright morning hours, ran to the market place, and cried incessantly 'I seek God! I seek God!'" This caused great merriment and laughter, as many in the square were nonbelievers. It is as though those in the square were the ones who needed to tell the news to the madman—have *you* not heard that "God is dead." No, instead they find this madman's crying quest for God, in the brightness of the public square, laughable because they are full of their own arrogant disbelief. They infantilize and mock the madman's search for the god who could have gotten lost, or gone on a voyage, or may be afraid to show his face. But as they deride him, the madman jumps among them, and says: "'Whither is God?' he cried; I will tell you. *We have killed him—* you and I. All of us are his murderers." God is not to be found because we, all of us, have killed him. Thus, the news is not just that God is dead; it is also, and perhaps principally as Vattimo underscores, that we have killed God. Then come a series of questions that disclose the dual character of Nietzsche's nihilism, and they merit extensive quotation:

> How could we drink up the sea? Who gave us the sponge to wipe away the entire horizon? What were we doing when we unchained this earth from its sun? Whither is it moving now? Whither are we moving? Away from all suns? Are we not plunging continually? Backward, sideward, forward, in all directions? Is there still any up or down? Are we not straying as through an infinite nothing? Do we not feel the breath of empty space? Has it not become colder? Is not night continually closing in on us? Do we not need to light lanterns in the morning? Do we hear nothing as yet of the noise of gravediggers who are burying God? Do we smell nothing as yet of the divine decomposition? Gods, too, decompose. God is dead. God remains dead. And we have killed him.[10]

The death of God is here a metaphor for the end of all metaphysical referents. Without God, then, we are without a sense of direction. We are immersed in a night that no metaphysical light will pierce. In the words of Zarathustra, those for whom the old god is dead suffer a *great nausea*, the nausea of nihilism.[11] But at the same time, we are the culprits of this killing. We alone are responsible for this darkness and void. We alone accomplished this "great deed." Indeed, there is no greater deed than theocide. But are we worthy yet of the greatness of this deed? Even if we accomplished it, have we yet awoken to its momentousness? We are not yet at the height of our accomplishment, namely, to have liberated ourselves to this metaphysical solitude, this utmost nihilism. "[W]hoever is born after us—for the sake of this deed he will belong to a higher history than all history hitherto."[12] The age of gods and humanity's credulity and infantile naïveté has come to an end by our own means. A new history is dawning, one that is higher than all history that has transpired.

After his long speech, the madman fell silent. His listeners were also silent and astonished. There is mutual incomprehension. The madman shatters his lantern in the public square, and proclaims: "I have come too early. . . my time is not yet." The deed of theocide has taken place, but they fail to recognize it. It is farther from them than the "most distant star." The parable, so to say, ends with the madman's words of justification when they called him to give an account of his *requiem aeternam deo*, which he chanted in several churches: "What after all are these churches now if they are not the tombs and sepulchers of God?"[13]

There are several themes running through these passages that are key for Vattimo's reading of Nietzsche. First, we have the theme that God's death is something we accomplished. God was not killed by another god or gods, but by humans. In Vattimo's language, theocide is part and parcel of metaphysics. Second, we have yet to recognize the importance of this theocide, and both belief and unbelief hinder us from rising to the height of the dead. In other words, mere atheism and theism are blinders that prevent us from recognizing God's death. And third, it is the "free spirits," the *Übermenschen* who can grasp the enlightening and liberating consequences of receiving this news in its fullness. For Nietzsche, the news of the death of God is also news about the need to abolish a certain form of humanity and to proclaim a new humanity. Zarathustra teaches the *Übermensch*: "Human being is something that must be overcome. What have you done to overcome him?"[14] For Vattimo, these three themes converge in the affirmation of nihilism, as the proclamation of the end of all metaphysical expectations, beliefs, or systems. Nihilism announces how the "world become a fable," a myth, and how once we have the story of the stages of this mystification we are freed from both the real and illusory worlds (DN 27–30). This is nihilism as radical metaphysical critique, or the total critique of metaphysics. But Vattimo discerns also another notion of nihilism, what he calls "accomplished nihilism" (EM 19–29), or "perfect nihilism," which refers to the "joyous and creative recognition of the fact that there exists no order, truth, or stability outside the will itself, and that nihilism derives precisely from having wished at all costs to find them" (DN 19). The accomplished nihilism, like the joyful and fully conscious theocide, confronts the absence of values as a possible source of value itself, as a challenge, as a creative opportunity, which is also our "only possibility for freedom" (EM 29).

Heidegger, or the God Who Refused to Die

Vattimo has pointed out correctly that most of the contemporary reception of Heidegger and Nietzsche has been mediated by Heidegger's engagement with Nietzsche's work. Heidegger's lecture courses on Nietzsche, published in two massive volumes, from the late 1930s and early 1940s, overlap the so-called *Kehre*. Thus, Heidegger's critical relationship to Nietzsche has been assumed to be metonymic for his relationship to Nazism, or rather, by rescuing Nietzsche from a Nazi appropriation, he also saved his own work from a similar implicating proximity. At the same time, it is through Heidegger's assimilation of Nietzsche to the last stage of metaphysics, and thus to the fated event of the forgetfulness of Being in Western philosophy, that Heidegger positions himself on the cusp of that moment that Nietzsche announced as coming after the death of God, a higher history to which we have yet to measure up.

Heidegger's project for *Being and Time* promised to accomplish two central things: first, to offer an analysis of *Dasein* in terms of temporality as a prolegomenon to an understanding of Being in terms of time as a transcendental horizon, and second, to develop a phenomenological destruction of the history of ontology that would disclose how Being has been concealed by that tradition's metaphysical propensities. *Being and Time* did deliver on the first task. The second, it can be said, would be accomplished in later works. In fact, it is in the Nietzsche lectures, and subsequent texts on Nietzsche, that Heidegger offers the most elaborate, detailed, and sustained analysis of what he called "Metaphysics as History of Being." It is also in these lectures that Heidegger offers "Sketches for a History of Being as Metaphysics."[15] Heidegger distilled the central arguments of these two volumes into a compact essay, "Nietzsche's Word: 'God Is Dead.'"[16] This essay is without question vintage Heidegger, for it shows the originality of his reading, while also assimilating Nietzsche to Heidegger's history of Being as metaphysics.

For Heidegger, Nietzsche's announcement of the death of God means that the supra-sensory world has no effective power any more. It is an error whose utility has been outlived, or rather it is a necessary error that is no longer useful. Instead, God has become a liability to the enhancement of life. With God's death is also announced the death of all metaphysics. Metaphysics for Nietzsche, in Heidegger's view, is Platonism, that is, the means through which the real world has been turned into a fable, a myth. Nietzsche thus understands his philosophy as a "countermovement against metaphysics."[17] But precisely inasmuch as Nietzsche formulates his "transvaluation of all values" as a countermovement against all Platonism, whether in the form of Christianity or as the metaphysics of truth as evidence, Nietzsche remains in the grip of metaphysics as such. "Since all it does is turn metaphysics upside down, Nietzsche's countermovement against metaphysics remained embroiled in it and has no way out."[18] In fact, claims Heidegger, it is so deeply embroiled in metaphysics that Nietzsche cannot think of the very essence of it, and much less recognize the nature of his own thinking. Nietzsche's blindness to his own remaining mired in the grip of metaphysics, notwithstanding the pronounced gesture of rejection, is best illustrated in the ambiguous meaning nihilism has for him. On the one hand, nihilism means: *"That the highest values devalue themselves."*[19] So, nihilism expresses the devaluation of all high values, among them God as the supreme and highest value, as a historical process, a process of the demystification of all metaphysically underwritten values. In this way, then "nihilism" names the inner logic of Western history. On the other hand, the attenuation, rejection, devaluation of the highest values as a historical logic, is to be followed by a new, higher history, one that will offer a new dispensation of new values. Nietzsche calls this the "revaluation of all values." But this affirmation of a new order of values, which presupposes the pronouncement of an emphatic "no" to all hitherto existing values, is also called nihilism by Nietzsche. As Heidegger puts it, "nihilism which, through devaluation, completes itself in a new and exclusively normative dispensation of value. This normative phase of nihilism Nietzsche calls 'fulfilled,' i.e., classic nihilism."[20] And thus, in Heidegger's reading, this deep ambiguity about nihilism shows that Nietzsche still remains within the grasp of metaphysics, because "fulfilled" nihilism is still a positing of Being as a value, as that which is posited by man and for man. "Value is value provided it is valid. It is valid provided it is posited as what matters. It is so posited by aiming and keeping one's sight on what must be counted."[21] The revaluation of all values is no more than a perpetuation of the enframing and calculating that continue to posit Being as a being, or at least as that which must be counted by and counts for humankind's ends. In fact, Heidegger notes that the place of the God that sustains the values that matter is taken over by the Overman, who is nothing more than the fully accomplished essence of the human being as a willing being. "The man whose essence is the essence that is willing and willed out of the will to power is the overman. The willing of the essence that is willing and willed in this way must correspond to the will to power as the being of being."[22] Thus, even the Overman, with whom Nietzsche calls us to reject metaphysics and all Platonisms, has not stepped outside the history of being as metaphysics. But, even if Nietzsche has not yet overcome metaphysics, his thinking is probably the expression of the essence of this thinking. Nietzsche's thinking epitomizes, according to Heidegger, how metaphysics is itself nihilism, and how his thinking remains the latest and last episode in its history.[23]

Yet, even as Heidegger accuses Nietzsche of ambiguity vis-à-vis his understanding of nihilism, a similar charge could be leveled against Heidegger inasmuch as he remains ambiguous vis-à-vis Nietzsche's madman, the figure with which Heidegger closes his essay. The madman is deranged, and thus is moved out of the space of reasons, but in moving out of the space of reasons, he moves back into the essence of man as *animal rationale*. Heidegger plays on the etymology of madness as de-rangement [*Ver-rückt*].[24] It is the madman, however, who returns out not to reason but to thinking, while those who are smug in their trust of reason no longer believe in God. Those "who did not believe in God" are not unbelievers. Instead, they "abandoned the possibility of faith since they are no longer able to seek God. They can seek no longer because they can no longer think. Those standing about in the public have abolished thinking and replaced it with gossip that smells of nihilism everywhere it fears its opinions are threatened."[25] The madman, in Heidegger's view, is the one who in crying out after God has cried out *de profundis*, is the truly thinking man. Heidegger then asks: "'and do we still hear this cry?' We can only hear it if we truly begin to think. But, the thinking needed to hear this call after God cannot get going until we have become conscious of its most 'stubborn adversary,' namely that which has been 'extolled for centuries, reason.'"[26]

This conclusion is astonishing, and turns on its feet Nietzsche's parable. It is the madman who calls us to faith, by evoking a form of thinking that is beyond the jealous and intolerant nihilism of a reason that fears threats to its opinions, claims, and valuations. It is those without faith, or beyond faith, because they are unthinking, who refuse to recognize that the call of God is a call beyond reason that heeds us to think properly, to proper thinking. If Nietzsche's madman proclaims the death of god, and our complicity in his death, Heidegger's madman calling out to God in the public square of *das Man*, with its deafening cacophony of gossip and idle talk, is a call that proclaims the possibility of faith as the possibility of authentic thinking.

Thank God We Are Atheist. God Is Dead, So That We May Have Faith

Even though Nietzsche and Heidegger remain the privileged sources of thinking for Vattimo, it is also evident how he differs from them. Vattimo removes every prophetic or messianic dimension from the announcement of God's death. Nietzsche's "madman" is not the last prophet, nor is his news an anticipation of the "gods to come." With Nietzsche, Vattimo also reads this highest of deeds, this theocide, as having been accomplished by "us." It is internal and integral to the history of the West. The advent of nihilism is the fulfillment of the tradition that has its beginning in the encounter of the Greek and Jewish that gives rise to the Christian. With Heidegger, Vattimo also reads the history of the advent of nihilism as the history of the event of Being. The history of Being as metaphysics is the history of the ascendancy of nihilism. But against Nietzsche and Heidegger, this nihilism does not summon us to another moment of metaphysics. Rather, the consummation of metaphysics in nihilism, what Vattimo calls the weakening of Being, allows us to stand on the edge of the *Abgrund* of the tradition that is its interpretation. Vattimo seems to be claiming that there is no being other than the Being that is recollected, *Andenken*, in the trace of the tradition itself. All that we have are interpretations, and the most important of them is that even this is an interpretation. As he puts it, "[h]aving 'listened to' Nietzsche, then, we do not want to, we cannot, we must not (any longer) limit ourselves to unmasking that inherited metaphysics in the name of a truer ground. Nietzsche has taught us to distrust the very idea of a true ground."[27] Indeed, Vattimo urges us to inoculate Heidegger's metaphysical nostalgia for Being with Nietzsche's nihilism. For Vattimo, Heidegger, as he in turn argued against Nietzsche, is still caught in the grip of metaphysics, in as much as he thinks that Being can be a giving and granting, the *Ereignis*, that irrupts from without. For Vattimo, Heidegger should have stopped at the giving and granting that take place in the tradition. For, as he writes: "if we could accede in some, albeit non-foundational, manner to Being by going *beyond* or *past* the events of Being (the *archai* that time and again, *je und je*, have dominated metaphysics), then the enterprise of overcoming metaphysics would end with a new metaphysics, a new 'representation' or conception (*Begriff*) of Being" (DN 188).

If for Heidegger phenomenology is at the service of ontology, in such a way that "*phenomenological truth (disclosedness of being) is veritas transcendentalis,*"[28] for Vattimo phenomenology is at the service of hermeneutics, in such a way that we have arrived at the realization that "not even nihilism must be understood metaphysically. . . . Being *is no longer*. And, in the end, nihilism too is an interpretation, and not a description, of a state of things" (BI 13–14). Ultimately, for Vattimo, the overcoming of metaphysics cannot be accomplished by a "destruction" of the history of ontology that reverses the forgetfulness of Being by the tradition. Rather, it is that very forgetfulness, *qua* tradition, that must be carried to its utmost logical conclusion: nihilism. Thus, we stand in relationship to the tradition not in terms of an impossible *Überwindung*, an overcoming and going beyond, but rather in terms of a *Verwindung*, a returning, twisting, a recovering after a long convalescence that "overcomes" pain and suffering without getting rid of them.[29] *Verwindung*, in fact, excises the traces of a violent prophetism that still lingers in Heidegger's metaphysics bringing him close to Nietzsche's "God is dead! And we have killed him."[30]

The history of hermeneutics is the history of both secularization and nihilism. Both are internal to the West. In fact, their exacerbation in terms of a postmodern nihilism turns out to be the very truth of Christianity and the West (see FR 47 and 51). But it is their very recrudescence and accomplishment (fulfillment) that opens up the horizon for a return of religion.

Paradoxically, as Vattimo puts it often, it is the corrosive effects of both secularization and nihilism that allow for religion to return. With no gods necessitated by metaphysics, since metaphysics has been dissolved, a purified relation of faith to a nonmetaphysical god is made plausible. To believe because one can believe, not because one must or is commanded, is thus both the realization of Christianity and the fulfillment of the Christian tradition, as a message that is always the trace of its appropriation and transmission. Now, it is this absence of metaphysically underwritten theologies and violent prophetic events that opens up the possibility for a religion beyond violence and coercion. Belief that is uncoerced (*Zwanglos*) is the response to the height of a divine incarnation as *kenosis*. *Credere di credere*, thus, as uncoerced coercion, is the gratuitous, felicitous, free response to the news of the tradition that announced a God who debased himself, withdrawing to make space for human freedom. But this affirmation of human freedom is not the affirmation of the pure will, à la Carl Schmitt's decision; nor is it the call for a despotic autarky that enshrines the godless human as a caricature of Nietzsche's Overman. Instead, it is an affirmation of human freedom, as both a gift and a responsibility, with and for others. Freedom, for Vattimo, is charity.

To conclude, one last exegesis forces itself on us, if only because of the evident similarities in forms of argumentation. Vattimo's "weak thought," which is so implicated in articulating the end of metaphysics and which, in making explicit the "nihilist vocation of hermeneutics," announces a form of post-metaphysical thinking at the service of a peace to come, converges with Habermas' own linking of post-metaphysical thinking to what he calls "post-secular reason."[31]

The obvious point of reference for Habermas' understanding of post-metaphysical thinking is his long essay "Themes in Postmetaphysical Thinking" from the late 1980s.[32] In this diagnostic and programmatic essay Habermas identifies three central aspects of metaphysical thinking: first, there is the theme of unity in the philosophy of origins; second, there is the theme of the equation between being and thought; third, there is the theme of the redemptive effect of contemplation. These themes are the gravitational centers around which identity thinking, the philosophy of origins, and a strong valorization of theory form a coherent constellation. These three themes, claims Habermas, converge and reach their highest sublimation in the philosophy of consciousness, especially as it expressed itself in German idealism. Due to social, but also internal, developments the philosophy of consciousness with its strong theoretical claims, its elevation of contemplation over social praxis, and the expectation of a hidden symmetry between being and thinking, was challenged and, in the end, dethroned. Habermas claims that the strong conception of reason was supplanted by a more humble conception that re-thinks rationality procedurally. Additionally, nineteenth-century historicism, along with criticisms of all forms of reified consciousness and forms of life, as well as the abandonment of the overvaluation of *theoria* over *praxis*, led to a shattering of all metaphysical claims within contemporary philosophy, resulting in a *de-transcendentalization* of thinking and a rethinking of consciousness as dialogically constituted and praxis rooted. In the wake of the collapse of metaphysics, we are left with: procedural rationality, a situated (thoroughly historicized) reason, a linguistified reason and intersubjectivity, and a "deflation of the extraordinary."[33] In this way, philosophy discovers its vocation as an "interpreter" (*Dolmetscher*)[34] that "mediates between expert knowledge and everyday practices in need of orientation."[35] This desublimated and *kenotic* rethinking of philosophy, as an interpreter, leads Habermas to offer a rereading of Marx's eleventh thesis on Feuerbach: "Marx's saying about the realization of philosophy can also be understood in this way: what has, following the disintegration of metaphysical and religious worldviews, been divided up on the level of cultural systems under various aspects of validity, can now be put together—and also put right—only in the experiential context of lifeworld practices."[36] This means philosophy ceases to be a mere interpretation of the world pronounced from the Olympian heights of theoretical abstraction, and dissolves itself in the practices of the life world that are oriented to reaching the uncoerced coercion of giving and asking for better reasons. But at this moment of philosophy's demotion and humbling, when it withdraws in order to coexist with religion, "philosophy, even in its postmetaphysical form, will be able neither to replace nor to repress religion as long as religious language is the *bearer of a semantic content* that is inspiring and even indispensable, for this content eludes (for the time being?) the explanatory force of philosophical language and continues to resist translation into reasoning discourses."[37]

What Habermas attributes to religion beyond its dissolution into the life world, namely that it is the bearer of *semantic contents* that are both "inspiring" and "indispensable" is what Vattimo calls the "explicit appropriation of our Christian historicity" (FR 54). In a stronger fashion than Habermas, yet along the same lines, Vattimo argues that we have entered "the age of interpretation" precisely as the full realization of the Christian message of the event of incarnation and creation, which unleashed a dual historicity.[38] On the one hand, we have the historicity of the event of creation, namely that creation took place at a specific time. On the other, we have the historicity of the appropriation of the announcement or message of incarnation. Both events are suffused with temporality and historicity. It is this Christian historicity that, as secularization and nihilism qua hermeneutics as *koine*, allows us for the appropriation of the Christian message as charity. We have entered the age of interpretation, realized nihilism, and accomplished secularization, because Christianity has "brought to bear its full antimetaphysical effect" (FR 49). Like Vattimo, at the same time, Habermas recognizes that it is the demise of metaphysics that allows thinking to take religion seriously, precisely because this latter remains the reservoir of "semantic" (hermeneutical) contents that are indispensable for philosophy and our social practices. Post-metaphysical thinking becomes post-secular reason just as secularization becomes nihilism, and nihilism turns into the unforced and free *credere* [believing]. For both Habermas and Vattimo, however, it is post-secular reason and unforced *credere* that are indispensable in the attainment and preservation of a cosmopolitan and ecumenical world in which many worlds of belief can abide in their charity.

Notes

1. Vattimo distinguishes two senses of nihilism in Nietzsche. There is a passive form of nihilism that merely reflects the general decadence of European culture. Here nihilism is the trace of secularization, in which values have become instrumental and do not evoke reverence or fail to incite us to great deeds. On the other side, there is an active form of nihilism, and this is the nihilism that embraces joyfully the obsolescence of all values in order to postulate its own. This second form of nihilism is the one that orients the *Übermensch*. See DN 134–141.
2. Jean-Luc Nancy, "Atheism and Monotheism," in *Weakening Philosophy: Essays in Honour of Gianni Vattimo*, ed. Santiago Zabala (Montreal and Kingston: McGill-Queen's University Press, 2007), 387–399.
3. Ernst Bloch, *Atheism in Christianity*, trans. J. T. Swann (New York: Herder & Herder, 1972), 9.
4. See Gianni Vattimo, "The Secularization of Philosophy," in *Writing the Politics of Difference*, ed. Hugh Silverman (Albany: State University of New York Press, 1991), 283–290.
5. Gianni Vattimo, "Conclusion: Metaphysics and Violence," in *Weakening Philosophy*, 401–421.
6. Friedrich Nietzsche, *The Gay Science*, trans. Walter Kaufmann (New York: Vintage Books, 1974), §108.
7. Ibid., §343.
8. Ibid.
9. Ibid., §125.
10. Ibid.
11. Friedrich Nietzsche, *Thus Spoke Zarathustra*, trans. Adrian Del Caro (Cambridge: Cambridge University Press, 2006), 241.
12. Nietzsche, *The Gay Science*, §125.
13. Ibid.
14. Nietzsche, *Thus Spoke Zarathustra*, 5.
15. See Martin Heidegger, *The End of Philosophy*, trans. Joan Stambaugh (New York: Harper & Row, 1973); see Stambaugh's introduction vi–xiv.

16. Martin Heidegger, "Nietzsche's Word: 'God is Dead,'" in *Off the Beaten Track*, ed. and trans. Julian Young and Kenneth Haynes (Cambridge: Cambridge University Press, 2002), 157–199.
17. Ibid., 162.
18. Ibid.
19. Ibid., 166.
20. Ibid., 167.
21. Ibid., 170.
22. Ibid., 188.
23. Ibid., 198.
24. Ibid., 199.
25. Ibid.
26. Ibid.
27. Gianni Vattimo, "Metaphysics, Violence, Secularization" in *Recoding Metaphysics: The New Italian Philosophy*, ed. Giovanna Borradori (Evanston: Northwestern University Press, 1988), 45–61, 46–47.
28. Martin Heidegger, *Being and Time*, trans. Joan Stambaugh (Albany: State University of New York Press, 1996), 34.
29. See Joan Stambaugh's discussion of *Verwindung* in Heidegger, *The End of Philosophy*, 84 n. 1. See also Vattimo's discussion in "Ontology of Actuality," in *Contemporary Italian Philosophy: Crossing the Borders of Ethics, Politics, and Religion*, eds. Silvia Benso and Brian Schroeder (Albany: State University of New York Press, 2007), 92–96. See also EM 176–181.
30. An entirely different essay could have been written where I would have explored the ways in which Heidegger and Vattimo's relationship to secularization and atheism at the service of faith both differ and complement each other. Perhaps the "could have been" is a promissory note. Yet, it is evident that Vattimo has sought to secularize Heidegger, as Gadamer sought to urbanize him, and thus, he has struggled with Heidegger's relationship to Christian thought for the last two decades. In *After Christianity*, Vattimo offers a reading of Heidegger's concern with the Christian faith that parallels Vattimo's own understanding of Christianity (see AC 123–137), which tellingly closes that beautiful book. Yet, it seems to me that Vattimo could have made stronger his critique and *Aufeindersetzung* with Heidegger's pious atheism if he had tracked the shift from Heidegger's essay "Phenomenology and Theology" (1927) to his *Der Spiegel* interview "Only a God Can Save Us" (1966). At the center of this trajectory is the question of the relationship between theology and philosophy, on the one

hand, and between religious experience and factical existence, on the other. Whereas in the 1920s Heidegger set theology and philosophy against each other, later in his life he sought to reconcile the experience of divinity with the experience of Sein's *Ereignis*. Be that as it may, Heidegger was highly critical of the ways in which metaphysics had contributed to making theology into a "positive science," one that in the process of thinking about God with the tools of philosophy betrayed God. Yet, Heidegger continues to talk about the "gods" and the "God" that is to save us. Vattimo is right, Heidegger's propheticism and crypto-fideism must be demystified. While Vattimo laments the insufficiency of extant engagements with Heidegger's relationship with Catholicism and Christianity in general, it is nonetheless the case that we already have some good starting points. See, for instance, John Macquarrie, *Heidegger and Christianity* (New York: Continuum, 1994) and Ben Vedder, *Heidegger's Philosophy of Religion: From God to the Gods* (Pittsburgh: Duquesne University Press, 2006). Vedder's work is probably one of the most comprehensive and up-to-date analyses of Heidegger's relationship to both theology and Christianity.

31. For Habermas on post-secular reason, see Jürgen Habermas, *The Future of Human Nature* (Cambridge, UK: Polity Press, 2003), 101–115. See also *Zwischen Naturalismus und Religion: Philosophischen Aufsätze* (Frankfurt am Main: Suhrkamp, 2005), especially part II, "Religious Pluralism and Civic Solidarity," 106–154. See also my analysis of Habermas' works on religion in "The Linguistification of the Sacred as a Catalyst of Modernity: Jürgen Habermas on Religion," in Eduardo Mendieta, *Global Fragments: Globalizations, Latinamericanisms, Critical Theory* (Albany: State University of New York Press, 2007), 141–167.
32. Now in Jürgen Habermas, *Postmetaphysical Thinking: Philosophical Essays*, trans. William Mark Hohengarten (Cambridge: MIT Press, 1992), 28–53.
33. See ibid., 34–52.
34. Compare Vattimo, "The Secularization of Philosophy," 288–289. See also his "Metaphysics, Violence, Secularization," 60–61, and BI 47–48.
35. Habermas, *Postmetaphysical Thinking*, 50.
36. Ibid., 51.
37. Ibid., italics added.
38. See Vattimo, "The Trace of the Trace," in R 84–85.

Part Three

Politics and Technology

10

Philosophy and Politics at the End of Metaphysics

JAMES RISSER

In his articulation of hermeneutics as the *koine* of contemporary thinking, Gianni Vattimo has established himself as a central figure not only in the current outlook for hermeneutics, but also for philosophy in general where today it must face its own question regarding its nature and its task. Vattimo's initial approach to hermeneutics centered on the idea of "weak thought," an idea that is more indebted to Heidegger and Nietzsche than to Gadamer. It is the idea of the end of metaphysics in which the stability of metaphysical structures—that is, those frameworks that put in place a universal structure of being, along with its related notions of objectivity and truth—undergo a weakening through the exposure to the historical. For Vattimo, what is really at stake in this idea is not at all a matter of replacing an old idea with a better idea, but a strong anti-authoritarian gesture that constantly worries about the establishing of foundations in which a sovereign power can take root. Under the heading of "weak thought" Vattimo's hermeneutical philosophy is thus oriented to emancipating philosophy from itself and from its pretension to be scientific, which holds its own form of sovereign power in relation to the production of knowledge.

And yet, Vattimo's hermeneutical philosophy is not opposed to an idea of truth and to a certain project of construction for coming to terms with our contemporary life situation. If such a statement comes as a surprise to some of his readers, that is because the subtlety of

Vattimo's position can be overlooked. It is not, ultimately, a position that results in nihilism, despite the fact that he wants to tie the truth of hermeneutics to a "nihilistic philosophy of history"; and, it is not, ultimately, a position that wants to efface the power of reason, despite the fact that he is suspicious of the ability of philosophy to "demonstrate" its truths. These subtle distinctions are easily accounted for once one recognizes that it is precisely the emancipatory interests in play in Vattimo's hermeneutical philosophy that will require that it adhere to a certain notion of truth and to the operation of reason in some form. In different words, we can say that there is some notion of truth and reason at work in Vattimo's hermeneutical philosophy because "there is *always* a political good at stake in philosophy,"[1] and as such, the philosopher, whether directly or indirectly, must speak for a truthfulness in relation to the political and argue for it. The subtlety of Vattimo's position can be readily seen, then, when one takes seriously his far-reaching and emphatic claim that philosophy cannot be separated from the political.

In more recent years Vattimo has refined his version of hermeneutics under the name of an "ontology of actuality" in order to provide a more specific and nuanced account of philosophy at the end of metaphysics and, at the same time, to better express this connection between philosophy and the political. Even more to the point, under the name "ontology of actuality" Vattimo wants to articulate the way in which a hermeneutical philosophy reflects the pluralism that is expressed in the political realm by democracy. Vattimo makes the argument for this position in a number of places, but it has its most thorough presentation in essays gathered together under the title *Nihilism and Emancipation*. Most instructive in this regard is his essay "Philosophy, Metaphysics, Democracy" (NE 81–89). The stated intention of the essay is to address the problem of the relation between philosophy and politics at a time when philosophy faces the crisis of the dissolution of foundationalist thought and when politics has witnessed the collapse of real socialism. While the dissolution of foundationalism in philosophy would appear to leave no place for philosophy within the political, because it can no longer contribute to the grand theoretical construction of it, philosophy's new self-understanding can be applied to political choice; and politics for its part, Vattimo notes, "is experiencing the impossibility of adhering to 'the truth'" (NE 83). Vattimo sees, in other words, that, as a result of the end of metaphysics and the expansion of democracy, "philosophy becomes intrinsically political thought" precisely in the form of an ontology of actuality.

Vattimo actually borrows this expression "ontology of actuality" from Foucault. In his late writings Foucault draws a distinction between two ways of proceeding in philosophy, either through an analysis of truth (*analitique de la verité*) or through an ontology of actuality (*ontologie de l'actualité*), in which the latter pertains to the question of who we are today. Vattimo insists that he does not want to use this term in the same way as Foucault, not because he does not want to extend philosophy into the ethico-practical sphere, which is connoted by the term *actualité*, but because what is important for Vattimo is the ontology in the expression "ontology of actuality." Accordingly, the "ontology of actuality" is for Vattimo the expression that will capture the character of Heidegger's philosophy of being at the end of metaphysics that Heidegger himself describes as the recollection of being. Obviously, what Heidegger has in mind here has little to do with a classical version of *anamnesis*, and, as Vattimo points out, it has little to do with a nostalgia for a return to a prior condition. According to Vattimo, the recollection of being is simply "a way of answering appeals which come down to us through the *Ge-schick*, through the history or destination of being."[2] And this is to say that the recollection at issue here cannot be located outside the actuality of the event, which bears within it the traces of the past as well as the voices of the present. In this sense, an *ontology* of actuality is simply what being means in our current condition.

Now, as Vattimo himself notes, one can legitimately ask at this point why a hermeneutical philosophy that wants to situate itself in the relation between philosophy and the political would make an appeal at all to an ontology, especially a Heideggerian one. Is not the continuation of the talk of being fundamentally an unpolitical philosophy? Somewhat surprisingly, Vattimo's answer is an emphatic "no," for the talk of being is ultimately connected to an experience of freedom. With no consideration of the event character of being in which the historical phases of our humanity are recomposed, we are susceptible to taking the present order of things as if it were absolute. Fully grasping the fact that the present order is not the only possible one requires a memory of different possibilities of being. Thus the emancipatory interest, even within a democratic politics, requires an understanding of the event character of being. Vattimo underscores this latter point by his insistence that the experience of freedom is not captured once and for all in the political when democracy for its part abandons "the truth" of political power, for a new power has intervened. It is the power residing in the vestiges of metaphysics in which its objectifying thought sets the stage for a society of total organization. It is the social power of the specialist who exerts control in the ethico-political sphere. If everything is left to the specialists, there is, in fact, no longer any democracy. Thus, at the end of metaphysics the anti-authoritarian gesture has to remain vigilant for we run the risk of losing our freedom by being subjected to a new supreme power for making life together possible.

But Vattimo actually wants to go further than this in the operation of an ontology of actuality. It is not just a matter of confronting a new authority that wants to rob interpretation of its liberty and contingency. Curiously, Vattimo thinks that an ontology of actuality must also confront the multiplicity of approaches and views (business, religion, science, for example) about being that, when taken at face value, hides from us a clear insight into the historical phases of humanity emerging in an interpretation of an epoch. An ontology of actuality wants to preserve the possibility of *connecting* the multiple notions of being as a necessary condition for clarifying what being means in the present situation. In this context, the notion of truth and reason at work in Vattimo's hermeneutic philosophy becomes apparent. Vattimo sees that the political sphere can be a possible place for the event of being as the setting into work of truth, not unlike the description that Heidegger gives for truth as opening in relation to the work of art. And in relation to this, an ontology of actuality "offers politics a certain vision of the ongoing historical process and a certain interpretation of its positive potential, judged to be such on the basis not of eternal principles but of argumentative choice from within the process itself" (NE 88). In sounding much like Heidegger—urbanized, to be sure—Vattimo claims that hermeneutical philosophy has the task of "corresponding" to the event of being, but in his own fashion this would mean to imagine a new role for the philosopher, one "closer to that of the artist and of the priest [without a hierarchical church] than to the one of the scientist and of the technologist." In such a role, this task of corresponding will be able to connect "the current experience with those of the past and with those of other cultures and societies, building and rebuilding a continuity which is the very meaning of the term logos, dis-course."[3]

One can readily see in Vattimo's position an attempt to not let hermeneutics become a mere *theory* of interpretation such that its truth would establish an authoritarian ground for interpretation. He keeps the paradox of self-reference at bay by an appeal to the Heideggerian idea of a recollection (*Andenken*) of being, an idea that Vattimo straightforwardly describes as "democratic thought" (NE 87), because he sees in it an experience of truth that does not issue from a stable ground. One has to wonder whether such an appeal is sufficient for the "strengthening of democracy," if only for the reason that it does not work from the inside, so to speak. To ask this question in another way: Is it sufficient to say that "the event teaches us how to defend against dogmatism"?[4] Are we still not left with the need for a further construction in order to avoid what Plato understood quite well about democratic life: "It is a constitutional bazaar, a harlequin's outfit such as is preferred by men for whom the great issue is the consumption of pleasures and rights. But it is not only the reign of individuals who do anything they please. It is properly the regime that overturns all the relations that structure human society: its governors have the demeanor of the governed and the governed the demeanor of the governors. . . ."[5] As a way of furthering Vattimo's position and attempting, at the same time, to provide a limited challenge to it, I would like to attend to these questions by considering a variation on the idea of hermeneutic recollection—one that I believe more adequately relates hermeneutical philosophy and the political.

The starting point for this variation on hermeneutic recollection comes from the trajectory of Gadamer's hermeneutics to which Vattimo's own thought remains indebted. In "Reflections on My Philosophical Journey," Gadamer tells us with respect to his own position that,

> my intention would not be to supplement the Heideggerian history of the increasing forgetfulness of being with a history of the remembering of being. . . . [Certainly] everywhere that philosophizing is attempted, one finds in this attempt a recollection of being takes place. In spite of this fact, however, it seems to me there is no history of the recollection of being. Recollection has no history. . . . Recollection is always what comes to one, and comes over one, so that something that is again made present to us, offers, for the space of a moment, a halt to all passing and forgetting. But recollection of being is not a recollection of something previously known and now present once again; rather it is recollection of something previously asked, the reclaiming of a lost question.[6]

The recovered question would be such that, in a way similar to what Vattimo maintains under the idea of the recollection of being, it would mirror the historicity of our thinking. But for Gadamer specifically this would be nothing less than a recollection that pertains to the interrogative opening of life to itself by thinking further and speaking further the language we speak. And this to say that for Gadamer all recollection takes place as dialogical conversation,[7] which is oriented to a practical task, understood as the actual work of *ethos,* of a self-relatedness (*Sich-Verhalten*) and a comportment (*Haltung*) within a life that is able to discourse about itself and be responsible for itself.[8]

To attend to this idea of recollection then requires an analysis of the specific character of the *speaking* appropriate to the justification of our practical living, that is, to the character of speaking that sustains communal life with others. It is this point that one could argue that Vattimo does not sufficiently develop. The issue here is not strictly speaking about the dialogical dimension of human speaking, which is so central to Gadamer's version of hermeneutics. Rather, the issue here concerns the rhetorical turn in hermeneutics and how this is configured in the practical task of hermeneutics, which concerns our moral, social, and political life. To state the issue in the form of a question: What constitutes the discourse of a pluralistic community, that is, democratic discourse, from the perspective of a hermeneutics in which there is a peculiar fusing of the rhetorical and the political?

What stands behind this question is the problem of democratic discourse itself. Democratic discourse is a discourse that supposedly holds *power* within itself that, on the one hand, makes possible the organized structure of human coexistence (speech employed for agreement, the speech of solidarity where the "logos is common to all"); but, on the other hand, democratic discourse is constituted by a genuine pluralism of antagonistic speech, a discourse constituted in terms of sovereignty in the subject. Vattimo is right to claim that with respect to the (Heideggerian) recollection of being the sovereign role of the philosopher is finished, but clearly a form of sovereignty remains in democratic life through which the emancipatory concerns are actualized. Now, it is precisely this issue of power and speech that Foucault thematically presents under his idea of an ontology of actuality. Foucault presents this issue through a historical analysis of the rise of Greek democracy in which the rhetorical and the political were inseparable, and in regard to this development Foucault makes use of a term, which we find embedded in his ontology of actuality, that I would like to borrow for hermeneutics. The term is "*parrhesia*," which means ordinarily "free speech," and as such it was considered an essential component of the art of persuasion necessary for political life. In the context of its original use, such speech activity could be mere chattering, but more positively could mean telling the truth; and with respect to such truth-telling, there is the added element of a risk in this speech activity.

It is the philosopher who readily comes to mind as a *parrhesiastes*—someone who speaks freely in a truth-telling discourse involving risk. The philosopher is a *parrhesiastes*, for example, when he "addresses himself to a sovereign, to a tyrant, and tells him that his tyranny is disturbing and unpleasant because tyranny is incompatible with justice. [Here] the philosopher believes he is speaking the truth, and, more than that, also takes a risk (since the tyrant may become angry, may punish him, may exile him, may kill him). And that is exactly Plato's situation with Dionysius in Syracuse."[9] And a similar situation holds for Socrates. He speaks in relation to truth and does so at the risk of his own life. The *parrhesiastes* is accordingly to be distinguished from the rhetorician, who, in speaking persuasively, does not necessarily believe what he says, that is, does not speak truthfully. At the same time, the *parrhesiastes* is also to be distinguished from the polemicist, who engages in critical discourse only for the sake of controversy. Such a philosopher, one would think, would be of interest to Vattimo.

In its historical use, the word "*parrhesia*" is associated primarily with the experience of freedom and has little to do with truth. The word first appears in Euripides' *Hippolytus* and *Ion* where it denotes freedom of speech in political matters.[10] *Parrhesia* is more specific than *eleutheria* (freedom) and, in the context of its more frequent use within Athenian democracy, it is equivalent to democracy (*isegoria*) itself. Its use in the Athenian *polis* constituted part of its unique form of social life. Speech, no longer relegated to the ritual word, meant open debate. And, more importantly, this debate was not simply the prerogative of the *basileus*, but was open to the entire *demos*. In the second half of the fifth century and during the greater part of the fourth century, every Athenian citizen had the right to speak at assemblies. As such, speech did not stand over against power, but was itself an instrument of power. Such speech presupposed a public to which the speech was addressed and, more importantly, decided. Understood in this way, speaking truly sets itself within the ability to speak freely. A show of hands measured the victory of a speaker, but the character of this public, open life was unique. As has been already alluded to, what stands under the public entailed risk. In this situation there was the possibility of being prosecuted if it was discovered later that people had been mislead by the speech, that is, if the speaker did not speak truly.

Something of the character of this speaking truly can be found in Thucydides. He referred to the democratic activity of free speech with neither the word *parrhesia* nor *isegoria*. Thucydides recognized that freedom of speech is inseparable from good faith, both in the speaker and the listener, and must for the sake of democracy be used to foster reason against unreason. If you attack not the objective validity, but the good faith of your opponent, you introduce an element that will poison democratic proceedings. Speaking truly is linked to what is said, and *parrhesia*, which retains this connection of the speaker to what is said and not simply to the audience, describes a political virtue. Accordingly, *parrhesia* comes to differ from *isegoria* in that the latter is associated with political institutions, while the former is not. When Socrates appears on the scene, *parrhesia* became a philosopher's virtue and in this context brought about a change in its use as a political virtue to a moral virtue.

Now, what interests Foucault in this change from political to moral virtue is the further attribute of *parrhesia* that emerges in connection with it. *Parrhesia* is now tied to the question of *who* we are, to the question of *who* we can be. For Foucault, what is behind this question is the issue of political spirituality, of how we can truly and freely make ourselves into certain kinds of beings. And with this question we return to Foucault's distinction between an analytics of truth and an ontology of actuality that Vattimo appeals to for the sake of his own position. In relation to this issue of our ethical being, Foucault sees that philosophical reflection can no longer be understood in its classical formulation as a discourse that is concerned with the "analytics of truth" through which it dictates the order of truth, that is, as a discourse that is able to say *what* is true and to say this in such a manner that it dictates the law to other discourses, telling them where its truth is and how to find it.[11] Philosophical reflection today can still concern itself with truth, but only in the form of a "critical attitude to the truth,"[12] that, as a *practice*, generates possibilities for moral and political choice—the production of truth relative to who we are. Up to this point I believe that Vattimo would be in agreement with Foucault. Where he would depart from Foucault is with respect to the "ethical" dimension that Foucault is after in all this. The question of the ethical being of the individual is accordingly a question of the practices "which permit individuals to effect by their own means or with the help of others a certain number of operations on their own bodies and souls, thoughts, conduct, and way of being, so as to transform themselves in order to attain a certain state of happiness, purity, wisdom, perfection, or immortality."[13] In this description one can readily see that Foucault is drawing on Hellenistic ethics, which is precisely where the development of the ethical *parrhesiastes* reaches its heights.

But before Rome there is Athens, and, for Foucault, it is Socrates who marks a decisive juncture in the development of the critical attitude to the truth, to the truth-telling practices that constitute this parrhesiastic tradition. The crucial question that Foucault attempts to answer in his analysis is that concerning *who* is entitled to speak the truth, and under what conditions is this truth spoken. The case of the philosopher is different from that of the sage and the prophet, for it involves a truth-telling with respect to the present situation. At the same time Socrates invents a new parrhesiastic game, one that, as previously noted, gives an account of the *who* by speaking to others at the risk of his life. In this new game, truth-telling shifts to the constitution of the subject. *Parrhesia* becomes a certain way of acting, an *ethos* of the individual. This shift occurs in part because Socrates discovers an incompatibility between truth-telling and democratic life. Democratic rule, as we know from the *Republic* would be such that "everyone would arrange a plan for leading his own life in a way that pleases him."[14] Socrates sees that *parrhesia* can degenerate into irresponsible freedom and thus needs to be thought in terms of the soul's relation to itself, where the order of life can be taken hold of. In effect, what occurs through Socrates is subtle displacement of the very duty that initially ties the *parrhesiastes* to democracy.

But as Foucault develops this idea, the issue is precisely not to secure the order of life that is envisioned in the *Republic*. Socrates the *parrhesiastes* is best when he is not essentially dialectical, but simply engaged in truth-telling practices—a "care of self" that Foucault believes opposes a political system of truth. For Foucault, and one would think for Vattimo as well, the attempt to engage in truth-telling is "the attempt to open an experience of the freedom that conditions our participation in the history that constitutes us as individuals, as members of communities, and of states."[15] Moreover, this experience of freedom would have both public and private uses, and in this particular doubling truth-telling is no longer equivalent to its Socratic expression. Interestingly, what Foucault does not give up in the Socratic truth-telling practice is the notion of duty relative to critical community. In an interview given in 1984, Foucault remarks:

> Nothing is more inconsistent than a political regime that is indifferent to the truth; but nothing is more dangerous than a political system that claims to prescribe the truth. The function of "free speech" doesn't have to take legal form, just as it would in vain to believe that it resides by right in spontaneous exchanges of communication. The task of speaking the truth is an infinite labor: to respect it in its complexity is an obligation that no power can afford to shortchange, unless it imposes the silence of slavery.[16]

The contemporary *parrhesiastes* then has the duty to speak freely as a refusal to participate in the prevailing system of thought. Again, Foucault, in response to the question whether a truth in politics exists, says:

I believe too much in truth not to suppose that there are different truths and different ways of saying it. To be sure, one cannot demand a government to speak the truth, the whole truth, nothing but the truth. On the other hand, it is possible to demand from governments a certain truth as to final aims, the general choice of tactics, and on a number of particular points of its program: that is the *parrhesia* (free speech) of the governed, who can and must summon in the name of knowledge and their experience and because they are citizens the government to answer for what it does, for the meaning of its actions and the decisions that it has taken.[17]

Given the above remarks, one has to wonder why Vattimo, despite his indebtedness to Heidegger, specifically refuses to let a hermeneutical philosophy follow more closely Foucault's ontology of actuality. It is not because he opposes the idea of truth-telling practices as such, but because he opposes the reduction of such truth-telling to a kind of ethical anarchism—an aesthetic (ethical) anarchism where everyone is free to construct selfhood as he or she pleases. What is clearly at stake for Vattimo is the exercise of a freedom that produces more than a harlequin's outfit, for in the end even a Hitler would be possible under these circumstances. For Vattimo, the exercise of freedom depends on the citizen "who would like his own moral ideas to carry the day in the social dialogue and puts them forward in the hope that others will be persuaded, what values do I profess and what reasons do I offer for preferring them" (NE 68). With this idea of social dialogue, Vattimo is in fact much closer to Gadamer's hermeneutics than he readily indicates. And with this idea we can return to the consideration of the variation on hermeneutic recollection. To pose the question again: How are we to understand, from the perspective of a hermeneutical philosophy, the character of speaking appropriate to the justification of our practical living? In view of the analysis just given, this question can be reformulated: How are we to understand hermeneutical philosophy as a parrhesiastic activity? The answer to this question follows from three brief considerations.

First of all, as a preliminary matter, we need to underscore the way in which hermeneutics in its Gadamerian orientation stands in relation to rhetoric. Because he draws so heavily on Plato and the art of Socratic conversation, and follows Heidegger's critical perspective on the status of the proposition for philosophical research, Gadamer has always insisted, even in relation to the experience of interpreting texts, that the experience of understanding follows a rhetorical line rather than that of classical argumentation. It is certainly the case, as Gadamer points out, "that rhetoric has been the basis of our social life since Plato rejected and contradicted the flattering abuse of rhetoric by the Sophists. He introduced dialectically founded rhetoric as in the *Phaedrus*, and rhetoric remained a noble art throughout antiquity. Yet one wonders why today everybody is not aware of it."[18] Simply stated, the *noble* art of rhetoric is for Gadamer the art of agreement concerning the *logos*, which is a hermeneutic task. This means that the rhetorical and the hermeneutical aspects of human linguisticality interpenetrate each other at every point. Rhetoric would not be needed if understanding was not fundamental in human relationships, and there would be no hermeneutic task if there was no loss of agreement between parties to a conversation.[19] Linking hermeneutics and rhetoric in this way is essential to a hermeneutics embedded in life. What Gadamer learns from Plato is the significance of the difference in speaking, a difference that was already noted in the analysis of *parrhesia*, namely, the difference between sheer argumentation and the speaking truly that involves coming to agreement about what is said. This coming to agreement in speech is really the effort not merely to convince, but to illuminate without being able to prove. In this, the aim of rhetoric is the same as the task of understanding: to speak relative to a truth claim that "vindicates the plausible, the *eikos*, and that which is illuminating to common sense";[20] that is, that "asserts itself by reason of its own merit within the realm of the possible and probable."[21] Both hermeneutics and rhetoric defend what is evident in contrast to truth that is proven and thereby known in the strongest sense.

But the significance of rhetoric for hermeneutics is not just that it identifies the manner of achieving insight in understanding. For Gadamer, the opening of insight is at once the opening of social life. In effect, the link between hermeneutics and rhetoric identifies for hermeneutics its character as a "practical science." The hermeneutical turn to rhetoric comes to serve social life as the antidote to the framework of modern science that would constrain social life to its form of order. According to Gadamer: "The rationality of the rhetorical way of arguing, which admittedly seeks to bring emotions into play but works with arguments and with probabilities, is and remains far more a determining factor in society than the excellence of science."[22] What modern science covers over in its applications within modern life is precisely an exercise of freedom whereby the individual is faced with determining what is real and feasible. But to determine what is real and feasible requires in fact the other, not as a transcendence that would dictate the conditions for a new moral law, but as the instantiation of a solidarity within the discourse of democracy. For Gadamer, the idea of solidarity pertains to the communal that arises in real speech. This distinctive (although entirely Greek) understanding of practical life, namely, that the speaking within it sustains communal life, is what separates in a fundamental way hermeneutic *parrhesia* from Foucault's care of self. This difference is a difference between speech that would communicate and thereby search for the other, *and* speech that expresses in an effort of the subject to tell the truth about itself. And would not Vattimo concur with this hermeneutics *parrhesia*? Is this not precisely the role of the new philosopher as politician who connects with others, in effect building and rebuilding a continuity, which is the very meaning of dis-course?

Secondly, it is not just that hermeneutics is a rhetorical phenomenon, but that the character of speaking appropriate to our practical living is parrhesiastic in the fullest sense: it is a truth-telling practice engaged in "the testing of life." In the case of Socrates, *parrhesia* demands the giving of an account of oneself so as to lead one to care for oneself. The testing of life in this context, as read by Foucault, must not be equated with veridiction on a metaphysics of the soul. Rather, the testing of life is the manner of living and of truth-telling that yields a certain form to this rendering an account of oneself. For Gadamer, the testing of life is found in the manner of living whereby what is real and feasible come to be disclosed. But this means that the testing of life is an accomplishment of speech, that is, the testing of life is found in the testimonial character of speaking. Gadamer notes in several places that Socrates saw clearly with respect to his own knowledge something that was relevant for rhetoric: He who is truly capable of speech is also the one who has acknowledged that of which he speaks; he recognizes the good and the right of which he is trying to persuade, and is thereby responsible for it. Being responsible for something literally means to be able to give a response, to answer; in speaking the answering requires that one is able to stand up for what is spoken about.[23] The testing of life is enacted through a *standing* for the truth. In this context, speaking truly minimally pertains to the strength rather than weakness of words. In conversation the point is not to attack the words of the other for the sake of sophistical persuasion, but to make the words of the other so strong that the truth of what one says becomes evident.

Truth-telling for hermeneutics, then, is this telling of the word, where the word is always something more than the word of the proposition and the word that commands by virtue of an outside force prescribing the law to discourse. The "truth of the word" is the appearing sense that comes to stand in the manner of *aletheia* as the unconcealed. But this is not to suggest that we want simply to repeat Heidegger here. The unconcealing at issue here does not concern historical epochs, but that which cannot be separated from the thematic of speaking, and within this parrhesiastic speaking, from the notions of singularity, decision, and risk. Singularity because the life goals, which are implicit in all social practice, must make themselves concrete; that is, the aims of social practice derive their determinacy by means of the singular not the universal. Coming to agreement, even for a dialogue with oneself, is that of which one must be persuaded here and now. This is why, as Gadamer notes, utopia is not a guide for action, but only a guide for reflection. Knowledge with respect to action is coming to know what must be done from the concrete demands of the situation. And obviously so, coming to know what must be done requires deciding for something against something else such that the truth-telling practice requires that the other must be convinced, while holding to the possibility that the opposite conviction could be correct. And in this resolve there is always risk, but not simply the risk that the resolution itself enacts. Gadamer tells us that the task of the human future involves "risking of one's own for the understanding and recognition of the other."[24] And perhaps here, to a lesser extent, we can also find Vattimo's new philosopher, for the philosophy that becomes political thought must, as he tells us, pass "from the ethics of the Other (with a capital O) to an ethics of the other (lowercase o)" where there can be an ethics of negotiation and consensus (NE 64).

The third consideration proceeds from the following question: How are we to understand the *duty* associated with the truth-telling practice in a hermeneutical philosophy? Granted that it is possible to speak truly—that our social world is not entirely under the domination of technical and anonymous powers—*why* should one speak freely? For Foucault, duty lies within critical philosophical activity in the task of maintaining limits on the excesses of political management of the state. In effect, duty is conditioned by the opposition to the practice of freedom, and thereby establishes in its own way a new authoritarianism in his version of an ontology of actuality. Vattimo wants to refuse such a structure of duty, describing it instead as "that which summons us as a value to be realized in a good action [in the] negation of the definiteness of the given" (NE 69–70). But here, I think, more needs to be said insofar as the very idea of duty would be linked to some form of political obligation.

Certainly democratic rule in its strict sense, where political power is assigned to each individual, does not necessitate the duty that would be attached to the strong sense of solidarity that follows the Gadamerian line—a duty conditioned by a "promise of payment of friendship, which is limited, like everything."[25] On the contrary, what is of *demos*, as we discover from the root word *dia*, is what is divided. This was already Socrates' insight. For Socrates duty is indeed seen in relation to communality, but this means for the sake of *who* we are, where the "*who*," stands as a *supplement* to democratic discourse.[26] In this supplementarity, the economy of debt that haunts all duty is curious. The duty of the new philosopher to speak cannot be understood as simple restitution, for it is not clear what the debt is and to whom it is owed. It is not a debt in the manner of Socrates' acknowledged debt to the polis in the *Crito*. And the "who," which arises in speaking truly is not to be understood as a "we" of a collective entity, one that concretizes itself through practices and in doing so begins to form an identity that separates one from another. The "who" in a real sense has not yet appeared, for I would think that it is there in speech and nowhere else. But mere speech by itself does not constitute this "we" for words are fragile and "who we are," as Hannah Arendt tells us, is in constant need of remembrance. The duty to speak freely, let me suggest, coincides with hermeneutic recollection: reactivating the moment of decision that underlies our sedimented lives. And here emancipation does not receive a new ground, because it only emerges in its enactment, leaving the question of its origin in darkness.[27]

Notes

1. This phrase is Vattimo's and quoted by Paolo Flores D'Arcais in "Gianni Vattimo; or rather, Hermeneutics as the Primacy of Politics," in *Weakening Philosophy: Essays in Honour of Gianni Vattimo*, ed. Santiago Zabala (Montreal: McGill-Queen's University Press, 2007), 251.
2. See Sebastian Gurciullo, "Interpretation and Nihilism as the Depletion of Being: A Discussion with Gianni Vattimo about the Consequences of Hermeneutics," *Theory and Event* 5, 2 (2001).
3. Gianni Vattimo, "The End of Philosophy in the Age of Democracy," *Le Portique* 18 (2006).
4. Quoted in D'Arcais, 260.
5. Plato, *Republic*, 562d–563d. Quoted in Jacques Ranciére, *Hatred of Democracy*, trans. Steve Corcoran (New York: Verso, 2006), 36.
6. Hans-Georg Gadamer, "Reflections on My Philosophical Journey," in *The Philosophy of Hans-Georg Gadamer*, ed. Lewis Hahn (Chicago: Open Court, 1997), 35.

7. "The 'recollection' that I have in mind is derived from myth and yet is in the highest degree rational. It is not only that of the individual soul but always that of 'the spirit that would like to unite us'—we who are a conversation." Hans-Georg Gadamer, "Destruktion and Deconstruction," in *Dialogue and Deconstruction*, eds. Diane Michelfelder and Richard Palmer (Albany: State University of New York Press, 1989), 110.
8. See Hans-Georg Gadamer, "Die Kultur und das Wort," in *Lob der Theorie* (Frankfurt: Suhrkamp, 1983), 17.
9. Michel Foucault, *Fearless Speech*, ed. Joseph Pearson (Los Angeles: Semiotext(e), 2001), 16.
10. A complete account of the history of this word is given by Arnaldo Momigliano in "Freedom of Speech in Antiquity," in *The Dictionary of the History of Ideas* (New York: Scribners, 1973), 252–263.
11. Michel Foucault, *The Use of Pleasure*, trans. Robert Hurley (New York: Random House, 1986), 9.
12. In an interview titled "An Aesthetics of Existence" Foucault responds to the question "Does a truth in politics still exist?" by saying "I believe too much in truth not to suppose that there are different truths and different ways of saying it." *Foucault Live*, trans. John Johnston (New York: Semiotext(e), 1989), 314.
13. Michel Foucault, *Technologies of the Self* (Amherst: University of Massachusetts Press, 1988), 18.
14. Plato, *Republic*, 557b.
15. John Rajchman, *Truth and Eros* (New York: Routledge, 1991), 119.
16. Michel Foucault, "The Concern for Truth," in *Foucault Live*, 308.
17. Foucault, "An Aesthetics of Existence," 314.
18. Hans-Georg Gadamer, "The Hermeneutics of Suspicion," in *Hermeneutics: Questions and Prospects*, eds. Gary Shapiro and Alan Sica (Amherst: University of Massachusetts Press, 1984), 55.
19. Hans-Georg Gadamer, "Rhetoric, Hermeneutics, and the Critique of Ideology," trans. Jerry Dibble, in *The Hermeneutics Reader*, ed. Kurt Mueller-Vollmer (New York: Continuum, 1985), 280.
20. Gadamer, "Rhetoric, Hermeneutics, and the Critique of Ideology," 279.
21. Hans-Georg Gadamer, *Truth and Method*, 2nd revised ed., trans. Joel Weinsheimer and Donald Marshall (New York: Crossroads, 1989), 485.
22. Gadamer, "Reflections on My Philosophical Journey," 30.
23. Hans-Georg Gadamer, "Hermeneutik als theoretische und praktische Aufgabe," in *Hermeneutik II*, Gesammelte Werke, vol. 2 (Tübingen: J.C.B. Mohr, 1986), 306.

24. Hans-Georg Gadamer, "The Future of the European Humanities," in *Hans-Georg Gadamer on Education, Poetry, and History*, eds. Dieter Misgled and Graeme Nicholson (Albany: State University of New York Press, 1992), 207.
25. Hans-Georg Gadamer, "Freundschaft und Solidarität," in *Hermeneutische Entwürfe: Vorträge und Aufsätze* (Tübingen: Mohr Siebeck, 2000), 64.
26. The notion of supplementarity brings Derrida to mind.
27. See Ernesto Laclau, *Emancipation(s)* (New York: Verso, 1996).

11

Deciding to Bear Witness

Revolutionary Rupture and Liberal Continuity in Weak Thought

LUCA BAGETTO

In February 2007 Vattimo published a new book titled *Ecce Comu. Come si ri-diventa ciò che si era* [*Ecce Commie: How One Becomes Again What One Was*]. Who could foresee the revolutionary turn of weak thought? I remember the debates in the 1980s, when Vattimo's postmodernism tried to purge violence from the Italian extra-parliamentary left. Within this most radical horizon, Vattimo was always questioned about the current order. He also had to defend himself from the suspicion of conservatism, that is, from the suspicion that his thought might fall back into an apology of the present time because of his insistence on the factual historical provenance, and of his claim to an always historically and culturally situated argumentation. For many, the rehabilitation of prejudice in postmodern hermeneutics carried the stigma of Gadamer's conservatism, despite Vattimo's passage through the roughest Heideggerian regions.

At that time, in Italy Heidegger was an author to whom the left paid attention. The question of his adhesion to Nazism did not prevail over his query about the order of being. Moreover, from a revolutionary standpoint it was easier, and also more dialectical, to launch an anti-systemic criticism not against Heidegger—who, on his side, had challenged the system innovatively—but against Gadamer's hermeneutics, which appeared more classically Hegelian, and therefore more conciliatory.

The revolutionary left at that time indeed also paid attention to weak thought for a while because of the large use Vattimo made of the term "nihilism." Later on, though, revolution and weak thought parted their ways. Revolution did not think it could do without dialectics as engine behind ruptures; conversely, weak thought aimed at continuity, even when trying to shake off Gadamer's classicist conservatism. Besides, Vattimo used the term "nihilism" in a refined and ultimately misleading way. The revolutionaries still thought of themselves within an anarchistic history, and they considered themselves nihilists if not like Dostoevsky's Stavrogin, at least like Ivan Karamazov. In their minds, "nihilism" meant militancy against a social order guaranteed by religion; that is, against a social order that claimed to assert itself as the order of being. Here anarchism converged with Marxist argumentation. To be nihilists meant to be atheists *and thus* open to the goals of social justice.

For Vattimo, on the contrary, nihilism did not come from the succession of dialectical reversals among Hegel, Feuerbach, and Marx. For Vattimo, nihilism was not atheism, but passage from a fixed order of being to a historical-eventual one. What is universal, and therefore counts as foundation, is not based on a steady natural essential being, in the presence of which there is nothing more to say. The universal rises instead in and from agreement among speakers, always in a historical and concrete situation (NE xxv–xxvi). Whereas the natural order is authoritarian, and denies the confrontation with the other, the nihilistic order is democratic, and encourages the search for social consent.

With this formulation, weak thought was set out for a left-reformist politics, in which the goal of emancipation went hand in hand with an acceptance of continuity; even, it relied on continuity. How does weak thought then come to the idea of the urgency of discontinuity, so that normal democracy would need "intense injections of subversiveness"? (EC 49).

The Interpretation of *Being and Time*

The revolutionary turn of weak thought has been, for me, too, a surprise. Before reading *Ecce comu*, I invited Vattimo to drop the absolute continuity weak thought shared with Richard Rorty's thought. Such a request easily assumes an existentialist tone, for it calls to the urgency of a decision—that is, a rupture—in order to give form to one's own existence. In the Turin school, it was precisely Vattimo's master, Luigi Pareyson, who had opposed neopragmatist continuity, which at that time was advocated, rather than by Rorty, by another master of the Turin school, Nicola Abbagnano. Through an interpretation of the condition of possibility in Kant's transcendentalism, Abbagnano had come to a radical criticism of all ontologies, which constituted the ground for all authoritarian dogmatisms. Abbagnano supported a neo-illuminist thought oriented toward the experimentation of always circumstantial and tentative techniques of reason. Its principle was to be determined by indefiniteness, that is, by the possibility of the possible. The principle of knowledge and action consisted in not making these acts impossible in the future, in a remarkable anticipation of Rorty's continuation of the conversation. Besides, Abbagnano's references were also Dewey and James.[1]

Pareyson reacted against this neutrality of choice and affirmed that the dignity of a free existence consists exactly in assuming the risk of choosing. Existence is not defined by the constant opening of possibility, in an eternal beginning state, but by the threat of closure and the risk of failure. Freedom is choice, which can lead either to an accomplishment or to a failure.[2] This is the tragic character of existence and of its choice of form, which Pareyson opposed to the vitalistic feature of neopragmatism.

My request to Vattimo that he abandon the continuity of tradition's infinite referrals had actually been spurred by the conviction that one must find the form of one's own existence; this can happen only by confronting decisions, that is, by exposing oneself to ruptures. What was at stake, however, was not only Pareyson's early existentialistic tragic orientation, which, through a choice, was supposed to break off the infinite referral of tradition's background/unground [s-fondo]. At stake was the interpretation of *Being and Time* that Vattimo had always proposed to us.

Vattimo's interpretation penetrated the sanctuary of Heidegger's thought through questions that indeed belong to hermeneutics, the historicity of comprehension, and existentialism as a critique of idealism. These were Pareyson's and Gadamer's questions—but they did not guide Heidegger's meditation. Heidegger had arrived at *Being and Time* through a long confrontation with neo-Kantianism and the logical mentalism of the theory of knowledge. Heidegger had opposed all this with phenomenology and its critique of psychologism, and with the attempt at bringing logic back to the question of being. It is not logic that sets beings into form through judgment; rather, it is being that gives itself in a form, in Dasein's existence.[3]

No one of us who studied in Turin was drawn toward any of this: either toward the logical problems discussed in Germany after 1850, from Lotze to Frege, from Lotze to neo-Kantianism, and from Lotze to Emil Lask; or toward Husserl's polemic against psychologism, and the opposition of phenomenology to the various formulations of idealism and realism.

With such premises, I had difficulties understanding the questions *Being and Time* wished to answer. In particular, I could not resign myself to the fact that Heidegger had simply introduced historicity into the *a priori*; that he had limited himself to adding the feature of temporality to the ways of ordering experience. If this were the only issue, then the *a priori* maintained a mentalistic, albeit social and super-subjective, feature: beings give themselves to us starting from "our" epochal way of ordering phenomena. Was the ambitious horizon of *Being and Time* so small? It dealt with time as if it were the expropriation of every ordering and reduction to disposable presence. Had that been the question, however, then Hegelian dialectics would have seemed more innovative than Heidegger's proposal thanks to its ability to join the mental with the ontological element. Yet, Heidegger's phenomenology aims at doing much more: it wants to rescue being from the mental and the objective elements.[4]

Moreover, if one held that Heidegger was just a more radical Dilthey, and that the *Geworfenheit* in *Being and Time* "was still liable to be understood as a sort of Kantian a priori" (NE 6), which became explicitly historical only after the *Kehre*, could one say to have really passed through Heidegger's interpretation of Kant? In the latter, transcendental is equivalent to ontological.[5]

In short, in reading Heidegger's critique of the notion of judgment, a broadening of the view was necessary: pre-judice does not mean only the historical-material conditions within which we formulate judgments. In Heidegger, "ante-predicative" does not mean the factual conditions "prior to language," but rather "prior to judgment."[6] In the critique of judgment as conformity between the proposition and the thing one should see not only the critique of a criterion of truth understood as objective and steady structure, but also Heidegger's entire movement, namely, his critique of the central position of the "cultural" and "mental" elements in neo-Kantianism and the formalism of logic.

The Notion of "World"

The question became clear for me once I passed through Cassirer.[7] The theme of symbolic forms articulates the Kantian heritage according to the conviction of mentalism: that is, that experience forms itself insofar as the human mind places the disorder of sensible impressions into some kind of order. The order can be logical, but also mythical, aesthetical, or logical-aesthetical, as in the case of the language of gestures. The *connexio* between representations, that is, the fact that something belongs to something else, is brought by the human mind, in conformity with a historical tendency toward an increasing abstraction from concrete existence. This is the tendency of language from its mythical forms, still bound to sensibility, toward the pure logical relationships of the mathematical science of nature. Cassirer's reading of the philosophical meaning of Einstein's theory of relativity[8] has the goal of confirming exactly in this direction one of the benchmarks of Marburg's neo-Kantianism, namely, Hermann Cohen's argument that space and time are already logical, mentalistic ways to order phenomena. In his *Critique of Pure Reason*, Kant would have ascribed them to the order of sensibility due to his loyalty to precritical positions. But for Cohen, when one says "this is here," "that is there," one is not receiving a form that gives itself in the phenomena; rather, one is constructing logically.[9] In Einstein, space and time indeed lose all sensible qualities and become constructions.

Being and Time clearly realizes that, if the connection of being is entrusted to the copula, that is, to the mental construction of judgment, then "being" means what is verifiable as actually present in reality, and reality becomes the logical result of the negation of negation—that which excludes the no-thing. In judgment, the ontological question is reduced to the verification of what is really there— what "exists"[10]—according to an anxious trait of modernity. Its need for reassurance transforms thought into a technique of control. Heidegger, on the contrary, tries hard to show that negation does not belong to judgment, and thereby neither does "reality." The reality of something does not reduce itself to its actual existence. These are the arguments of "What is Metaphysics?,"[11] which disconcert Carnap's logicism so much. Nothingness opens the way to an ontology no longer subjected to domination by judgment.

Vattimo paid no attention to this critique of logicism. This huge underground river in *Being and Time*—namely, the confrontation with Leibniz regarding impulses, interpreted starting from being (the *Sorge*) and not from the statement on being (the monad); negation as key to the objective reality of Kant's categories, so that they present themselves as *real* determinations of things without being empirical properties, and so on—was disregarded by weak thought. Heidegger ended up being the thinker of the radical historicity of the conditions of possibility of our argumentations. The conditions of possibility lost the meaning they had in *Being and Time*, namely, that of being ecstatic openings to the beyond, freedom, and excess; instead, for Vattimo they became the factual conditions of discourse.

Philosophical discourse then takes up residence in the historicity of absolute continuity, of which weak thought seeks a total representation. Radical historicity must become the criterion by which to interpret historicity itself. Since historicity is no longer a condition of possibility that opens discourse but it is discourse itself, then philosophy becomes the narration of how all *a priori* have become narration (NE 94–95; 87–88; 25). This is a thesis in which being is made available to language in an idealistic and neo-Kantian, and not a Heideggerian way. The subject is admittedly weakened to the role of interpreter of the signs of the time; however, precisely like the idealist subject, such weakened subject creates meanings by introducing culture where there was nature. An ontology of actuality understood in this way risks repeating Hegelianism plus a vigorous injection of interpretation, in the attempt to avoid all conclusive encounters with a no longer consumable presence, capable of finally silencing the voice of culture (NE 88).

It is true that Heidegger seems to introduce the notion of "world" in terms of a cultural context, for example when he indicates the difference of worlds within which one can experience such a being as the solar sphere. The world of mathematical physics has a comprehension of it that is different from the natural understanding of everyday perception.[12] Vattimo, however, used to explain to us this "world," that is, this way in which being gives itself, in the terms of Thomas Kuhn's centrality of consciousness:[13] that is, the cultural change in our scientific image of the world modifies our sensory perception.[14] Conversely, the notion of "world" in *Being and Time* is phenomenological and tries to overcome the distinction between mental and material. Through such a notion Heidegger fights against the neo-Kantian conviction that only judgment, as activity of the mind, gives knowledge by agreeing with a representation or rejecting it. The phenomenological world is instead that framework that explains to us why we can have a familiarity with things that lets us grasp them not through judgment, but through the way we directly direct ourselves toward them—in perceptions, in hallucinations, in simply having something in mind, in hating, in loving, and so on.[15]

The difficulty for Heidegger himself admittedly consists in specifying the relation between the self-giving of a thing (the way in which it is understood) and this thing itself. "How the being-intended of an entity is related to that entity remains puzzling."[16] The phenomenological space is precisely this problematic remaining-*between-two*, between thought and being. In intentional correlations there is not something that comes first, whether conscience or world. Thus the *a priori* does not have to do primarily with subjectivity, and it does not consist in enclosing the world into language as if into a shell. Otherwise, the fall into neo-Kantianism is unavoidable. The opening as background/unground [*sfondo*] and provenance, that is, the throwing of being as thrown project, does not coincide with the actual historical-cultural horizon; rather, it indicates the ability to grasp the form of the experience as something that gives itself to me. "This means that the continuum of the perceptual sequence is not instituted supplementally by a supervening synthesis."[17] The synthesis is *a priori*. The structures of orientation of experience are "given" of a new kind: they are "donated." They give themselves, and give the object, that is, they make it accessible. This is what is at stake in categorial intuition. Heidegger shows how in it the ideal (nonsensible) element can avoid being identified with the element that conforms to consciousness, with the subjective—as it happens in neo-Kantianism at the peak of modern mentalism.[18]

If, conversely, for hermeneutics the matter is that of becoming aware of the interpretive-narrative character of all categorial frameworks, and such awareness is called to "a giving-form to widely felt sentiments about the meaning of being alive in a certain society and in a certain historical world" (NE 87–88), then the *a priori* becomes again a character of a being and not of the being of beings.[19] Philosophy becomes again a subjective, now more aware *Weltanschauung* (NE 25). As image of the world, weak thought then participates to the will to control Heidegger denounces. Vattimo must in fact argue for his position by appealing to the power of culture—a power that is not alien to some imperialism and hegemony. He indeed appeals to the fact that "westernization is a destiny that even the 'other' cultures . . . are unable to escape" (NE 33). Interpretation, too, becomes something that imposes itself together with the present time. In it, reality becomes now representation, and representation imposes itself as matter of fact. Through this path, escaping the logic of hegemony is very difficult, even, is impossible.

Representation

If one accepts the neo-Kantian position, representation will certainly be able to substitute itself for the hardness of reality, lightening, and spiritualizing it. But it will be necessary to remain within the dichotomy between mind and reality, so that the mind can become the hardest and most despotic reality.

For Heidegger, on the contrary, the articulation of reality does not come from language. If something did not have a meaning already from the beginning, it could not be expressed and made explicit.[20] Heidegger is precisely the most radical destroyer of the idea of language as a conceptual scheme organizing our experience.[21] Weak thought runs instead the risk of lightening reality in conformity with an idealistic history of culture. It narrates the story of how reality lightens itself in the narration of reality. This way, it takes part in the Hegelian grandiose movement of the history of humanity, that is, in the consumption of the immediacy of nature.

If Heidegger's *Ge-Schick* is weakened into a history of culture, then continuity prevails, and the necessity to proscribe all interruptions even imposes itself. If something interrupts the accumulation of cultural stratifications, it could only occur in the name of the rescue of a natural, silencing, and thus violent essence. This point, automatic within a *neo*-Kantian horizon (dogmatism is precisely before Kant and the Enlightenment; *afterward*, there is a *neo*progress of emancipation that should not be interrupted), is articulated by Vattimo at a central moment of his interpretation, when he develops his critique of the foundation of universal validity. For weak thought, it is particularly relevant to retrieve Hume's argument against necessary universality. Moving "without explicit reasons" from the description of a matter of fact to the formulation of a universal principle is not allowed (NE 39).

With Hume's law, Vattimo embraces provenance, which ultimately amounts to embracing habit or custom. In this way, Vattimo intends to historicize the *a priori*, which for him (who pays so little attention to the transcendental in Heidegger) is equivalent to a silencing presence. Here the evocation of Hume does not go in the direction of an empiricism of the particular. It does not interrupt the repetition that leads to idealization, according to Derrida's sophisticated interpretation. The ontology of weakening continues to hold, like Cassirer, that the repeated connection between particulars is something mental,[22] albeit historicized in continuity. Thus, it is not facts that are raised to legitimacy, but rather interpretation, in its historicity. The universal principle is given by the cultural stratifications built by the accumulation of interpretations and their mutual reference. In such a cross-reference of interpretations the primary violence of an essential-natural-silencing foundation is consumed.

As I stated earlier, however, if one remains on the level of cultural aspects, in their cross-reference the different interpretations have anyway the tendency to impose themselves, that is, to reach the status of "habitual facts." The destiny of Westernization and of post-mechanical dissolution of material objectivity into the pure abstractions of media communication (NE 15–16) is admittedly an interpretation; yet it is an interpretation that "emerges as dominant" (NE 40).

Such an imposition and command (*Ge-stell*) tell us that the mutual referral of interpretations, if it remains on the level of the neo-Kantian/idealistic ordering of the world, is not at all a mere background/unground game. The mutual referral presupposes the fight for mutual recognition, which is the result, not to be taken for granted, of a hard fight for predominance. The fact that the interpretive practice is a *procedure*, consisting in finding again and again a precedent, without ever stopping at an absolute beginning, must be brought to a confrontation with the fight between master and servant, between master and student. The coming-before and the coming-after describe a procedure that is not peacefully continuous. They imply tension, a comparison of testimonies, the confrontation between an Old and a New Testament. They involve the labor of recognition and the difficult overcoming of the logic of the new, and of simple substitution. The *Verwindung* of metaphysics is not only a resumption that involves torsion and distortion, as if it were the case of a story of differences among accents. What is at stake in *Verwindung* is the critique of traditional substitution.

Here is the political theme in postmodern weakening: representation and the question of substitution—of the old with the new, of the particular with something more universal, or of the single citizen with a political representative. My thesis is the following: If the founding-unfounding [*fondamento-sfondamento*] is configured in the form of a procedure and of the retrieval of a precedent, and if principles are a matter of pure inheritance, and thus of historicity and contingency, then it becomes difficult to give form to representation and to its political space, to its theater as public space. In pure cultural immanency, where everything is subject to dealings, the common space receives no form. In this limited sense Carl Schmitt is right: the immanency of continuity is a category based on pure economics and founded on the immanency of interests and their power. Pure economics is not only the naturalism of the law of the strongest—as Vattimo asserts (NE xxix, 129; EC 37,

108–109). Economism is also the culturalism of idealistic-subjective appropriation.

In the ontology of actuality, such an appropriation is expressed by the word "interest." Vattimo for example intends to weaken the natural foundation of justice into the historical contingency of an interest. What we define as "right" is to be weakened in the interest of the preservation of social life, which is the *factual* condition of the possibility of finding a precedent—the factual condition of continuity. Is it, however, legitimate to say that there is an *interest* in social life? Interests do not legitimate. Interests correspond to the subjective appropriation and will to control and to reassurance expressed by neo-Kantian judgment.[23] There is no interest in social life—only responsibility for it. The public space of representation is not related to the immanency of consciousness, to subjective interest; rather, it gives itself as something preceding us, and calling us to responsibility.[24]

The *responsibility* for the precedent indicates toward a notion of representation that is new in a new way. It is not the tradition's mental notion, which culminates in neo-Kantianism and the liberalistic economism of subjective appropriation. "*Aliquid stat pro aliquo* [something stands for something else]" does not define, in the neuter genre of reification, the act of substitution belonging to private law—someone stands for someone else. In terms of constitutional law, this is simple *Vertretung*.[25] In the political sphere, the phenomenon of representation (*Repräsentation*) regards a category that gives order and form. These order and form are not ontic properties of existing things; rather, they are a *trascendens* that gives itself to be seen only to the one who lets it be. The synthesis is *a priori*. Such a perspective is not the same as the absolutism of representation in Hobbes and Schmitt, for whom the space of representation, in order to give form to the unformed game of interests, takes all power upon itself, and expropriates the citizens of it. Heidegger's being *is* not but gives itself, and thus it is a form that escapes all appropriation. Despite Heidegger's misunderstandings, it does not lead to the Nazi State. It *is* not the exceeding and inaccessible;[26] rather, it *gives itself* according to a vertical representation, in which the represented idea is phenomenologically linked to the spectator[27] and is present only through the citizen-spectator's eyes.

"*Aliquid stat pro aliquo*" then does not mean "in the place of," but rather "in front of," in the sense of what precedes but also in the sense of something that sets itself in front of the particular and protects it. The sign takes upon itself the blow that the universal, like a despotic master and Moloch, tries to strike on the particular.[28]

Only through vertical representation is it possible to maintain the difference between political representation—which gives a figure to the *trascendens* of the common space—and rank-representation, which is the bearer of specific interests, albeit the interest in the expression of interests. This difference is today at the center not only of the Italian tensions, that is, of the tensions occurring in a country that has always had difficulties understanding that which transcends subjective appropriation. It is also at the center of the world tensions concerning globalization as domination by greedy multinationals, and concerning the necessity of a political governance of globalization.

The Politics of Testimony

Vertical representation introduces the outdated question of legitimacy within the comfortable absolute continuity of the immanent set of norms and their mutual referrals. Even in Vattimo, vertical representation introduces a doubt about the world of aesthetization and total representation, which is now the *loisir* [leisure] of the cultural industry dominated by the United States (EC 74). I recall that, at the time of the ayatollah Khomeini, Vattimo suggested weakening Khomeini's fundamentalism exactly through the power of the media, from movies to *Baywatch*, from consumerism to porn. Now it has become clearer to everyone that, in strong doses, *loisir* makes people stupid.

In weak thought the conviction remains that the products of culture save us. This is so, for example, in the belief that philosophy finds an affinity with religion in the project of a diffuse intensification of the meaning of life (NE 36). This continuity, too, is not convincing. The demand for an intensification of the meaning of life can be better satisfied through means that have nothing to do with a radical interrogation of meaning. It can be satisfied through rites of the artificial, which, precisely as such, show how distant the dimension of interrogation of faith is from being a simple artificial consumption of the natural, first of all of the natural character of death (NE xxix). The experience of faith proper to the Christian transmission is not situated within the alternative between nature and culture as the cultural element par excellence, which would have generated also socialism (NE xxix, 31–32, 116; EC 11, 37). Christianity, as history of the Christian faith, places itself not at an ontic but rather at an ontological level as the appeal that space be made for being and that the *polis* become more habitable. This is humanization according to the Gospel; it is not humanism. On the level of cultural history, is it possible to say that Christianity as culture has made the world better? Or that Christianity has reduced the world's violence? And is it really possible to say, as Vattimo wants to do, that faith helps to reassemble a coherent meaning of experience (NE 9, 87–88), as if it were the original plot of all narrated stories? Perhaps not even faith settles life; as Christ's cry on the cross warns us, faith simply renders the quest, and the hope, more burning.

We are responsible for the other, not for culture. Heidegger's opening of being is not a historical-cultural opening. His is not a neo-Kantianism like Dilthey's or Cassirer's, for which the universal is built by the mind. The universal—being-with—comes first: the synthesis is *a priori*.

On such premises of absolute cultural continuity, weak thought was perhaps inevitably bound to develop nostalgia for the revolutionary rupture.[29] Yet Vattimo continuously tries to tie the revolution to factual and actual conditions of possibility, as if the historical continuity itself were to produce its own interruption. It is an actual revolution that arises from the provenance of the situation itself: it is a matter of "doing what one finds" (EC 95), of "accepting to assume the claims for freedom and emancipation as they manifest themselves" (EC 97). Since the legitimation of rupture comes from continuity, then it is necessary that continuity itself becomes unbearable so as to lead to the revolution. Vattimo continues to refuse the arguments of the appeal to some natural essence of humanity, to some metaphysical evidence, to some human authenticity and profundity, as reasons for the revolution (EC 75): *it is the situation that is not normal* (EC 58). The legitimacy of revolution is found in the demand for legality, for the normality of the norm. It is the situation that has changed: this is the condition of possibility of the revolution. "Something has happened that has changed us while it has also changed the world around us" (EC 75). Even when it disposes itself toward the revolution, postmodernism remains an ideal that is admittedly normative, but is also the result of an immanent cultural interpretation (NE 11).

The burden of the rupture and discontinuity, which in the political dimension describes the responsibility of an act of government (that is, the ability to respond to the unpredictability and gravity of events), shifts entirely onto the representation of personal coherence. It bears witness to a continuity through which one becomes again what one was, and one opposes a treacherous and disappointing historical continuity. Political representation, emptied out of all decisive elements capable of transcending immanent interests, becomes a representation based on the immanency of life and its force of negation. Since such a negation does not know a *trascendens*, it becomes a force of absolute negation; it becomes the testimony of the martyr, who is ready to die for some ideals. It is a question of "building a world where everyone is free to choose, in all freedom, the value, the God, in whose name to live one's life or even to sacrifice it" (EC 24).

So triumphs modern consciousness such as we described it: the ideal element is to coincide with the element that conforms to consciousness. Dangerously, this is also the logic of terrorism. With its last step, weak thought risks turning upside down the position it had so courageously defended in the 1970s. This testifies to the fact that absolute continuity is always on the verge of capsizing into will to power.

It is at this point that the figures of the master and servant, and the insufficiency of the Marxist revolutionary interpretation are to be investigated.

> The ideals for which one sacrifices oneself historically change, yet a radical difference remains: it is the difference Hegel philosophically theorized in the analysis of the relation between Servant and Master: the Servant frees himself of his slavery only when he has the courage to risk his life in the fight for freedom. And if he does not die in the fight, his life changes, and becomes the life of a free man. (EC 25)

As long as Vattimo remained bound to reformist continuity, the figures of the master and servant entered his thought as demands for the recognition of differences. Whereas a globalized society is reluctant to recognize differences, reformist politics pursues the mutual recognition of the different communities composing the state. The stage of recognition is reached only by claiming the primacy of politics over economics, that is, the primacy of the common space over the principle of appropriation. I clearly remember Lukács's passages where, from an orthodox socialist point of view, the category of recognition is rejected as regressive because it is juridical and conservative, whereas the economic category of transformation, bound to the idealism of work, is progressive.[30] Vattimo, on the contrary, still in 2002 preferred recognition to revolutionary transformation:

> I prefer to believe that the recurrent crisis of the capitalist system, which have become more devastating as the globalization of the economy has advanced to new levels, are proofs rather of the need to restore the independence of politics from economics. This autonomy, well expressed in the slogan "from each according to her abilities to each according to her needs,"

is still the living and relevant substance of the socialist message. ... And "socialism" in the sense I have used the term here has to mean a conception of the state as guarantor of the multiplicity of the communities that compose it, communities in which individuals confer recognition on one another because they are not all homogenized into an indistinct mass of citizen-subjects. (NE 128–129)

At a deeper analysis, however, also the thesis that Vattimo has asserted more recently from a revolutionary standpoint remains faithful to recognition: namely, to a recognition of the self that leads to become again what one once was, without any emancipation from the economic and idealistic category of appropriation. The recognized servant turns himself into the master of appropriation. This way he forces the master, who preceded him, to recognize him. So the servant substitutes for the master. The servant wins by taking possession of the master, and by forcing him to recognition.

The Master and Servant Struggle

It is true, as Hannah Arendt and Jürgen Habermas (and the prerevolutionary Vattimo) emphasize, that recognition among differences within the *polis* must transcend all problems of survival.[31] But this implies a perspective that goes radically beyond consciousness—an anti-idealist and anti-neo-Kantian perspective. Conversely, when one still speaks of revolution and fight between master and servant, the point of departure is ever again a philosophy of consciousness.

In Hegel, master and servant must recognize each other, but at the beginning only one is recognized. There will be truth if the object (that is, what one is for the other at this level) shows through its doing that it reaches the level of the "for itself," that is, when the consciousness of the self and that of the other are brought into unity.[32] One rises in level exactly by showing that one does not fear death, which is the Other from oneself. But the two self-consciousnesses cannot stop here, otherwise they remain in their indifference. The two self-consciousnesses must gain experience of the fact that for them not only self-consciousness, but also life is essential. Life is where negation *is*: where every thing assumes *a form*.

Hegel says that this is the sphere of work, in which the will to negate and transform the material is held back by the ontological quality of the object to be transformed. Work on an object must follow the way in which the object wants to be worked. The dignity of the object halts in a specific form the process of working transformation.

I have become convinced of the rightness of Axel Honneth's thesis, as a hard-fought upshot of the Frankfurt School, that work is not sufficient to reach recognition. This thesis not only upsets the proletariat's role as bearer of the direction of history because it has no interests to defend; it also upsets all ideas of revolution as founded on a disinterested representation of interests. Honneth arrives at such thesis through a meditation on the historical-political experience of the Marxist liberation of the servant. He tries to understand how it happened that a logic of liberation turned into the production of a new despotic and engulfing master, in real socialism.

Work does not suffice to reach self-consciousness as a juridical person.[33] Work in Marxism, or the work of concept in dialectics, is the conciliation of subjective and objective from the point of view of consciousness.[34]

Such tenacity in the role of consciousness operates here, too, when weak thought seeks the revolution. As it happens in all philosophies of consciousness, in the end the servant is ready to die exactly like the master is, and with the very same thoughts.[35] In Vattimo's case, such logic may lead him to proximity with terrorism—a proximity that his beautiful intellectual history does not deserve.[36] Consciousness shows in fact its supremacy by affirming the universal in the form of negation. The universal is what denies life, and the testimony of the universal imposes itself because it is ready to die. Here is the anti-political essence of terrorism, which does not recognize but deny. Terrorism is a way of the master's self-affection, is a self-feeling in which the master becomes aware of himself so as to make sure that, when the time to die comes, he has not yet died.

In all philosophies of consciousness, the servant, too, is caught in a logic of dominant negation. The servant obtains recognition because he wins, and wins when he gets the other to desire his own desire. A logic of seduction, of bringing (*ducere*) the other to the self (*se*), of full mastery over the other, forces the other to recognize us.[37] The desire for desire is the permanent revolution; it is revolution as absolute continuity, which in the end feels attraction for the fury of disappearing.

The issue, however, is not forcing the other to recognize us as subjects of rights. The political problem consists in the expropriation of the solipsism of consciousness. Only in this way can the state stop being negation; that is, it can stop overruling the members of the society. Consciousness is called to recognize that it is preceded by the universal, the being-with, and that it must primarily confront not the disavowal it suffers from the others, but its own tireless resistance to recognize its own will to power.

As said, it is difficult to escape the domination of hegemony. Vattimo accuses Michael Hardt and Toni Negri of proposing once again, in *Empire*,[38] a hegemony of the multitudes in revolt. Such multitudes would still be guided by an organic model of society, by the beautiful ethicity of the *polis* in which the individuals' will coincides, totally and effortlessly, with the will of the whole (EC 22–23). It would be a hegemony that has no problems of representation, a hegemony *à la* D'Annunzio, searching for "new dangerous figures of global redeemers" (EC 23). What does Vattimo propose to substitute for the multitudes? I say "substitute" because for him institutional democratic representation is corrupted by money. What remains then is only a representation that is explicitly aware of its being an expression of an interest, namely, the interest in the expression of interests. What looked like an essential category of things now reveals itself as simply a way of narrating them—and such a revelation, too, is a narration. In the same way, what transcends representation reveals itself as representation of a representation. As the representation imposes itself as a fact, however, in the same way the interest in the representation of interests leaves a free hand for the imposition of the strongest. Against this logic, one must say that the proletariat will not free itself thanks to a representation of rank (of interests), but thanks to the political representation of the common space and the demand for openings for those who are excluded. This will be the way of the revolution.

The revolutionary turn of weak thought, too, participates in the difficulty (experienced by the Marxist left) of distinguishing political representation from class representation. Marxism does not have a notion of political representation because it is bound, through the concept of class, to economic representation and the idea of a direct and limited mandate by voters. Marxism knows the political commissary, and not the representative of some *transcendens* such as the common space. Hence come the difficulties of an opening of the political space, and the continuous recourse to the instance of consciousness, as if the action of political representation should find its own tribunal in individual consciousness, and not in responsibility toward the common space.[39]

The testimony of consciousness, *martyria,* is this: According to the logic of negation, the witness is ready to put his own life or his own political representation at stake so as to denounce the present; the imperialism of money. But political representation is never *one's own*. Today the new martyrs bring to paroxysm such logic of appropriation, of absolute negation, of the fury of dissolving—perhaps a Western logic of consciousness. For all those who remember the numerous martyrs in the years of Italian terrorism, and look with terror at the new martyrs, listening to the times suggests a move away from the continuity of cultural history.

Notes

1. Nicola Abbagnano, *La struttura dell'esistenza* (Turin: Paravia, 1936); and *Scritti esistenzialisti*, ed. Bruno Maiorca (Turin: UTET, 1988).
2. This thesis of Pareyson was influenced by Pietro Chiodi, the Italian translator of Heidegger, and student of Abbagnano. Chiodi, who had been a partisan commander in the Italian war of liberation from Nazism and fascism, developed the ontological aspect of possibility as risk of failure. On this topic, see Luca Bagetto, *Il pensiero della possibilità. La filosofia torinese come storia della filosofia* (Turin: Paravia, 1995), especially "L'ontologia della possibilità in Pietro Chiodi," 88–107, and "Luigi Pareyson: la realizzazione della libertà," 128–151.
3. Pareyson's existentialism, too, never relied on a subjectivism of a neo-Kantian kind, for which the subject gives form to its own existence through decision. See Luigi Pareyson, "L'esperienza religiosa e la filosofia," in *Ontologia della libertà* (Turin: Einaudi, 1995), 127–128: "For personality, there is nothing more lethal than misrecognizing the occult articulation that, deep down within ourselves, turns the existential choice not into an operation of the conscious will, but into an originary contact with transcendence, which arouses profound essences."
4. For Heidegger, Hegelian dialectics is just a loophole to reduce time to the presence of being. See Martin Heidegger, *The Metaphysical Foundations of Logic*, trans. Michael Heim (Bloomington: Indiana University Press, 1984), 204.
5. Ibid., 170.
6. Vincenzo Costa, *La verità del mondo. Giudizio e teoria del significato in Heidegger*, (Milan: Vita e pensiero, 2003), 272.
7. I remember that, during a course on Cassirer at the beginning of the 1990s at the University of Turin, one day Vattimo remarked on the classicism and great style of the neo-Kantian philosopher, in comparison with which Heidegger's language was surely more

broken and disquieting. Yet in these lectures Vattimo did not go thoroughly into the question of the copula and judgment.
8. Ernst Cassirer, *Zur Einsteinschen Relativitätstheorie. Erkenntnistheoretische Betrachtungen* (Berlin: Bruno Cassirer, 1921).
9. Hermann Cohen, *Kants Theorie der Erfahrung* (Berlin: Dümmler, 1871). On this topic, see Michael Friedman, *A Parting of the Ways. Carnap, Cassirer, and Heidegger* (Chicago: Open Court, 2000), 142–144.
10. In Italy this is the position supported by Vattimo's student Maurizio Ferraris against the prevailing of interpretation over *reality* in weak thought. Ferraris, however, does nothing but carry on Vattimo's misunderstanding about judgment. Exemplary in this sense is Maurizio Ferraris, *Goodbye Kant! Cosa resta oggi della Critica della ragion pura* (Milan: Bompiani, 2004).
11. Martin Heidegger, "What Is Metaphysics?" in *Pathmarks*, ed. William McNeill (Cambridge: Cambridge University Press, 1998), 82–96.
12. Heidegger, *The Metaphysical Foundation of Logic*, 170–180.
13. Thomas Kuhn, *The Structure of Scientific Revolutions* (Chicago: University of Chicago Press, 1970).
14. Costa, *La verità del mondo*, 206.
15. Martin Heidegger, *History of the Concept of Time: Prolegomena*, trans. Theodor Kisiel (Bloomington: Indiana University Press, 1992), 31.
16. Ibid., 47.
17. Ibid., 61.
18. Ibid., 66.
19. Ibid., 74.
20. Costa, *La verità del mondo*, 261.
21. Vincenzo Costa, *Esperire e parlare. Interpretazione di Heidegger* (Milan: Jaca Book, 2006), 73, n. 29.
22. Ernst Cassirer, "On the Theory of the Formation of Concepts," in *Substance and Function* (Dover Publications, 1980), Part I, chap. I, 18–25 especially.
23. Martin Heidegger, *Logik: Die Frage nach der Wahrheit, Gesamtausgabe*, vol. 21 (Frankfurt a.M.: Klostermann, 1976), 62–88. The reduction of being to the "is," that is, to the logical account of the copula, marks the continuity from Descartes to neo-Kantianism: truth is no longer the disclosing of what is, but is the reassurance given by the more constant representation. Starting from here, the distinction between ideal and real develops and becomes, after the

Copernican revolution, the distinction between subjective and objective.
24. Heidegger, *History of the Concept of Time*, 60.
25. See Carl Schmitt, *Constitutional Theory*, ed. and trans. Jeffrey Seitzer (Durham: Duke University Press, 2007), 239; Gerhard Leibholz, *Das Wesen der Repräsentation unter besonderer Berücksichtigung des Repräsentativsystems* (Berlin und Leipzig, 1929), later revised as *Das Wesen der Repräsentation und der Gestaltwandel der Demokratie im 20. Jahrhundert* (Berlin: Dunker & Humblot, 1966). On this problem see Giuseppe Duso, "La rappresentazione e l'arcano dell'idea," in *Il Centauro*, 15 (Napoli: Guida, 1985), 35–70 (esp. 45–46).
26. Heidegger, *The Metaphysical Foundation of Logic*, 165, n. 9.
27. Hans-Georg Gadamer, *Truth and Method*, trans. Joel Weinsheimer and Donald Marshall (New York: Crossroads Publishing, 1989), 121–123.
28. On this point I take the liberty of referring to my "Ontologia del declino e ontologia del riconoscimento. L'interpretazione nello spirito hegeliano," in Luca Bagetto, *L'espressione del servo muto. Mente e mondo dopo Kant* (Turin: Trauben, 2005), 73–98.
29. "If by now democracy is, as it is increasingly clear, a question of liquid assets . . . does it make sense to call the respect for the system's rules 'morality'?" (EC 68).
30. György Lukács, *Der junge Hegel und die Probleme der kapitalistischen Gesellschaft* (Berlin-Weimar: Aufbau-Verlag, 1986), chap. 3, §7, on the limits of Hegelian economics.
31. Vattimo, "Globalization and the Relevance of Socialism," in NE 125–126.
32. Georg W. F. Hegel, *Phenomenology of Spirit*, trans. A. V. Miller (Oxford: Oxford University Press, 1977), 110.
33. Axel Honneth, *Kampf um Anerkennung. Zur moralischen Grammatik sozialer Konflikte* (Frankfurt a.M.: Suhrkamp, 1992), 104.
34. Alexandre Kojève, *Introduction to the Reading of Hegel*, trans. James Nichols (Ithaca: Cornell University Press, 1980), 24.
35. Honneth, *Kampf um Anerkennung*, 49.
36. EC 59–60: "If [the Enlightenment] is deprived of its intimate eschatological reference—according to the ways Hegel inaugurated in the *Phenomenology*, which denounces the fatality of Terror as excess of political rationalism—then the appeal to the Enlightenment works simply as plea for a 'liberal' reasonableness that, like

all 'moderate' positions, seems preferable especially to those who would have 'something to loose' in a revolutionary process"; EC17: "What if we were finally to acknowledge that all revolutions, or resistances, began under the guise of 'terrorist' acts?"
37. Kojève, *Introduction to the Reading of Hegel*, 6ff.
38. Michael Hardt and Antonio Negri, *Empire* (Cambridge, MA: Harvard University Press, 2000).
39. As it is perhaps known, in 2007, together with Chomsky and other intellectuals like the director Ken Loach, Vattimo signed an appeal in support of senator Turigliatto, who was ready to make the Italian center-left government led by Romano Prodi fall in the name of a "question of conscience" over international politics.

12

Emancipation and the Future of the Utopian

On Vattimo's Philosophy of History

SILVIA BENSO

Philosophy, History, and Politics

"The opening of an epoch is also the French Revolution. Of course! Then why should not one also say that truth happens also in electoral results—in addition to in some other mysterious word that only few can understand?" So writes Gianni Vattimo in his almost autobiographical work titled *Non essere Dio* [*Not to Be God*].[1] The underlying conviction is that of a deep connection, even continuity between philosophy and politics, or at least the political. In the contemporary world, Vattimo claims, philosophy "becomes intrinsically political thought" (NE 86). The connection explicates itself at two levels, as it were: hermeneutical, that is, the theoretical level of interpretation, and practical, that is, the level of philosophy as concrete project of emancipation.

For Heidegger, from whom so many of Vattimo's reflections move, truth and Being give themselves in art and poetry (whereas politics is left out of the picture after the brief active experience with Nazism in the 1930s); Being is language, but it is in the poets' words, mainly the great poets of the German tradition, that the voice of Being reveals itself. For Vattimo, on the other hand, truth, with which philosophy, even in its postmodern, weak version, concerns itself (the truth of

Being and historical events, the hermeneutic truth of historical openings rather than the truth of absolutes and objective certainties), does not disdain political events, as one reads in the opening sentence. This is part of the conviction that philosophy cannot exempt itself from a reflection on the current times. Philosophy can only be, in Vattimo's expression, "an ontology of actuality," "the effort to grasp what is meant by Being—the word itself and virtually nothing else—in our experience now" (NE 86; see also EM 3).

Vattimo's (verbally confessed) "weakened Hegelianism," his "obviously taking a 'Hegelian' stance" (NE 88) in the formulation of an ontology of actuality is apparent.[2] The Hegelianism of the position, which is nevertheless coupled with a powerful injection of empiricism, lies in the fact that here "philosophy makes a commitment vis-à-vis history" (NE 88). The justification for such historicism is found in the historical character of Being itself. Unlike many traditional metaphysical positions that include also contemporary thinkers such as Levinas and Derrida, for whom history remains marginal, for Vattimo there is no incompatibility between history and ontology because it is Being itself that gives itself in history. "If Being is truly event, then Being itself is history, time, and happening," Vattimo in fact claims (VRF 75). Furthermore, not only does Being give itself in history, as others (from Christianity to Hegel) before Vattimo have maintained, but also Being can be described only in terms of the history of Being. "There is ontology, there are things, there is a Being that 'there is'; yet this *ontological* gives itself only within a history; if I speak of ontology, I can only speak of history of Being" (VRF 97). Being, which gives itself within a history, gives itself as language, as provenance from a tradition that the self lives and assimilates precisely as linguistic, that is, within a dialogue with others—in the community of a *polis*. That is, Being is linguistic, historical, and political at the same time.

Heidegger's and the existentialist insistence on the historicity and finitude of human beings meets in Vattimo with the originally Nietzschean theme (also filtered through the teachings of Vattimo's own teacher, Luigi Pareyson) of the interpretative, that is, once again historically determined character of all truths, including the interpretative truth itself—"all facts are a matter of interpretation," Nietzsche claims, and Vattimo emphasizes how this, too, is an interpretation. As clearly stated in *Beyond Interpretation*, hermeneutics, which for Vattimo has become the philosophy of modernity (BI 11) and the philosophical *koine* of our times, is "not only a theory of the historicity (horizons) of truth: it is itself a radically historical truth. It cannot think of itself metaphysically as a description of one objective structure of existence among others, but only as the response to a sending, to what Heidegger calls *Ge-Schick*. The reasons for preferring a hermeneutic conception of truth to a metaphysical one lie in the historical legacy of which we venture an interpretation and to which we give a response" (BI 6).

The reconfiguration of philosophy as an ontology of actuality does not, however, turn philosophy into an *expression* of the current times, as "the spirit of the age" (NE 88) in a purely Hegelian mode. This is so because all foundational pretensions to be able to provide an adequate description of reality, and hence to be an expression, have collapsed precisely as a result of the historical times. That is, nowadays the theory of truth as correspondence has lost its explanatory power. But so has also the claim that there are essences and foundations the knowledge of which would place philosophy in a privileged position to provide politics with guidelines for programs and actions. Far from supplying programmatic directives or accurate descriptions, that is, far from being foundational in a political or philosophical sense, an ontology of actuality is rather an *interpretation* of the current epoch, "a giving-form to widely felt sentiments about the meaning of being alive in a certain society and in a certain historical world" (NE 87–88). In this sense, an ontology of actuality resonates with deeply political undertones.

As with all interpretations, the present one is also risky, free, and contingent and can count in its support only its own experience of what the epoch may mean. Such an experience, however, is filtered through and thereby legitimated by its passage through the historical times themselves rather than by appeal to eternal principles. Thus, the clear and admitted "historicism" explicating itself in the commitment to history in the double sense of loyalty to historicity as fundamental category of human finitude as well as attention to the historical legacy (the tradition) mandating the commitment itself is accompanied by the caveat that this is "not a deterministic historicism" in the sense of any "historiographical objectivism that mistrusts all . . . epochal categories" (BI 11). Vattimo's historicism is rather aware of its being only an interpretation whose current value lies "in being able to establish a coherent picture we can share while waiting for others to promote a more plausible alternative" (BI 11). The validity itself of the ontology of actuality is dependent on its validation within the *polis* (hence the importance of persuasion). In other words, the historical legacy demands not only the hermeneutic character of philosophy and the related ontology of actuality, but also the political stance as the current "vocation and responsibility" of philosophy.[3]

Vattimo's theoretical commitment to history (and the political) finds a correlate in the concrete project of emancipation, which inspires the content of his philosophy. Already autobiographically, Vattimo recognizes that he "began to study philosophy because [he] felt himself involved in a project of human transformation, in a program of emancipation" (VRF 113). The liberating project immediately characterizes philosophy as a political enterprise. As Vattimo writes, "I think that in any event the philosophical vocation is deeply linked to the *polis*; it is not by accident that philosophy is properly born in the 'political' context opened up by Greece" (VRF 115). This, in turn, justifies the philosopher's involvement, and even duty to participate in the political events of the age. The Platonic flavor of the philosophical vocation to politics does not go unrecognized by Vattimo (VRF 115). "I think that in philosophy what is always at stake is a political good; it is always a question of political community, which justifies both philosophy as teaching, and philosophy in the newspapers, and also, I think, philosophy in politics" (VRF 113). These are the activities in which Vattimo consistently engages.

The differences between a philosophical profession oriented to politics and the properly political profession are not indifferent; first of all is the critical attitude toward the present that philosophy can afford more easily than politics in its more decision-oriented, pragmatic needs to govern (VRF 117). But not indifferent are also the affinities, which indicate a fundamental "unity in the life of spirit that specifies itself in the individual vocations and yet maintains a certain continuity" (VRF 118), as Vattimo's teacher, Luigi Pareyson (but also Dilthey and Heidegger), understood clearly. Both philosophers and politicians "work in the same direction, albeit at a different level" (VRF 117–118). The direction is that of promoting transformation—"the transformation of human beings prior to the transformation of structures" (VRF 117), which properly belongs to politicians. This human transformation, which also bespeaks the non-Marxian presupposition in Vattimo's philosophy, is what Vattimo pursues under the title of emancipation.

Emancipation, Nihilism, Democracy

How does Vattimo characterize emancipation? "The only emancipation I can think of is an eternal life in charity, that is, in the listening of, and replying to the dialogue with others," he writes (VRF 103). In a return to the Christian origins of his philosophizing, Vattimo claims that the matter is that of a project of emancipation through truth. The Evangelical precept that "the truth shall set you free" is reinterpreted by Vattimo to mean that truth itself is emancipation in the sense that "that which . . . liberates is true" (VRF 103).

In Vattimo's perhaps most political book so far, *Nihilism and Emancipation*, one reads that the Pauline expression "'*Veritatem facientes in caritate*' . . . [is taken to mean], in terms of today's philosophy, that the truth is born in consent and from consent, and not, vice versa, that agreement is reached when we have all discovered the same objective truth" (NE xxvi). Issue of the objective nature of the truth aside, Vattimo's well-established line of interpretation, developed throughout much of his production, understands emancipation as "a process in which constraints are shed and we gain greater freedom, autonomy, and opportunity to choose" (NE xxv). The perspective of freedom and liberation is then connected to the history of nihilism.

Vattimo's consolidated idea is that "the terms 'nihilism' and 'hermeneutics' are . . . synonyms" (NE xxv) insofar as "hermeneutics is the thought of accomplished nihilism" (NE xxvi). This coincidence of terms becomes clearer if, following Nietzsche, one distinguishes between positive (or active) and negative (or reactive) nihilism. Whereas negative nihilism expresses the nostalgic "desperation of those who continue to cultivate a sense of mourning because 'religion is no more'" (NE xxvi), active nihilism, which Vattimo also qualifies as "constructive" (NE xxviii), means "the dissolution of any ultimate foundation, the understanding that in the history of philosophy, and of western culture in general, 'God is dead,' and 'the real world has become a fable'" (NE xxv). Such a dissolution of any ground or foundation, which in itself "brings freedom" (NE xxvi) insofar as it also dissolves any authoritarian archaic principle, runs the risk of hardening itself into a new form of foundationalism, into a new metaphysics. It is at this point that hermeneutics, based on "the principle of the plurality of interpretations, in other words respect for the freedom of everyone to choose" (NE xxviii) and offering "a concept of the world as conflict of interpretations" (NE 90), can constitute a powerful corrective against the foundationalist aberrations of nihilism.

Hermeneutics, which explicitly theorizes the existence of a "manifold of interpretations," is not simply one philosophical position among many, but rather it is "the philosophy of modernity and modernization *tout court*" (NE 90), Vattimo claims. That is, hermeneutics contains within itself a (nonmetaphysical) philosophy of history "that views hermeneutics as the result of a 'nihilistic' process, in which metaphysical Being, meaning violence, consumes itself" (NE 94). This process, which can also be thought of as a phenomenon of "secularization" (NE

32) and as the "destiny" or "destination" of the West (NE 33), requires the "reconstruction of an idea of universal rationality that, if [one has] to distinguish it from rationalism and metaphysics, [one] can do no better than describe as weak and secularized" (NE 30). It is precisely the weakening of strong structures attested in contemporary philosophical thought, which also implies a "reduction of claims" (NE 35), that will bring about human emancipation and liberation, since the truth will no longer be given by an objective standard established a priori, or as a one-to-one correspondence, but rather as the outcome of "an affair of consensus, listening, participation in a shared enterprise" (NE 35). A nihilistic hermeneutics is a "thought that knows it can only regard the universal by passing through dialogue, through consent, if you like through *caritas*" (NE xxvi). In this sense, a nihilistic hermeneutics is the philosophical parallel of the political notion of democracy (NE 90 ff), with its idea that truth is a matter of consensus rather than the imposition of an authoritarian principle. Vattimo summarizes his general position by claiming that, for him, "philosophy, project, historicity, *theoresis*, and emancipation mean one and the same thing" (VRF 116); that is, the fundamental continuity between philosophy (in its hermeneutic and nihilistic variation), politics (in its projects of emancipation), and history (as the commitment to the current times) is reasserted throughout.[4]

Utopian Thinking?

In the Foreword to the English translation of *Nichilismo ed emancipazione*, Richard Rorty describes Vattimo's philosophy as one that "takes the form of historical narrative and *utopian speculation*," and continues: "for leftists like Vattimo and Dewey, [philosophy] becomes ancillary to sociopolitical initiatives aimed at making the future better than the past" (NE xiii).[5] If utopian speculation simply means thinking of, or imagining "a future better than the past," then certainly Vattimo is a utopian thinker. Likewise, if one were to associate utopian thinking with having an ethical, social, and political commitment geared toward a general future transformation of human existence.[6] There is no doubt that Vattimo's thought is oriented by strong ethical and political inspirations of a leftist kind.[7] Is this enough, however, to gain Vattimo the appellation of "utopian thinker"? Or, and more generally, is Vattimo a utopian thinker?

The purpose of the question is neither (critically and polemically) taking issues with Rorty's qualification nor (in an argument *ad personam*) labeling Vattimo with some sort of "objective" classification, but rather (philosophically) assessing the kind of philosophy of history that supports Vattimo's overall position. Ultimately, underlying the question of the utopian is the question of the possibility of the future and its unexpected nature; that is, whether there is a place for ruptures, breaks, and discontinuities—some form of radical alterity, of which the future and the utopian would be a mark, interrupting the process of historical thinking—in Vattimo's epochal thinking of a weakening of the structures of Being that finds its parallel in a very specific political project and commitment.

Vattimo on Utopias

A fundamental distinction should be drawn between thinking utopias and utopian thinking; that is, between the imaginative process of devising a perfect model of society to live in and a mode of thought that is inspired by the desire for a just society yet with no representation of how such a community would be.

Vattimo's contribution to the dismissal of the possibility of thinking utopias in the traditional sense emerges clearly in several of his essays.[8] In *Etica dell'interpretazione*, referring to the great modern utopias of Thomas Moore, Tommaso Campanella, and Francis Bacon, Vattimo associates the concept of utopia to the narratives of modernity marked by a rationalism that reads history according to a unitary line of continuity. Utopia, claims Vattimo, is not simply an image of a "happy world," a "*paese di Bengodi*," a "pleasure island" and a mythical golden time where everything is perfect. Vattimo writes that "considered in its specifically modern origins, utopia is actually an aspect of the will to system belonging to metaphysics; one could say that it is a metaphysical rationalism, or a Hegelianism, projected in the dimension of the future" (EI 66). Bloch's utopian future *telos*, which is grasped by the anticipating consciousness,[9] as well as Adorno's iconoclasm with his prohibition of representation of the utopian *telos* are for Vattimo equally linked to an idea of "totality, and hence [to] the metaphysical will to a system" (EI 67). Nor do dystopias or counter-utopias escape such an association with totalizing, rationalistic metaphysics, Vattimo maintains, because they merely reveal the awareness of the counter-finalities of reason, that is, the inability of reason to achieve the ideals of rationalism and the Enlightenment. In other words, utopian thinking is bound to modern metaphysics as an accomplishment or a disillusion thereof. To delineate a new utopia (of whatever kind) is still being part of such a horizon.

Is there any place for utopias then, in a postmodern world that accepts the legacy of the metaphysical deconstruction operated by Nietzsche and Heidegger? There is, claims Vattimo, but it is not the thetic position of any (possible or impossible) utopia. Rather, he says, "the ironic-nostalgic inventory of the fetishes of progress is perhaps the only still possible 'utopia,' the only imaginable and in a sense desirable future condition for human beings in late modernity who have seen the hopes in a rationalization of the world, in the ever fuller *Aufklärung*, dissolve under their eyes" (EI 71). In many senses, this is not utopian at all; it is neither the delineation of a final state, nor the possibility of a state to come. As Vattimo says, "not only, at the end of metaphysics and faith in progress, must utopia have as its only content an inventory, nostalgia, and revival; moreover, also from the standpoint of its emotional value, this condition can no longer appear as a 'fulfillment,' as the *achievement* . . . of a condition [deemed] desirable or in any event final in the teleological sense of the term" (EI 71). What remains of thinking utopias once it is understood in terms of an ironical-inventorial revisitation of past utopias?

The critique of ideologies, of which Karl Löwith's thinking is an example, leaves us with the concept of disenchantment, Vattimo claims (EI 131). When applied also to utopias, disenchantment leads to the recognition that there is no (singular) utopia, but a plurality of utopias—that is, "from utopia to heterotopia," as the title of the section contained in *The Transparent Society* states (62). That is, no utopist description can be idealized or idolized as the model of utopia. All utopias are, in this sense, merely an interpretation. If traditional thinking of utopias was linked to a will to systems and totality, thinking of heterotopias is more in tune with the contemporary epoch marked by nihilism. Yet, both are simply interpretations corresponding to their respective historical times.

Is there any meaning left for utopian thinking once we have realized the historically interpretative character of all thinking of utopias? The impracticability of thinking utopias in what Vattimo characterizes as "the end of modernity" actually opens the way for the possibility of a different understanding of utopian thinking.

What Concept of Utopia(n)?

Many discussions surround the concepts of utopia, utopian thinking, and the modes of utopian realization. It is not the intention of this essay to enter such complex debate, which involves philosophical, political, ideological, sociological, literary, and even theological (if not openly religious) aspects. It is important, however, to clarify the specific understanding of the notion of utopia(n) for which Vattimo's overall philosophical position clears the way, and with which this essay will in fact work.

As is well known, the term "utopia" is coined by Thomas More in 1516 with a double albeit equally Greek derivation. On the one hand, "utopia" comes from *eu-topia*, and thus signifies "the good place" where it is desirable to be, or to live. On the other hand, however, "utopia" derives from *ou-topia*, and therefore indicates the nonplace, that is, I would argue, the place that is not and will never be (nor ever was)—the place of an impossibility, as it were. As Derrida writes, "go there where you cannot go, to the impossible, that is at bottom the only way of going or coming. To go there where it is possible, that is . . . to be there already and to be paralyzed in the in-decision of the non-event."[10]

According to the Greek double meaning, which is at play in the etymology of the word, the real sense of the utopia(n) is, I argue, the one that keeps open the gap, the difference, the discontinuity between good-place and nonplace; that is, between what is concretely realized or even realizable and representable as good and what still ought to be realized, the real and the ideal, the good and its remnant (without thereby ascribing the status of objective reality to what is, and of normative rule to what ought to be. They can both, as Vattimo claims, be the work of interpretation, and therefore retain a high level of contingency and hence nonobjectivity). The utopia(n) in the sense of the absolutely good-place is always a nonplace—the place of an impossibility, as in Derrida's expression—not in the sense that it does not exist, but rather in the sense that it is always a not-yet; utopia(n) is that more desirable place that continuously comes to interrupt, and thereby judges the alleged goodness of any constituted historical and political situation. The utopia(n) is the possibility that comes and calls into question the goodness of the actuality. In other words, utopia(n) is the name that the political good takes up.

This political good, however, like Plato's good, is always beyond being, that is, beyond representation. Therefore, unlike Bloch's concrete utopia(n), which is founded on objective conditions and therefore ripens within reality, utopia(n) comes here to name the political transcendent, what in all politics constantly remains futural, yet to come—like in Bloch's ontology of the being-that-is-not-yet, like Derrida's democracy, which is always to come first of all because there is always more democracy that can be instituted, like, ultimately, in messianism, where the expectation for the Messiah is always beyond fulfillment. In this sense, utopia(n) is neither pure (individual or communitarian) projectable ability geared toward the future (as a dream or a fantasy) nor simply any program (political or otherwise) aimed at the future realization of a more just society, which might in fact merely reveal the presence of an ideology (there are leftist as well as rightist utopias and utopian thinking). Utopia(n) is the alterity that comes and abruptly breaks the continuity of history, progress, development, even of the best kind. As in Max Horkheimer's later atheist theology, as it were, utopia(n) is the longing for "the wholly other" and the "absolutely unrepresentable" that nevertheless inserts itself in history and causes its discontinuity. Utopia(n) is the remnant of all political goodness, what suspends the metaphysical claim to ultimate truth of any historical judgment or realization. It is, as Vattimo phrases it in one of his most recent works, "the dream of the 'barbarians' who at a certain point, coming from the outside, will force us to a harsh restructuring of our ways of life and consumption" (EC 124).

Is there a place for such utopian thinking inspired by the stranger (the "barbarian" or even the Messiah) in Vattimo's philosophy? What is at stake here is, among other issues, the possibility of the new, of which the concept of the utopian as delineated above would be an instance. That is, the issue is whether the new is a matter of radical novelty (as in Messianism) or rather the consequence and the consignment of a legacy, and therefore does not properly exist as new. In other words, is revolution or reformism at work in Vattimo's philosophy? That is, is there the possibility of breaks, ruptures, and interruptions (which also enable the presence of a radically other), or is it rather a matter of transformation (that does not let the novelty of the other manifest itself as other)? Vattimo's philosophy is a philosophy of continuity, not of ruptures. This alone already casts some doubts on the possibility that a true utopian thinking of a messianic kind in which utopian is that which comes from the outside to interrupt in a radical manner the current course of political events may find any place in Vattimo's thought.

Postmodernism, Metaphysics, and *Verwindung*

Vattimo's discourse often refers to the situation of postmodernity in which we find ourselves, and devotes one of his fundamental books from the mid-1980s to the concept of "the end of modernity." It is important to realize, however, that in Vattimo's consideration of (at least philosophical and cultural) history, the idea of "post" (modernity, but also metaphysics, history, or anything else) does not imply the absolute break required by the concept of the utopia(n) evoked earlier. Rather than seeing postmodernity as "something new in relation to the modern," Vattimo in fact considers it as "a dissolution of the category of the new—in other words, as an experience of 'the end of history' [understood as a unitary process, see EM 7–9]—rather than as the appearance of a different stage of history itself" (EM 4). That is, for Vattimo postmodernity does not configure a new horizon of thinking, a new epoch, or even less a new reality, but rather a different attitude toward the modern that is however indebted to the modern.

The major link between modernity and postmodernity is represented by the philosophies of Nietzsche and Heidegger, whose "apocalyptic" and "prophetic overtones" (EM 11) fade once one realizes, as Vattimo does, that "both philosophers find themselves obliged, on the one hand, to take up a critical distance from Western thought insofar as it is foundational; on the other hand, however, they find themselves unable to criticize Western thought in the name of another, and truer, foundation" (EM 2). Like and thanks to Nietzsche and Heidegger's philosophies, postmodernism enables an attitude, or even better an interpretative posture, that allows us to understand the objectivist conditions that guided the philosophies of modernity; therefore, we can "tak[e] leave of modernity" [EM 3]. The taking leave, however, is a matter of a recovery from modernity, as if from a disease, and not of a "leaving-behind" (EM 164, 172), Vattimo clarifies.

An analogous discourse can be applied to Vattimo's concept of metaphysics. Every age has its own metaphysics, Vattimo claims. So, in a sense, we can never completely abandon the horizon of metaphysics to move beyond its existence. We are never out of metaphysics (see EM 172–173). What after Nietzsche and Heidegger's deconstruction of Western values we can and need to engage in is, instead, a different metaphysical attitude, a different interpretation that is marked by the "adventures of difference" rather than by unitary principles of explanation. Vattimo expresses all this through his peculiar interpretation of the Heideggerian notion of an "overcoming" of metaphysics, which he understands in terms of *Verwindung*, and not *Überwindung* (EM 164, 172–173). Whereas *Überwindung* denotes a Hegelian process of *Aufhebung*, an overcoming that goes beyond and leaves behind,[11] the term *Verwindung* for Vattimo implies a distortion, a twisting in new directions, a resigning to and an ironical acceptance of something—in the specific, of metaphysics. For Vattimo, we are never beyond metaphysics, we are never beyond modernity, but we can look at them in an ironical manner. And this is an act of interpretation, which justifies the overall insistence on the hermeneutic dimension in Vattimo's thought.

Ethics of Provenance, Tradition, and Legacy

When Vattimo speaks of an "ethics of provenance" (NE 37–48) or of the *pietas* that we should exert toward the past from which we come, that is, "the devout attention for what has nevertheless only a limited value" and "the love for the living and its traces" (EI 20), he means precisely this horizon of continuity entrusted to us through the notion of *Verwindung*. The contemporary times teach us that we have exited the period of modernity as the period of the vision of history in terms of a single, unitary principle leading (according to different interpretations) either to progress or to regress of a cultural or a technological kind; we have moved instead to a consideration of history in terms of the multiplicity and plurality of histories. What we have thereby abandoned, however, is certain historical interpretations of history, but not history *tout court*. Hence, the fact remains that we cannot escape the tradition or traditions (*Über-lieferung*) to which we belong and from which we come. It is precisely our (rationalist, metaphysical, modern) tradition that consigns us, that destines us to the tradition—as Heidegger says, and Vattimo repeats, we are a "*Ge-schick* in the sense of a *Schickung*, a sending" (BI 109), a destiny and a destination in the sense of having been destined, or sent by the past to our present and, one assumes, but I think correctly, to our future. A leap outside of history—our history—is impossible; the historical character constitutes the finitude of human existence.

This bears some relevance also on the possibility of a consideration of the utopian as a thought of the impossible. Messianism (ultimately, of a Jewish kind) is not part of Vattimo's religious "beliefs," which rather privilege the concept of the Incarnation not in terms of the abrupt insertion of the divine into human history, or of the scandal and interruption of the cross, but in terms of *kenosis*, of a progressive emptying out, of a process of secularization, which he identifies with a weakening of the structures of being.[12] Once again, the very concept of weakening implies continuity and not rupture.

Not revolutions then but rather reformism[13] moves Vattimo's political thinking, and his project of emancipation is also inspired by reformism (despite his latest outcries against the reformism in which the Italian left has fallen, see, for example, EC 126). After all, even at the anecdotal level, Vattimo's political career has always taken place not among the ranks of the Italian extra-parliamentary or radical left, but rather within institutional organizations, albeit generally of an oppositional kind (the youth movement Catholic Action, the European Parliament, the Democrats of the Left). Vattimo's formulation of weak thought is precisely the courageous attempt (one should give Vattimo full credit for this courage, given the heaviness of the times in which it was formulated) to deflect the violence potentially inscribed in all projects of revolutionary liberation, that is, of bringing about a rupture in history that may well (although not necessarily) result in terrorism. One should not forget that some of the individuals arrested in Italy on charges of terrorism during the 1980s were also Vattimo's students who had read his 1974 *Il soggetto e la maschera. Nietzsche e il problema della liberazione* [*The Subject and the Mask: Nietzsche and the Problem of Liberation*], perhaps Vattimo's most "utopian" book, in which the ideal of a "Nietzschean overmanly revolutionary subject" had been upheld.

Vattimo's most recent book, published in Italy in February 2007, may in this sense come as a surprise. It is titled, appealing to Nietzsche's *Ecce Homo*, *Ecce comu*, that is, *Ecce Commie*. Perhaps one can find here a place for a utopian thinking of the revolutionary rupture? Not really, as it becomes immediately clear in the Nietzschean subtitle, although twisted in an ironical sense: *How One Becomes Again What One Was*. Although in a specific variant named "catho-communism" (*cattocomunismo*), that is, a communism instilled with Catholic values (but here, too, Vattimo's Catholic values are twisted values, at least according to the Catholic hierarchy's values), communism, Vattimo claims, does not come as a rupture in his own personal biography; rather, it is part and parcel of the heritage, the legacy, the cultural and personal tradition from which Vattimo comes. And communism is well rooted in the Italian political, institutional, cultural, and even religious environment, even if one has to admit that those very parties for which communism was essential have now moved toward centrist political positions—hence the need, voiced in Vattimo's subtitle, to go back to what one was although through a twisting distortion of what one was. Vattimo in fact advocates a communism purged of the alleged economic foundation (economy as science) present in theoretical communism and leading to its historical degeneration in the countries of the so-called real-socialism. As Vattimo says, "a 'weakened' Marx is what we need to rediscover the truth of communism without reticences of a liberal nature."

For this reason of legacy and tradition, I would advance the possibility that what in Vattimo's concrete political proposals may be considered as a "utopian" project in Rorty's eyes, that is, in the eyes of a thinker who belongs to a country where someone who is openly registered in a communist party (if there are any left) may not even enter, may not at all appear as "utopian" in a country like Italy where communism is instead well rooted in the tradition. In this sense, there is nothing utopian in Vattimo's project of emancipation, which may appear as "utopian" only from the outside, from a different tradition of belonging. Vattimo's are simply the projects that the leftist legacy of the country of which he is part has consigned to him once (most of) such a left has itself lost memory of its own tradition of belonging. Again, no utopian rupture but only (albeit twisted) continuity is what is at work here.

Hope, Archaeology, and Resistance

Where does this understanding of metaphysics, history, and tradition in terms of continuity of *Verwindung* leave us with respect to the notion of utopian thinking? It clearly leaves us neither with a new utopia (a new political configuration that inhabits the space of the impossible and somehow makes it possible), nor with a new model for thinking utopias, nor with the possibility of utopian thinking *tout court*; rather, it leaves us with a different, *verwundene* way of interpreting the only utopias we have, which are the utopias consigned to us from the past from which we as cultural tradition come. That is, no proper space for utopias (whether as thinking new utopias or as utopian thinking) opens up. Vattimo's explicit ethical and political afflatus might lead some such as Rorty to characterize him as a utopian thinker. But we should recall that Vattimo's sense of ethics is peculiar (and Heideggerian); his is indeed an "ethics of interpretation," yet it is "ethics insofar as *ethos*, customs, culture that an epoch and a society share" (EI 135). Ethics is a matter of cultural belonging, that is, of the political, and the spur toward it comes from the past and its legacy to the present, not from the future and a futural good that remains transcendent in its being beyond representation. That is, in Vattimo ethics refers to a dimension of belonging or historicity (immanence) that is always finite.

What leads Vattimo's ethical and political agenda if it is not utopian thinking in the sense of a thinking from the future that works as a directing beam? In *Ecce comu*, Vattimo speaks of "the rediscovered (or to be rediscovered) communist hope" (EC 4). I would argue that it is precisely hope, rather than utopian thinking, that guides Vattimo's (ultimately optimistic) stance, and that Vattimo is better qualified as a hopeful thinker rather than a utopian one. This is not the place to develop the theoretical advantages of a philosophy of hope over the utopian. Let me conclude by saying that, if what Protestant theologian Jürgen Moltmann writes is true—namely (although paraphrasing) that hope is what we are left with when there is no longer hope, then perhaps Vattimo's position is, in a sense, a philosophy of the possibility of the impossible. But the crucial element of differentiation lies in the "origin" of such possibility of the impossible, whether it is in the legacy of the tradition or in some unfathomable anticipation of an unrepresentable future. The difference is between archaeology and eschatology—and Vattimo is undoubtedly an archaeologist, although an anarchic one. It should be emphasized that this element of anarchy is crucial because it is precisely what opens the tradition to innovation rather than to the conservativism of the essences; there are no essences to realize, neither the essence of democracy nor the essence of human nature and the related human rights. But innovation is measured in comparison with the past, so it is not properly new in the sense of what comes from the future as unexpected.

In the "Theses on the Philosophy of History," Benjamin claims that the memory of the enslaved ancestors nourishes the ideal of free future generations. *Denken* is *An-denken* and not *Vor-denken*, for Vattimo as well as for Heidegger (and Benjamin). What is required in and by the current age, Vattimo claims, is not utopian thinking, but rather "a great inventive and 'subversive' imagination" (EC 52), that is, an imagination capable of taking its move from a subversion of what the tradition has consigned to us in terms of actual conditions. It is a resisting thinking, a thinking of the resistance that finds its place in and is justified by "the situation of emergency" (EC 115) in which we find ourselves. "It is the same issue that the majoritarian right always opposes to the Italian left: you always simply say no, you do not have projects. And the untimid and compromising left is right when it answers: the project is that of destroying the right and its liberticidal laws, and then we will see," Vattimo writes in *Ecce comu* (EC 84).

The political experiments Vattimo proposes as instances of such resisting thinking are Chavez's Venezuela, Morales' Bolivia, and Castro's Cuba, where a "high energy democracy" (as in Unger's terminology, EC 112) is in place (EC 114–117). In these forms of democracy the state apparatus is not destroyed but is "repaired" by paralleling state bureaucracy with volunteer participation from citizens whose political allegiance is transversal to traditional parties, "members of local communities who perhaps do not even belong to a party but follow Chavez," for example (EC 114). Again, what is at work here is not any utopian model of civil organization, but rather a *Verwindung*, a distortion of the inherited structures of democracy that are not replaced but simply subverted, twisted in different directions in conformity with the demands of the actual times. In conclusion, the continuity of resistance and not the eschatological discontinuity of the utopian revolution leads Vattimo's political agenda and his philosophy of history.

The doubt remains whether this continues the legacy of Nietzsche's active nihilism, or rather falls prey of what Nietzsche would have called "spirit of *ressentiment*." Perhaps, after all, Vattimo has not entirely accepted the Nietzschean legacy, and what he should rather do is to return to the Nietzschean origins of his own philosophizing. After all, and against Vattimo's trajectory of thinking, the *Übermensch*, that is, the one who, regardless of his (or her) identity, with the power of his (or her) yes-saying is the truly liberated being, is not the result of human evolution. As *Thus Spoke Zarathustra* tells, the *Übermensch* is the one who, by biting off the head of the snake, interrupts the continuity of the tradition. What Vattimo's philosophy attests in its being an ontology of actuality is perhaps the fact that our age is neither the time of the *Übermensch* nor the time of the utopian. This we already knew. Yet, what we need the most is perhaps precisely what we lack the most—not only *caritas*, which, however, remains fundamental, but passion for the utopian or, as Levinas might say, Desire for the wholly Other. That this wholly Other is to retain "all the features of the metaphysical God—'ultimate,' peremptory foundation beyond which one cannot move" (B 84; translation modified) is, as Vattimo teaches us, a matter of Vattimo's own interpretation. What features might characterize a nonmetaphysical yet wholly Other corresponding to the current times is not a theme for us here to elaborate.

Notes

1. Gianni Vattimo and Piergiorgio Paterlini, *Non essere Dio. Un'autobiografia a quattro mani* (Reggio Emilia: Aliberti, 2006). The volume is "almost" an autobiography because it has been written by Paterlini (so it is not properly an autobiography), but Vattimo countersigns it and speaks in first person (so it is not a simple biography either).
2. On a possible subscription to Hegel's philosophy, see VRF 52, where Vattimo states, "if Hegel did not demand a completely determined, completely rational destiny for reason—but it is not clear how far he demanded this—there would be nothing to object to the Hegelian vision of philosophy."
3. *Vocazione e resposabilità del filosofo* [vocation and responsibility of the philosopher] is the title of one of Vattimo's works from 2000.
4. On this issue, see Paolo Flores D'Arcais, "Gianni Vattimo; or rather, Hermeneutics as the Primacy of Politics," in *Weakening Philosophy:*

Essays in Honour of Gianni Vattimo, ed. Santiago Zabala (Montreal: McGill-Queen's University Press, 2007), 250–269.
5. Many of the considerations that follow were first originated in conversation with Greg Johnson, at Lutheran Pacific University, whom I would like therefore to thank.
6. Whether this transformation should be for the better or the worse would imply some form of normative criterion, which might also require some objective standard of evaluation—all notions highly arguable, when not openly criticized, from Vattimo's standpoint.
7. One could debate whether the ethical-political interest is a recent accomplishment, as the more recent political books seem to attest, or is present already at the beginning of Vattimo's philosophizing—I would argue for the latter.
8. In his 1989 volume *Etica dell'interpretazione*, Vattimo devotes a chapter (published in the English translation of *The Transparent Society*) to the themes of "Utopia, Counter-utopia, and Irony." Some of its points are addressed in a condensed form also in the section of *The Transparent Society* titled "From Utopia to Heterotopia" (TS 62–74).
9. On Bloch's utopianism, see also Gianni Vattimo, "Il pazzo e il profeta," in Gianni Vattimo, *Le mezze verità* (Turin: Editrice La Stampa, 1988), 101–104.
10. Jacques Derrida, *On the Name*, trans. David Wood, John Leavey Jr., and Ian McLeod (Stanford: Stanford University Press, 1995), 75.
11. As it has been done, one may question the character of such leaving behind and claim that in fact everything is carried along.
12. On this theme, see especially the chapter "Secularization versus tragic thought" in B 80–84.
13. It should be noticed that not all revolutions need to be of a violent kind, and as the Indian experience of the Mahatma Gandhi attests, there also exists nonviolent revolutions. Thus, invoking the revolution as a moment of interruption is not tantamount to advocating violence and the use of force in political contexts.

13

"Postmodernity as the Ontological Sense of Technology" and Democratic Politics

ERIK M. VOGT

Reflections regarding the existence of correspondences between theses about the end of modernity and the new communicational and informational technologies have produced a variety of impressionist postmodern accounts of technology or of technological accounts of postmodernity, without, however, providing a coherent philosophical-historical frame that, by being mindful of its own provenance, addresses their ontological meaning for the present constellation of thought. It is for this reason, says Gianni Vattimo, that only a postmodern "ontology of actuality" that recognizes and affirms the end of metaphysics and the epochal essence of Being will reveal the historical-ontological relation between the new technologies and the end of modernity (NE 4). This end of modernity is itself to be understood as a condensation of several ends: the end of a progressive conception of history; the end of colonialism and imperialism; the end of each and every notion of (self-) transparency (TS 2–4). Moreover, only by carefully attending to the "aperture of Being typical of modernity" can one reveal within it "the traits of a new aperture" (NE 12). Consequently, the first question to be asked is: how and where has the aperture of Being become visible that has characterized the truth of modernity?

Taking Theodor W. Adorno and Martin Heidegger as principal reference figures, Vattimo suggests that philosophical theories of modernity usually focused on the question of technology. That is, the concepts of the culture industry and of administered society on the one hand, of the *Ge-stell* on the other hand, are indicative of the fact that both Adorno's as well as Heidegger's versions of a "sociological impressionism" (NE 4) rendered the essence of modernity in terms of the question of technology. Adorno and Horkheimer's *Dialectic of Enlightenment* presented a twentieth century that was marked by total technological domination. That is, Adorno and Horkheimer formulated as their task to identify the spell cast over the twentieth century not simply in terms of a mere symptom of decline of bourgeois society; rather, this very decline was to be reconstructed in terms of the catastrophe of technological rationality that had been effective since primordial times. Although the first signs of technological reason announced themselves already in the initial detachment from myth as domination of nature, as self-preservation through rational practices that, precisely in their instrumental rationality, remained trapped in deception, the "sun of calculating reason, beneath whose icy rays the seeds of the new barbarism is germinating,"[1] reached its theoretical conclusion at the point at which enlightened thought metamorphosed into a technological rationality that was utterly functional and instrumental. This reduction of reason was accompanied by the reduction of all things to mere exploitable objects. In the light of this technological rationality, the world could thus appear only as a collection of exploitable and disposable objects; that is, objects became, as a matter of fact, nothing more but this exploitability and disposability without remainder, casting their image on calculating thought. Adorno remarks: "Things, under the law of their purposiveness, take on a form which limits intercourse with them to pure manipulation and which tolerates no surplus, either of freedom of conduct or of the thing's independence, which would survive as the core of experience because it would not be consumed by the moment of action."[2]

At the same time, this reduction of all things to pure purposiveness dialectically affected the status of the subject-pole, in that human subjects found themselves reduced to the nodal points of exploitation, equally without remainder. Reifying technological reason was now itself reified, and this self-reification of technological rationality culminated in the "culture industry" or "administered society." In other words, culture industry or administered society completed a process of technological rationalization by means of which human subjects became mere secondary appendages of a machinery of calculation and instrumentalization, mere exploitable material reflecting the very material they exploited. Adorno and Horkheimer drew a panorama of the history of modernity in which progress appeared as the triumphal procession of permanent technological disaster. Modernity's dialectics of instrumental rationality—a form of rationality characterized by a reductionist calculus of means and ends—carried within itself a negative teleological continuum, ending with and in modern mass media. Vattimo comments:

> On the basis of his experience in the United States during the Second World War, Adorno . . . predicted that radio (and only later TV) would produce a general homogenization of society. By virtue of a kind of innate propensity for the demonic, this in turn would permit and indeed favour the formation of dictatorships and totalitarian governments capable . . . of exercising widespread control over their citizens by the diffusion of slogans, propaganda (commercial as well as political) and stereotypical world views. (TS 5)

It is thus not surprising that Adorno insinuated as the only alternative to the technological world of the culture industry "advanced" artworks that refuse closure and totality by insisting on and exhibiting those gaps that prevent any form of forced reconciliation, thereby keeping open the space for a redemption whose possibility is ultimately based on the impossibility of its actualization. Vattimo emphasizes this metaphysical aspect of Adorno's aesthetics when he states about the auratic artwork: "That the harmony is utopian and belongs within the realm of appearance . . . does not mean a true change in essence, however, but only its location in an indefinite future, where its role remains that of a regulative ideal" (TS 46–47).

For Martin Heidegger, the catastrophe that took on its ultimate figure in the *Ge-stell* of the twentieth century could only be rendered fully legible by reinscribing it into the history of Western metaphysics as history (of the thinking) of Being. "That which makes our history 'Western,' according to Heidegger, is metaphysics, and metaphysics culminates in the age of technology. The truth of our Western conception of what it means to know is revealed in modern science, and is completed as techno-science."[3] It is the *Ge-stell* as the essence of modern technology that crystallized the particular form of rationality characterizing and determining the history of Western metaphysics. To be more precise, it was the principle of reason codified by metaphysics that authorized planetary technology: "Modern technology pushes toward the greatest possible perfection. Perfection is based on the thoroughgoing calculability of objects. The calculability of objects presupposes the unqualified validity of the *principium rationis*. It is in this way that the authority characteristic of the principle of reason determines the essence of the modern, technological age."[4] Thus, the essence of modern technology revealed itself as calculative thinking that, similar to Adorno and Horkheimer's account of instrumental rationality, pointed to a fundamental transformation of the nature of man's relation to beings, and to the world as a whole, in that entities were reduced to mere standing-reserve. Planetary technology involved therefore not only the reduction of entities to objects to be mastered, administered, and controlled, that is, to exploitable and disposable objects, but, more radically, they were ultimately transformed into mere raw material vanishing into objectlessness. That is: "Now, the object has dissolved into the merely available, into the stockpile. It is entirely on hand. The subject-object dualism . . . underwent its own dissolution."[5]

Moreover, this dissolution of the subject-object dualism indicated clearly that the human being could no longer maintain a distance toward the process of technology, but rather became subjected to its challenging and summoning. The following two quotations attest to Heidegger's claim that this processing fundamentally transformed the being of man: "As soon as what is unconcealed no longer concerns man even as object, but does so, rather, exclusively as standing-reserve . . . then he comes to the brink of a precipitous fall; that is, he comes to the point where he himself will have to be taken as standing-reserve."[6] And:

> The subject-object relation thus reaches, for the first time, its pure "relational," i.e., ordering, character in which both the subject and the object are sucked up as standing-reserves. That does not mean that the subject-object relation vanishes, but rather the opposite: it now attains to its most extreme dominance, which is predetermined from out of Enframing. It becomes a standing-reserve to be commanded and set in order.[7]

But it is precisely at this extreme point of danger generated by the stance of technological Enframing that Heidegger repeatedly invoked Hölderlin's words: "But where the danger is, grows the saving power also."[8] As is well known, it is because of the demand imposed on us by the *Ge-stell* to think the essence of (the hidden truth of) technology that Heidegger could identify this danger itself as the saving power.[9] He writes, "The experience in Enframing as the constellation of Being and man through the modern world of technology is a prelude to what is called the event of appropriation."[10] This "decisive turning" concealed in the *Ge-stell* announced a different kind of gathering designated as *Gelassenheit*:

In *Gelassenheit*, it is a different kind of gathering, and of cohesion, that prevails: not that of the total capture and seizure of all things actual, but that of letting-be and releasement of such things from out of their essence (the essence of truth). *Gelassenheit* signals an attitude and comportment toward the world that is altogether different from that of *Ge-stell*. It is an attitude of releasement of beings *for* their being, of letting beings be in their being.[11]

Thus, the calculability of the *Ge-stell* seemed to cast the shadow of the incalculability of *Gelassenheit*—a shadow that came to the fore in that realm, which "is akin to the essence of technology and . . . fundamentally different from it. Such a realm is art."[12] It is from the perspective of art, says Heidegger, that one could thus gain a distance to calculative thought, technology and technological devices. "We must learn to leave them in their right place, to let go of them as something inessential, as something that does not affect us in any decisive manner. In letting go of them, we turn to the world, and to the beings in its midst."[13] That is, the catastrophe of the *Ge-stell*, when turned in the right manner, might harbor the saving power of a poetic thinking preparing for *Gelassenheit* that was supposed to lay the ground for the possible arrival or return of something altogether different.

It is here, perhaps, that one should recall Heidegger's involvement with National Socialism that, according to Slavoj Žižek, can be understood as the attempt to identify a concrete ontic engagement that would suit best and is closest to the ontological truth of the essence of technology. Žižek remarks:

> Until about 1935, he thought that Nazism did provide a unique solution of how, on the one hand, thoroughly to embrace modern technology, work, and mobilization, while simultaneously including them in an "authentic" political act of a people choosing its fate, acting on a decision, and so on. So we have technology, not aseptic traditionalism, *but* combined with roots, *Volk*, authentic decision, not *das Man*—in contrast to the Russian and American versions, which, each in its own way, betrays this authentic dimension (either in liberal individualism or in mass mobilization).[14]

And as Žižek immediately adds, even after 1935, when Heidegger provided Nazism no longer with some kind of transcendental "dignity," he continued to appreciate it "as the most radical version to enable modern man to confront technology."[15] What is more, even Heidegger's famous turn toward *Gelassenheit*, supposedly marking his philosophical disentanglement and turn away from his former involvement with National Socialism as the culmination of the metaphysics of subjectivity, might remain complicit with what it attempted to overcome. For *Gelassenheit*, "the humble subordination to and listening to the voice of Being,"[16] only exacerbates this problem, insofar as it is ultimately a fetishistic attitude: it suggests that one should fully accept the technological world; however, this engagement occurs on the basis of a fetish (the fetish of poetic thinking) that supposedly allows for some kind of distance, thereby not only weakening the impact of technology, but also preparing silently for the possible arrival of the gods.[17]

Both Adorno and Heidegger seem to argue that the catastrophe that instrumental rationality and technological calculative thought have brought onto mankind is so total that it is no longer possible even to imagine alternatives within the framework of technology. The only "alternative" left is that between a surrender to a "quasi-totalitarian" administered society and *Ge-stell* on the one hand, and a passive waiting, prepared by the exceptionality of advanced art or poetic thinking, for some messianic light to intrude upon contemporary closed society on the other hand.

Here is precisely the point at which one can locate Vattimo's novel, *verwinded* appropriation of Heidegger's conception of *Ge-stell*. First, Vattimo concedes that Heidegger ultimately "confined himself to the aperture that takes place in poetry" (NE 13). Moreover, it is no longer possible to appeal to another or different foundation for some return of Being, even if that foundation were a poetic one, since this would conceal precisely the achievement that marks Heidegger's *Ge-stell*: the letting-go of all principles, authorities or foundations. In short, Vattimo does not subscribe to Heidegger's move to install poetry as the very realm in which the question of Being, which "the reign of technology renders universally unpronounceable,"[18] has been preserved. Similar to Alain Badiou, Vattimo no longer sees thought under the exclusive condition of the poet. Although Badiou acknowledges the strength of Heidegger's reflections on poetry when he writes that his "thinking has owed its persuasive power to having been the only one to pick up what was at stake in the poem, namely the destitution of object fetishism,"[19] he immediately adds that "it is no longer required today that disobjectivation and disorientation be stated in the poetic metaphor. Disorientation can be *conceptualized*."[20] And in a certain sense, the age of the poets is completed for Vattimo as well. What takes its stead is aesthetic experience that, however, is to be reconceptualized in a novel manner via the productive constellation of Heidegger's notions of *Ge-stell* and *Stoss* and Walter Benjamin's notion of *shock*.[21] Only this aesthetic experience can correspond to the contemporary society of generalized communication, in that it leaves behind concepts of origin, authenticity, aura and reconciliation by insisting on and keeping alive "the experience of disorientation" (TS 51) and of unfounding.[22]

Furthermore, Vattimo locates the saving power of the *Ge-stell* not in its concealed *Wink* toward a different (poetic) opening, but rather in the *Ge-stell* itself. That is, Heidegger's *Ge-stell* is not only "the highest point of the metaphysical oblivion of being," but also "a first, oppressing flash of *Ereignis*, that is of the event of being, beyond the metaphysical oblivion of being" (TS 56). Vattimo continues: "Precisely in the *Ge-stell*, that is, in the society of technological and total manipulation, Heidegger sees an opportunity of overcoming the oblivion and metaphysical alienation in which Western man has lived until now" (TS 56). Since the *Ge-stell* is that event in which, ultimately, "there is nothing to Being as such (*es mit dem Sein selbst nichts mehr ist*),"[23] insofar as technology exerts its power of objectification and representationalism not only on entities, but also on human beings, it can free "Being and humanity from the subject and object of metaphysics."[24] However, this opportunity indicated by Heidegger regarding this flashing of the "new" in the midst of the *Ge-stell* remains at the same time somewhat schematic. Vattimo explains: "The brevity and failure to expand upon this indication, which . . . should be seen as an essential gap in Heidegger's thought is probably motivated . . . by the fact . . . that Heidegger . . . never escaped from a vision of technology dominated by the model of the motor and mechanical energy" (NE 14). The actual ontological sense of technology can only be disclosed through a "radical shift in our vision of technology" (NE 15). Thus he continues:

> The technology that actually does give us a glimpse of a possible dissolution of the rigid distinction between subject and object is not the mechanical technology of the motor . . . but it might very well be the technology of modern communications, the means by which information is gathered, ordered, and disseminated. To speak more plainly: the possibility of overcoming metaphysics, which Heidegger describes obscurely in the *Ge-stell*, really opens up only when the technology . . . ceases to be mechanical and becomes electronic: information and communication technology. (NE 15)

Only this updated, nihilistic vision of the *Ge-stell* can provide new meaning to Heidegger's other definition of modernity as the "age of the world picture." The reduction of the world to a world picture, says Heidegger, that constitutes the essential trait pertaining to the increasing specialization of science and technology, is accompanied by a certain shadow of incalculability. Instead of simply releasing this shadow into *Gelassenheit* as an alternative beginning, Vattimo suggests that, far from extricating it from the web of the *Ge-stell*, it rather has to be grasped as its immanent and nihilistic consequence in form of a proliferation of conflicting images of the world. "It is this conflict that sets in train a massive enlargement of the system of calculation and prediction, to the point where this movement to the extremes of calculability leads to a general incalculability: the image of the world picture gives way to the dissolution of this image in a Babel of conflicting images" (BI 25–26). In other words, Heidegger's analysis of the modern production of the *Weltbild* must therefore be extended "from the field of science and its languages . . . to the more general sphere of social communication as it has developed thanks to print, radio, television, an everything that we now include under the heading of the Internet" (NE 16). Vattimo concludes: "We can recognize in the *Ge-stell* a first flashing of the new event of Being to the extent that it brings with it a dissolution of the realistic traits of experience, in other words what I think we might call a weakening of the principle of reality. It is probably only the shift from its mechanical stage to that of electronic information that is determining the advent of postmodernity" (NE 16).

This weakening or erosion of reality may be understood as the fulfillment of a Nietzschean "prophecy": "in the end the true world becomes a fable. . . . For us, reality is rather the result of the intersection and 'contamination' . . . of a multiplicity of images, interpretations and reconstructions circulated by the media in competition with one another and without 'central' coordination" (TS 7). Therefore, one must reject any ideological-critical account of mediatic mass culture that claims that "the manipulation of consensus and the errors of totalitarianism *are* . . . the only possible outcome of the advent of generalized communication, the mass media and reproduction" (TS 59). The dream of a society of transparency is left behind in light of the recognition that "the society of human sciences and generalized communication has moved towards what could, in general be called the 'fabling of the world.' The images of the world we receive from the media and the human sciences . . . are not simply different interpretations of a 'reality' that is 'given' regardless, but rather constitute the very objectivity of the world" (TS 24–25). The reality of this world "presents itself as softer and more fluid"; what is more, "experience can again acquire the characteristics of oscillation, disorientation and play" (TS 59).

Recasting the objectivity of reality in terms of a complex, dense, chaotic and nontransparent web of images of the world also has consequences for the traditional metaphysical conception of the subject. Similar to the weakening of reality and world into "a sort of residue, a crystallization of the 'conflict of interpretations'" (NE 17), the subject can be less and less conceived of as "a centre of self-consciousness and decision-making, reduced as it is to being the author of statistically predicted choices, playing a multiplicity of social roles that are irreducible to a unity" (TS 117). That is, since the "subject [is] just the geometrical site of a multiplicity of roles that can never be fully unified,"[25] its constitution is best rendered in terms of multiple narratives that are to be interpreted hermeneutically without giving in to some desire for their unification. It is here that Vattimo suggests as the possibility of a weakened subject for a world constituted and inhabited by multiple interpretive agencies Nietzsche's figure of the *Übermensch*. This weakened subject, "derived from the artist, he who knows how to experiment with a freedom derived,"[26] is "the most moderate," "a new human subject capable of living without neurosis" (TS 26). Characterized by self-irony, he "has the capacity to move about like a tourist in the park of history, in other words one who is able to look at many cultures with a gaze more esthetic than 'objective' and truth seeking" (NE 55). Moreover, this new subject may have appropriated "the variety of ideas, sometimes labeled 'delirious,' that were in the air in the late 1960s" (NE 101).[27] Ultimately, this massified, post-humanist *Übermensch* who is able to extract a chance for freedom from the Babel of mass culture by being "even more Babelic than it is,"[28] represents a kind of collusion of "the two figures of Abraham and Don Giovanni in Kierkegaard's philosophy: a blend of, or perhaps a wavering between, religious faith and aesthetic existence."[29] Without examining in more detail Vattimo's condensation of the aesthetic and the religious,[30] it can certainly be maintained that the aesthetic plays a dominant role in his ontology of actuality; after all, "the salvation of our postmodern civilization can only be an esthetic salvation" (NE 56). What is more, there must be a certain priority of aesthetics (an aesthetics that has come to terms with the pluralization of the beautiful) over Enlightenment ethics, if "the variety of lifestyles and the diversity of ethical codes" are to "coexist without bloody clashes" (NE 58).

But the new technologies of communication and information have not only generated a society marked by an aesthetic plurality and a dissemination of utopia into heterotopias, but they have also brought about "a radical transformation . . . in the nature of political power."[31] By dissolving metaphysics, they have also enabled liberal democracy to come into its own. The essential link between contemporary mass technologies and liberal democracy can be discerned in their respective emancipatory possibilities, in that both partake "in the dissolution of the strong, centralized, authoritarian structures of political power, thus contributing decisively . . . to create the chance for being to give itself (to occur, to presence) outside metaphysics' violent and objectifying patterns."[32] Hence Vattimo's declaration: "The end of metaphysics has its genuine political parallel in the strengthening of democracy" (NE 83). It is only this postmodern "ontology of the weakening of Being" that can supply "philosophical reasons for preferring a liberal, tolerant, and democratic society rather than an authoritarian and totalitarian one" (NE 19). Its emancipatory force is no longer associated with a politics of truth, but rather with a hermeneutic politics that promotes not only the "letting-go of foundationalism and the letting-loose of a conflict of interpretation" (NE 92), but "also entails a philosophy of history . . . that views hermeneutics as the result of a 'nihilistic' process, in which metaphysical Being, meaning violence, consumes itself" (NE 94). Again, this nihilistic process appears as a process of weakening, "on many levels, of all strong structures," leading to the "acceptance of an array of cultural universes" (NE 96–97). That is to say, the emancipatory force of Vattimo's hermeneutic-nihilistic politics is a "liberation of differences, of local elements . . . that finally speak up for themselves" (TS 9). It is not only a liberation and recognition of diversity, but also provides minorities and subcultures with a microphone "in the limelight of public opinion" (TS 5), accompanied by an acknowledgment of the "historicity, contingency and finiteness" (TS 9) of all the plural voices weaving the web of a multicultural world.

Of course, Vattimo does not deny that there are threats to this radically polytheistic, ontologically plural world and its "prime mover," the "principle" of reducing violence. He identifies two of those threats: "the supermarket culture and the forms of reactionary foundationalism opposing it" (NE 99). While the "supermarket culture" is briefly described as a pluralism without nihilism,[33] the various religious, ethnic and communitarian revivals of foundationalism are best grasped as "neurotic defenses of identity and belonging in reaction to the indefinite widening of horizons entailed by the culmination of the epoch of the world picture" (BI 39–40). Both, Vattimo suggests, are to be countered, "criticized" and dissolved by the faithfulness to the nihilistic "guideline of reducing violence" (NE 99).

But what steps should be taken to practically implement and safeguard this principle of reducing violence? In light of current globalization, the current encroachment of the social and economic on the political realm, Vattimo considers two options: the populist and the federalist. While he associates the populist option with Hardt and Negri's politics of multitude that, however, constitutes at best "a sort of anarchic shadow of globalization" (NE 126),[34] he seems to lean toward a federalist model as counterweight to the "homogeneous universal state" (NE 127). However, this federalism would have to ensure not only the guarantee of livability (the avoidance of both repression and populism), but also that of a charitable and open recognition of multiplicity. Hence Vattimo's appeal to giving priority to politics over economics. In short, what is needed is a restoration "of the independence of politics from economics"—a restoration, that is, of the "truth" of socialism as "a program for setting politics free of the laws of economics, especially the laws of globalized economy" (NE 129). A politics, moreover, that could gain its necessary distance from the economic realm by heeding to an ethics of nonviolence, of (aesthetically informed) recognition of plurality and of compassion: that is, this politics would do well "to introduce the notion of 'compassion' to the culture of the left, and in general replace the critique of ideology with an explicit commitment to ethics as the capacity to transcend the logic of the struggle for life" (TS 103).[35]

Vattimo's hermeneutical-epochal interpretation of postmodernity as "the ontological sense" of contemporary technology intimates thus humanity's free relation to technology, with the "collateral benefits" of the possibility for a renewed thinking of an advanced democratic politics. This free relation is distinguished by a supposedly non-neurotic response to the dissolution both of the principle of reality and of the concept of the subject. Of course, a psychoanalysis contributing to this dissolution of neurosis will no longer be one that stands under the dictate of either "realistic self-representation" or "Habermasian/Apelian "self-transparency."[36] Instead, it will be (a Jungian) one that finds in the heart of the human subject only multiple "*mythologies*" and "narratives."[37] However, does Vattimo's hermeneutic-nihilistic logic, that enters the continuous process of dissolving or weakening of all "hard psychic and societal kernels" in order to show that the epoch of technological postmodernity must be grasped as its end result, not produce some "collateral damages" of its own? The remainder of this paper will examine this question, written in the haste of a shorthand text.

Vattimo's description of electronically generated communication and images in terms of Nietzsche's "truth as fabling" implies that the metaphysical concepts of (true) reality and of appearance are no longer applicable; after all, Nietzsche stated that the loss of (the concept of) reality entailed at the same time a loss of (the concept of) appearance. This simultaneous loss of "true" reality and appearance suggests thus a theory of simulacrum as the only viable cognitive mapping for the world of postmodern technology.[38] Moreover, as Mario Perniola demonstrates, a proper conception of the electronic image as simulacrum must be distinguished from the "iconophiliac approach by realists and hyper-realists" on the one hand, and the "iconoclastic approach by hyper-futurists" on the other hand,[39] insofar as both constitute a return to reality in terms of "exaggerated and extremist assertions of a present of future reality."[40] Both still operate within a metaphysical framework that "posits a relation between image and original, whether this is a relation of identity, or of difference."[41] However, since images today are always already generated under the technological condition of reproducibility, neither the iconic nor the visionary approach hold any longer, and their pretense to still be able to render some "original" or "authentic" reality (in the present or future) must be deciphered as a manipulation and predetermination of reality. That is, "Hyper-reality and hyper-vision resemble each other because they both *advance the claim to be other than images*, they claim to represent a present or a future substance, an original."[42] Only if one gives up the metaphysical distinction between image as appearance and reality, can one liberate the electronic mass media and their images as simulacra from the metaphysical frame, according to which these are mere "mirrors of reality."[43] However, Perniola's examination of the potential of the contemporary electronic mass media does not simply end on that note; on the contrary, a later text seems to effect a kind of dialectical reversal in that the virtual media of mass communication are now presented as the foreign and disquieting "real . . . of technological and economic devices."[44] Perniola specifies: "The crucial moment of this extreme realism is . . . the meeting place between human and machine . . . people and commodities. The harsh reality that we are obliged to confront is . . . the human capital."[45] Thus he concludes: "The virtual body, invaded and disseminated in networks, becomes the object . . . irreducible to the imaginary and symbolic dimensions."[46] Whereas Perniola's perspicacious remarks ultimately only point to the necessity of critically examining this "return of the Real" *in* and *by means of* virtual reality through the lens of the Lacanian triad of Imaginary, Symbolic, and Real, the most comprehensive Lacanian ideology critique of technological postmodernity as, perhaps, the key symptom of the current socio-ideological constellation can be found in Slavoj Žižek's writings on the (foreclosed) Real of cyberspace and virtual reality.[47]

The following question frames Žižek's investigation of cyberspace: "Does it not involve the promise of false opening . . . as well as the foreclosure of the social power relations within which virtual communities operate?"[48] Žižek seems to agree with Vattimo when he concedes that, regarding technology, the shift from modernity to postmodernity is one from transparency to nontransparency. For the "interface screen is supposed to conceal the workings of the machine, and to simulate our everyday experience as faithfully as possible;"[49] this means that we "'become accustomed to opaque technology'—the digital machinery 'behind the screen' retreats into total impenetrability, even invisibility."[50] But Žižek adds immediately that what gets lost is precisely "the Real behind the screen; that is to say, we are never submerged in the play of appearances without an 'indivisible remainder.'"[51] In other words, this postmodern mode of engagement with virtual communication reveals as its hidden presuppositions a "foreclosure of the Real."[52] It is therefore not surprising that he identifies Vattimo's position with regard to technological postmodernity as a regression to "pre-symbolic psychotic immersion."[53] Describing Vattimo's stance in terms of the "postmodern assertion of a Brave New World of universalized simulacra as the sign that we are finally getting rid of the metaphysical obsession with authentic Being," Žižek points out that, here, it is not "'reality,' which is dissolved in the multiplicity of simulacra, but, on the contrary, *appearance* itself."[54] This retreat of "appearance," that is, of symbolic efficiency, characterizes as well the other central thesis in Vattimo's account that technological postmodernity "opens up the domain of shifting . . . identities," thereby announcing not only "the end of the Cartesian *cogito*," but also an "ideology of aesthetic self-creation."[55] Once again, to Žižek, crucial distinctions might have been lost: that between imaginary and symbolic identification[56] and, more importantly, that between subject and self: after all, "the Lacanian 'decentred subject' is *not* simply a multiplicity of good old 'Selves', partial centres."[57]

Moreover, Vattimo's reduction of the Symbolic to the Imaginary universe held together by the decentered proliferation of nontotalizable differences entails a multicultural virtualization of the Other, in that the encounter with the Other is always already in danger of being "replaced by a screen spectre"[58]—a "screen spectre" that is marked by the imaginary filling of the gap separating the symbolic Other from some fantasy of the Other. This general availability of the Other, effected by the virtualization of his or her "traumatic *presence*," "will induce unbearable claustrophobia . . . an unheard-of imposition of radical closure" in form of a "return to a symbiotic relationship with an Other in which the deluge of semblances seems to abolish the dimension of the Real."[59] And it is this multicultural, imaginary virtualization of the Other that engenders its own form of racism; that is, far from grasping the current returns of racism as archaic "aberrations" (NE xviii) that have not yet exposed themselves thoroughly to the liberating force of postmodernist nihilism, they have to be interpreted precisely as postmodern racism.[60] This speculative identity between multiculturalism and racism (in that both cannot come to terms with an Other that is not always already desubstantialized, deprived both of his/her symbolic spectrality and of his/her Real) would question Vattimo's (at least implicit) claim that some emancipatory force is directly inscribed into the technological properties of postmodernity; rather, it hinges on the "social conditions of late capitalism"[61] overdetermining the effects of postmodern technology.

Finally, could one not say that there is a certain "democratic fundamentalism" in Vattimo's thought?[62] When he states that the "legitimacy of liberal democracy is hardly contested any longer by anyone" (NE 85), he implies that liberal democracy is the ultimate horizon of contemporary political practice, a horizon apparently immune to contestation and interpretation. His liberal-pragmatic approach resembles, precisely through its infusion of politics with an ethics of nonviolence, compassion, and plurality, a pure politics.[63] By ascribing to postmodern technology the weakening force that creates the conditions for the democratic proliferation of multiple, fluid narrative identities, communities and cultures, he might not only neglect white capital's continuing force of deterritorialization providing the horizon for the affirmation of colorful differences playing across boundaries, but also subscribe to a kind of economic fundamentalism based on a rather totalizing account of late capitalism that might actually be a repetition of capital's own fantasy. That is, Vattimo's presentation of late capitalism as closed economic structure might appear as the very mirror image of the way late capitalism wants to appear to itself. A depoliticized economy as the "disavowed fundamental fantasy"[64] of Vattimo's democratic politics could then explain his suspension of the political significance of the economic realm, his dismissal of economy as the site of political struggle and intervention. Therefore, what these two fundamentalist tenets of his ontology of actuality would exclude is both the possibility that liberal democracy might have to be conceptualized as the political form of capitalism covering up the antagonism traversing the economical-political process of late capitalism,[65] and the possibility to do interpretive justice to Marx's term "political economy" that opens up a space not only for the problematic (and historically obsolete) gesture of economic determinism based on some alleged necessary economic process, but also for the gesture of a *re*-politicization of economy. The formidable task of Vattimo's ontology of actuality, its reinterpretation of the historical constellation of contemporary technologies of communication and information, of the postmodern multicultural universe of globalized contingency and of the steady proliferation of a politics of difference might be in need of a supplementary articulation of the nihilistic potency of Capital, concealed by the hegemonic role of liberal democracy.

Notes

1. Max Horkheimer, Theodor W. Adorno, *Dialectic of Enlightenment*, ed. Gunzelin Schmid Noerr, trans. Edmund Jephcott (Stanford: Stanford University Press, 2002), 25.
2. Theodor W. Adorno, *Minima Moralia*, trans. Edmund Jephcott (London: New Left Books, 1974), 44.
3. Miguel de Beistegui, *The New Heidegger* (London and New York: Continuum, 2005), 106.
4. Martin Heidegger, *The Principle of Reason*, trans. Reginald Lilly (Bloomington and Indianapolis: Indiana University Press, 1991), 121.
5. Beistegui, *The New Heidegger*, 110.
6. Martin Heidegger, *The Question Concerning Technology and Other Essays*, trans. with an introduction by William Lovitt (New York: Harper & Row, 1977), 26–27.
7. Ibid., 173.
8. Ibid., 28.
9. Ibid., 42.
10. Martin Heidegger, *Identity and Difference*, trans. Joan Stambaugh (New York: Harper & Row, 1969), 36–37.
11. Beistegui, *The New Heidegger*, 120.
12. Heidegger, *The Question Concerning Technology*, 35.
13. Beistegui, *The New Heidegger*, 125.
14. Slavoj Žižek, *The Parallax View* (Cambridge, MA: MIT Press, 2006), 284.
15. Ibid., 284.

16. Ibid., 280.
17. Ibid., 273–284.
18. Alain Badiou, *Manifesto For Philosophy*, trans., ed., and with an introduction by Norman Madarasz (Albany: State University of New York Press, 1999), 50.
19. Ibid., 74.
20. Ibid.
21. See TS 45–61.
22. However, this is not to suggest what would be a false affinity between Badiou and Vattimo; for Badiou's "de-suturing" of philosophy from its poetic condition strictly opposes not only any hermeneutic *Verwindung* of both thought and poetry into some aesthetic experience informed by technology, but Badiou does not even accept Vattimo's thesis according to which technology can "designate the essence of our time, nor that there be any relation useful to thought between 'technology's planetary reign' and nihilism;'" see Badiou, *Manifesto for Philosophy*, 53. For him, the contemporary epoch is neither technical nor nihilistic; what is more, the word "techno-science" conceals that "science does not belong to the same register of thought as technology"; ibid., 54. This may explain why Vattimo is, for Badiou, ultimately a "minor sophist"; ibid., 137.
23. Gianni Vattimo, "Conclusion: Metaphysics and Violence," in *Weakening Philosophy: Essays in Honour of Gianni Vattimo*, ed. Santiago Zabala (Montreal and London: McGill-Queen's University Press, 2007), 400–421; 415.
24. Ibid., 419.
25. Ibid., 420.
26. Ibid., 403.
27. In this context, Vattimo mentions explicitly and seems to affirm the anti-oedipal and anti-symbolic politics of both Deleuze and Guattari's free flux of desire and Marcuse's "esthetic-instinctual" revolution.
28. Gianni Vattimo, "Democracy, Reality, and the Media: Educating the *Übermensch*," in *Democracy and the Arts*, ed. Arthur M. Melzer, Jerry Weinberger, M. Richard Zinman (Ithaca: Cornell University Press, 1999), 146–158; 155.
29. Ibid., 157.
30. Unfortunately, it is not possible to examine Vattimo's writings on Christianity in the context of this essay. Suffice to say that he develops there a rather intriguing interpretation of Christianity in terms of the process of secularization leading from a weakening of monotheism to an affirmation of polytheism.

31. Vattimo, "Democracy, Reality, and the Media," 150.
32. Ibid., 154.
33. See NE 99.
34. The politics of multitude is anarchic because, as Vattimo remarks, it leaves unresolved the important question of political organization. In short, his question is: What would be a multitude in power? In addition, Vattimo seems to suggest that, precisely as a theoretical articulation of contemporary anti-globalization movements, it does not escape the cycle of violence generated by the reduction of politics to economics; and this inherent violence of Hardt and Negri's multitude can only lead to some version of permanent revolution that mimics the violence of economic globalization.
35. This is the reason why Sebastian Gurciullo concludes that the corollary of "Vattimo . . . inclining us ethically toward an ontology destined to dissolve . . . seems to be a demise . . . of the *political* aspiration that once motivated thinkers in the Enlightenment tradition. Emancipation comes now to be understood . . . as resignation in making the best of a less than ideal situation." See Sebastian Gurciullo, "The Subject of Weak Thought: There Are Only Interpretations and This Too Is an Interpretation," in *Theory and Event* 5, 2 (2005). http://muse.jhu/journals/theory_and_event/v005/5.2gurciullo.html
36. See NE 150, and TS 24.
37. See TS 43, 36.
38. Interestingly, Slavoj Žižek makes the claim that a reading of Nietzsche's epistemological stance regarding truth in terms of a postmodern passion for semblance would not only have to be supplemented by a notion of truth, also found in Nietzsche's texts, as inaccessible Real, but that one would have to go further and interpret the presence of these two opposed notions of truth in Nietzsche in terms of a certain deadlock. In his *The Puppet and the Dwarf* (Cambridge: MIT Press, 2003), 78–79, he writes: "Everything is not just the interplay of appearances, there is a Real—this Real, however, is not the inaccessible Thing, but the *gap* that prevents our access to it, the 'rock' of antagonism that distorts our view of the perceived object through a partial perspective. . . . The site of truth is not the way 'things really are in themselves,' beyond their perspectival distortions, but the very gap, passage, that separates one perspective from another. . . . There is truth; everything is not relative—but this truth is the truth of the perspectival distortion as such, not the truth distorted by the partial view from a one-sided perspective. . . . Both terms have to be fully asserted: there is,

among the multitude of opinions, a true knowledge, and this knowledge is accessible only from an 'interested' partial position."
39. Mario Perniola, *Ritual Thinking: Sexuality, Death, World*, Foreword Hugh J. Silverman, trans. with an Introduction Massimo Verdicchio (New York: Humanity Books, 2001), 163.
40. Ibid., 163.
41. Ibid.
42. Ibid.
43. Ibid., 170.
44. Mario Perniola, *Art and Its Shadow*, trans. Massimo Verdicchio, Foreword Hugh J. Silverman (New York and London: Continuum, 2004), 4.
45. Ibid.
46. Ibid.
47. These writings are his *The Plague of Fantasies* (London and New York: Verso, 1997), and "Is It Possible to Traverse the Fantasy of Cyberspace," in *The Žižek Reader*, ed. Elizabeth Wright and Edmond Wright (London: Blackwell, 1999), 102–124.
48. Žižek, *The Plague of Fantasies*, 130.
49. Ibid., 131.
50. Ibid.
51. Ibid., 132.
52. Ibid.
53. Žižek, "Is It Possible to Traverse the Fantasy of Cyberspace," 111.
54. Žižek, *The Plague of Fantasies*, 111.
55. Ibid., 112–113.
56. See Žižek, *The Plague of Fantasies*, 136–138.
57. Ibid., 141. It should be mentioned that Žižek describes other modes of engagement with cyberspace: a neurotic one in which cyberspace is read in terms of a strengthening of the Symbolic; a strictly perverse one in which the subject identifies itself not with the big Other, but rather with its hidden point of *jouissance*; and, finally, that of a "traversal or disturbance of the subject's fundamental fantasy;" see Žižek, "Is It Possible to Traverse the Fantasy of Cyberspace," 122. Thus, the last mode, by staging the subject's fundamental fantasy in/through cyberspace, seems to suggest some kind of emancipatory potential lying dormant in cyberspace; however, what should not be overlooked is that Žižek speaks here of an artistic appropriation of cyberspace, in that "traversing the fantasy" involves "our *over-identification* with the domain of imagination" (ibid., 122). What is more, at more than one occasion do Žižek's ideological-critical analyses proceed in a manner that

strongly suggests an indissoluble link between cyberspace and capital.
58. Žižek, *The Plague of Fantasies*, 154.
59. Ibid., 154; 156. For Žižek's brilliant "spectral" reading of the Other in Imaginary, Symbolic, and Real terms see his "Neighbors and Other Monsters: A Plea for Ethical Violence," Slavoj Žižek, Eric L. Santner, Kenneth Reinhard, *The Neighbor: Three Inquiries in Political Theology* (Chicago and London: University of Chicago Press, 2005), 134–190.
60. See Žižek, *The Plague of Fantasies*, 154. See also my *Zugänge zur politischen Ästhetik* (Vienna: Turia + Kant, 2003).
61. Žižek, *The Plague of Fantasies*, 156.
62. I take this term from Jodi Dean, *Žižek's Politics* (New York and London: Routledge, 2006), 95–133.
63. In this context, it would be of interest to examine the affinity between Vattimo's ethical politics and Richard Rorty's pragmatist politics aiming primarily at the avoidance of suffering.
64. See Slavoj Žižek, *The Ticklish Subject* (London: Verso, 1999), 355.
65. Vattimo's pure politics, cleansed from all economic traces, remains therefore close to both Adorno and the late Heidegger's disavowal of politics. What Žižek (with Miguel de Beistegui) says about Heidegger's thinking of technology, might also be relevant with regard to the absence of economy in Vattimo's linkage of postmodern technology and politics; "When Heidegger talks about technology, he systematically ignores the whole sphere of modern 'political' economy, although modern technology is not only empirically, but in its very concept, rooted in the market dynamics of generating surplus-value. The underlying principle which impels the unrelenting drive of modern productivity is not technological, but economic: it is the market and commodity principle of surplus-value which condemns capitalism to the crazy dynamics of permanent self-revolutionizing" (Žižek, *The Parallax View*, 277). At the same time, what distinguishes Vattimo from Adorno and Heidegger (as well as from Jacques Derrida) is his explicit refusal to engage some figure of messianic politics. On Adorno, Heidegger, and also Giorgio Agamben and the question of political economy see my "Catastrophic Narratives and Why the 'Catastrophe' to Catastrophe Might Have Already Happened," in *Tickle Your Catastrophe: On Borders, Cuts and Edges in Contemporary Theory*, ed. Dominiek Hoens, Sigi Jottkandt, Gert Buelens (Hampshire: Palgrave MacMillan, 2007), forthcoming.

14

What's Wrong with Biotechnology?
Vattimo's Interpretation of Science, Technology, and the Media

MARTIN G. WEISS

Introduction

"The world has become a fable,"[1] Vattimo states with Nietzsche, meaning that Plato's dualistic model of two worlds, the one being that of timeless ideas up in the *topos huperuranios* and the other that of mere appearance, is no longer valid. But if there is no more real world behind the appearing one, we have to give up the whole difference between a true and an only apparent world, because the only world that remains is the apparent one, our concrete *Lebenswelt*, which is never objectively given but always mediated by our interpretations. Thus Vattimo denies that there is a (hidden) objective reality that philosophy has to discover and describe as it really is, because according to him, our interpretations are not based on any kind of hidden substratum or Kantian *Ding an sich*, which we would have to discover beneath or behind mere appearances.

The productivity of Vattimo's hermeneutic beginning becomes clear when we look at two phenomena, which his concept opens to completely new possibilities of interpretation: science and technology. On the basis of Gadamer's hermeneutics, one might think that only the *Geisteswissenschaften*, the humanities, may access "hermeneutic" truth conceived as interpretation within a historical horizon, while the natural sciences are unable to get rid of the concept of truth as *adaequatio intellectus et rei*. Following Heidegger, Vattimo argues though that modern technology does not necessarily lead to reification and solidification of phenomena. Rather, Vattimo argues that the straight striving of modern science for absolute availability and predictability turns into absolute incalculability, because in the attempt to control nature, science dissolves its object into interpretations. So, according to Vattimo, philosophy's fight against the natural sciences in the name of hermeneutics is anachronistic, because today the straight natural sciences are the most striking argument against reification.

The Absolute Meaning of Interpretation

Vattimo shares the opinion with Nietzsche and Husserl that there is no "real world" hidden behind our interpretations and that our interpretations are the only appearance, that is, the being of reality. Interpretation is here used in the same sense we speak of an interpretation (meaning the performance) of a piece of music, where the interpretation *is* the music. Although there are many possible interpretations of this specific piece of music, every single interpretation is this very music and not only an imitation of it, because speaking of the objective, perhaps never attainable, music behind all interpretations would be nonsensical. The concept of interpretation Vattimo proposes and which he adopted from his teacher Luigi Pareyson,[2] is similar to what Rudolf Boehm, referring to Husserl's *Konstitution*, calls *absolute Bedeutung* [absolute meaning].[3] The absolute meaning has no origin in an "objective" reality because of the *Korrelationsapriori* of *Bewußtsein* [consciousness] and *Gegenstand* [object], to use Husserl's terms. There is no reality "outside" consciousness because there is no unmediated access to reality. In other words, to be real means to be mediated. The only reality is the reality of the phenomenon. To be means to appear. The essence of objectivity is subjectivity. This must not be confused with some sort of subjectivism or relativism, however, because for Vattimo the subject is also a phenomenon and not a last *fundamentum inconcussum* [unquestionable ground]. Like Nietzsche, Vattimo thinks that there are no "facts": "*Tatsachen gibt es nicht, nur Interpretationen,*" as Nietzsche puts it.[4]

Vattimo insists that the statement that everything is interpretation is itself no metaphysical, stable truth but only interpretation itself; otherwise his thesis would be self-contradictory. The true world has become a fable, but even this statement is nothing but a fable. The truth is only given in interpretations, but this too is only an interpretation. Vattimo remarks that the skeptical sentence "everything is *interpretation*" turns into the dogmatic sentence "everything *is* interpretation" as soon as it is uttered, because every definition turns, because of its form, necessarily into a metaphysical, stable statement. The sentence "everything is *interpretation*" simply means to emphasize the impossibility of objective statements, but it automatically becomes an objective statement itself because of its grammar, inherited from metaphysics but the only one we have. But if the necessarily dogmatic form "everything is interpretation" is destabilized again by saying that this sentence too is only a possible interpretation, then we are forced into an infinite wavering movement similar to classical skeptical indecision or the *reductio ad infinitum* of Romantic irony.

Nevertheless, even if we say that we do not believe any longer in objective *Dinge an sich* [things in themselves] behind our interpretations, we cannot deny that there are certain relatively stable starting points for our interpretations, which we are in the habit of calling "facts." But what are these relatively stable "facts" on which interpretations build, if they can no longer be seen as something objective? Vattimo writes that "'facts' are not interpretations only in the sense that when registering them we are not aware of our prejudices. These facts constitute themselves as facts only in a symbolic world" (SM 310). Facts are naturalized prejudices.

At first glance it seems that the skeptical sentence is only another metaphysical definition of the objective essence of the world (incidentally, Heidegger's criticism of Nietzsche's "eternal recurrence of the same" as the essence of reality is based on just such a misinterpretation). However, this is just the opposite of what Vattimo and Nietzsche want to say; otherwise they would only really be "reverse Platonists." The statement that there is nothing but interpretation is not yet an overcoming of metaphysics because, as a dogmatic statement about the "truth" and timeless essence of reality, it remains within the stable structures of metaphysics. To preserve the skeptical and destabilizing content of this thought, it is necessary to weaken it by adding that also the statement that everything is interpretation is itself an interpretation.

The supposed facts thus turn out to be not given timeless objects, but only implicit "prejudices," which mask the conditions of our inquiry.

The destabilizing fact that every interpretation starts with certain prejudices allows Vattimo to explain the peculiar phenomenon of the limits of interpretation without requiring the introduction of facts, or unreachable *Dinge an sich*, behind the apparent. Vattimo's concept of prejudices allows him to take into consideration the evident limits of interpretation without introducing an objective interpreted behind the interpretation and therefore falling back into objectivism.

Vattimo asks whether there is a position toward reality, which does justice to both the phenomenon of the limits of interpretation and the basic insight of modern (hermeneutic) philosophy, namely, that there is no objective truth or unquestionable fundament that could be seized directly. Vattimo tries to work out just such a third position, which neither dissolves reality into infinite interpretations nor freezes it into objectivity. In Vattimo's view, there is no interpreted text underling the interpretation, or more precisely, every interpreted text already is an interpretation itself and so on *ad infinitum*. Vattimo maintains that there is no "object" of interpretation, because every supposed object, once examined, proves to be itself "only" an interpretation of a previously supposed object and so on and so forth.

Similarly, Günter Figal tries to think together the inexhaustibility of interpretation and the phenomenon of the limits of interpretation when he defines "the substrate" of interpretation as the *Freiraum* or *Spielraum* (scope or play) of all possible interpretations.[5] Thus, every single possible interpretation becomes the representation of the interpreted itself, which is nothing beyond its interpretations. So in this model we find, at the basis of interpretation, not some kind of a metaphysical substance but instead a space of possible appearances. This model, which takes the interpreted "text" as the *Spielraum* of interpretation, allows us to explain the phenomenon of the limits of interpretation without reifying the text.

Like Jean Baudrillard, Vattimo identifies "reality" with power, or with violence, and this in turn is identified with the kind of speech that allows no contradiction. By reality, Vattimo means the violent immediacy of the "immediate pressure of the given, the incontrovertible imposition of the *in-itself*" (BI 93). This reality is violent as violence, according to Vattimo, is definable only as the evident ground that excludes all contradiction. Vattimo identifies violence with a brute fact, naked actuality, "an ultimate instance beyond which one does not go and which silences all questioning and thereby closes the discourse" (BI 85).

Vattimo does not locate violence in the dominance of the general over the particular, as existentialism did, but rather in rendering free contradictions (in the widest sense of the expression) impossible. According to Vattimo, this nonquestionable, and therefore by definition violent *real*, namely, the objective, surprisingly is being increasingly weakened by the findings of modern science. "It is modern science, heir and completion of metaphysics, that turns the world into a place where there are no (longer) facts, only interpretations" (BI 26).

The productivity of Vattimo's beginning becomes clear when we look at two phenomena, which his concepts open to completely new possibilities of interpretation: technology and mass media.

The Biotechnological Dissolution of Human Nature

This dissolution of objectivity through science currently affects also the notion of human nature, as new biotechnological practices are undermining the concept of a stable and given human nature conceived as biological basis of human *ratio*. Defined as *animal rationale*, or *rationabile*, as Kant puts it, the human being is traditionally considered the animal that is not yet what it is, but has yet to become itself. Up to now this process was limited to the *ratio*, whereas the natural side remained unaffected. The human being was manipulable, but never producible; and this because human nature remained untouchable. But with the uprising of biotechnology, this last constant term is also no longer stable. In the age of biotechnology the expression "human nature" has lost its meaning. What consequences does this loss of "essence" have for human self-conception? When the difference between growing and producing becomes unclear, then it is no longer possible to consider human nature as something given. Is this the beginning of post-humanity?

Concerning this question, the contemporary philosophical discourse offers two different approaches. The first could be described as "conservative technophobia" driven by the fear of losing the "essence" of what is human, whereas the second may be defined as "progressive technoeuphoria," given the fact that this position celebrates the achievements of biotechnology as the ultimate liberation of humans from the boundaries of nature, conceived as arbitrary. The exponents of the first approach try to maintain the concept of human nature as some sort of unchangeable norm, although the arguments often differ considerably. Whereas Francis Fukuyama's position for instance is openly naturalistic, Jürgen Habermas' critique focuses more on the consequences that manipulating the human genome and similar interventions may generate on the social level.

In *Our Posthuman Future: Consequences of the Biotechnological Revolution*, Fukuyama defines human nature as "the sum of the behavior and characteristics that are typical of the human species, arising from genetic rather than environmental factors."[6] The naturalistic background of his approach is evident, as Fukuyama identifies human nature with our specific genetic asset, which according to him determines our interaction with the environment, especially our emotional reactions. These patterns of emotional responses encoded in the genome of the human species and transmitted from generation to generation for Fukuyama represent a sort of safe haven, as in his view our emotional reactions are the common ground of human behavior and therefore the basis of all social interaction. According to Fukuyama, emotion and not reason is the ground on which social interaction and politics are based. For Fukuyama, emotions rather than arguments guarantee the pacific coexistence of humans, at least of members of the same ethnic group to which, according to Fukuyama, one feels viscerally attached "by nature." To interfere in this more or less good working system of instinctive behavior may lead to disastrous consequences, Fukuyama fears. Thus, for Fukuyama the victory of the mind over the body, now possibly within reach due to biotechnologies, bears the risk of ending in a situation of general violence, a violence that today is held back by our inherited instincts.

A second problematic outcome of (liberal) eugenics observed by Fukuyama is the danger it allegedly poses to democracy, because for him it threatens to undermine the basic equality of humans. Fukuyama fears that the genetically modified "will look, think, act, and perhaps even feel differently from those who were not similarly chosen, and may come in time to think of themselves as different kinds of creatures."[7]

This fear is shared by Jürgen Habermas. For him the great difference between genetic inequality and all other possible (economic, social, political) inequalities among people is that in contrast to all these traditional inequalities, the genetic one is not reversible. Whereas all social and political differences are contingent, because at least in theory the relation between master and slave may be reversed, the relation between the "enhanced" and the "naturals" is irreversible. According to Habermas the problem with liberal eugenics is that it threatens to fix the power-relations once and forever.

A second problematic consequence of liberal eugenics Habermas focuses on regards the image that a genetically modified person may develop of herself. According to Habermas, a genetically modified person, who is aware of her condition, would no longer be capable of conceiving of herself as of the sole actor of her actions, for she would always have in mind that perhaps she acts the way she actually acts only because someone else made her the way she is. According to this argument, a genetically modified person would be incapable of seeing herself as an autonomous subject and therefore would also be incapable of making responsible decisions. From this Habermas concludes that with an origin that is not natural—the German word Habermas uses is *Naturwüchsigkeit*—a person would be unable to conceive of herself as of an equal and autonomous individual. Thus, according to Habermas, biotechnologies risk undermining the two most important pillars of liberal democracy: equality as well as autonomy.

The "progressive technoeuphoric" position instead embraces the dissolution of human nature as ultimate liberation and emancipation from the biological boundaries that obstruct human freedom, which for this position constitutes the essence of humans. In this view, which is advocated by authors such as Gregory Stock[8] and Nick Bostrom,[9] the human animal represents only a transitory stage in the evolutionary history of this species, which has not yet reached its end. The human animal is not yet what it has to be, but must achieve its essence by enhancing its proper nature. Max More, a popular exponent of the transhumanist movement, writes:

> Transhumanists take humanism further by challenging human limits by means of science and technology combined with critical and creative thinking. We challenge the inevitability of aging and death, and we seek continuing enhancements to our intellectual abilities, our physical capacities, and our emotional development. We see humanity as a transitory stage in the evolutionary development of intelligence. We advocate using science to accelerate our move from human to a transhuman or posthuman condition.[10]

In this respect "post-humanism" is not different from classical humanism, which identifies the human being as the animal whose specific essence consists in not having a given essence at all. Humans are the only beings, which are not what they are but which, as essentially free, have to decide by themselves what to be. According to Stock, director of the Program on Medicine, Technology, and Society at the School of Medicine of the University of California at Los Angeles, even if humanity is not actively pursuing the goal of genetic enhancement, this possibility will come forward as a side effect of already widely accepted therapeutic practices: "The fundamental discoveries that spawn these coming capabilities will flow from research deeply embedded in the mainstream, research that is highly beneficial, enjoys widespread support, and certainly is not directed toward a goal like human germline engineering. The possibilities of human redesign will arrive whether or not we actively pursue them."[11]

In accordance with others,[12] Stock points out that the concept of a given natural nature, with which humans ought not to interfere, is quite problematic, as it is based on the assumption that the human being itself is not part of nature: "To some, the coming of human-directed change is unnatural because it differs so much from any previous change, but this distinction between the natural and the unnatural is an illusion. We are as natural a part of the world as anything else is, and so is the technology we create. . . . Remaking ourselves is the ultimate expression and realization of our humanity."[13]

The brief analysis that I have offered above shows that the technophobic rejection of biotechnology as well as the technoeuphoric embracing of the new technology is problematic. The first one because it tries to maintain a concept that risks being overruled by the developments of biotechnologies; the second one because by standing in the tradition of Descartes and the enlightenment, it is subjected to the "dialectics of enlightenment" described by Theodor Adorno and Max Horkheimer: what started as liberation from the boundaries of the biological nature of humans turns into reification of the entire human being.[14] So the pretended liberation from nature risks ending in a new form of manipulability, as the alleged liberation of the subject from its corporeal limitations finally proves to be a new sort of oppression of humans, who thus tragically learn that the body is not the grave of the soul, to quote Plato, but the only mode in which the mind exists.

Given all of the above, perhaps there is a third way to read biotechnology. This alternative interpretation of biotechnology, I suggest, results from a historical contextualization of these new technologies, which shows that they belong to the discourse of emancipation and its idea that human freedom is based on mastery over nature. Biotechnologies follow the paradigm of fabrication, the "*herstellendes Verhalten*" [producing attitude] that according to Heidegger dominates the Western concept of Being since Plato. In the perspective of the metaphysical paradigm of fabrication, to be means to be objective, and objectivity is identified with being made. This is an idea that Heidegger sees exemplified in the Christian concept of creation, which according to him openly equates being and fabrication.[15]

Today we are experiencing the overcoming of this objectifying approach paradoxically because of the radicalization of the discourse of emancipation. This occurs on a theoretical level in the philosophical discussions on postmodernity, and on the level of practice in the dissolution of human nature by means of biotechnology. In the same way that the consequences of the discourse of emancipation, which allays reification, in the end lead to a destabilization of the idea of objective substance, biotechnologies, which originally aimed expressly at the complete control of the objective body by the subject, also lead to the insight that this mastery of the subject over its body is not possible, simply because there is no self-transparent, autonomous subject beyond its bodily incarnation. The attempt to pursue total mastery over animality by means of biotechnology thus turns into the insight that humans are constitutively "unavailable" (*unverfügbar*).

Thus the dissolution of human nature, which is an effect of pharmacological, prosthetic, and genetic manipulations of the human *bios*, can be read as an aspect of the weakening of Being diagnosed by Vattimo (see especially BI).[16] Vattimo states that it is possible to detect in Western thought and history a tendency to weaken the traditional concept of timeless and unchangeable objectivity. In the age of hermeneutics truth is no longer conceived as monolithic evidence, but as accessible only through personal perspectives. Thus, on a theoretical level the philosophical discourse of postmodernity is dissolving the objective notion of Being—traditionally conceived as presence, evidence, substance, and timeless meaning—into discursively mediated interpretations. Biotechnologies are doing the same, but more concretely dissolving the metaphysical objectivity of the body into the product of a general Nietzschean will to power, which has nothing to do with subjectivism, but which is more an "event" of Being than an expression of individual will.

To recapitulate, one could say that in the field of philosophical anthropology biotechnologies lead to the same dissolution that has already taken place in epistemology. This weakening also of the biological nature of humans, which on the one hand risks ending in a new form of oppression, on the other hand could, according to Vattimo, also be interpreted as another sort of liberation: not as liberation from nature through reification but as liberation from unquestionable objectivity. This is so because the paradoxical effect of the technical attempt to control human nature by means of reification operated by biotechnologies, finally results in the intuition of the essential *Unverfügbarkeit*, that is, "unavailability," of the human *phusis*, as Heidegger puts it. So the unintentional effect of biotechnologies, which were based on the uncritical assumption of a dualistic model of humans (which defines human beings as connection between objective nature and subjective *ratio*), consists in the demonstration that this dualistic model is no longer suitable. A consequence of the mind-body dualism, biotechnology finally leads to the conclusion that the human being is an indivisible psychosomatic unity. This also means that the aim of total control over the human *bios* ends in the demonstration of the constitutive "unavailability" of human nature, here in the sense of human essence. In this sense, biotechnology fulfills a destabilizing, derealizing function aimed at freeing human beings from the yoke of unchangeable fact, and it can thus take the notion of nature out of the cave of the natural sciences and give it back to the open space of politics, to speak with Bruno Latour.[17] As for Vattimo, according to Latour, the "crisis of nature" we are experiencing today is more precisely a "crisis of objectivity." What is becoming more and more evident is that the realm of objective *Dinge an sich* that are accessible only to natural sciences, does not exist. In our days it is evident that nature, the allegedly mute object, is not a given eternal entity, waiting to be discovered and described by natural sciences; rather, it is a product of human discourse, and that means it is a product of politics.

The Media and the Proliferation of Reality

The same destabilizing, derealizing function that Vattimo ascribes to the sciences in general, he also locates in the media. Vattimo arrives at his surprising assessment of the mass media in his attempt to critically rethink Heidegger's essay "The Age of the World Picture."[18] According to Heidegger in this essay, modernity was the epoch of *Weltbilder* (images of the world), the epoch in which the world became an image (of the subject) in the name of boundless domination (of nature). Here, the Turin philosopher shifts the common reading of this passage to its opposite. Vattimo understands image-becoming not as rendering disposable, but—in view of the postmodern duplication of world images—as a symptom of the weakening of traditional Being (understood as presence and structure) and therefore as a positive step toward a "weak ontology," which unhinges even the supposed certainty of reality:

> In actual fact, the increase in possible information on the myriad forms of reality makes it increasingly difficult to conceive of a *single* reality. It may be that in the world of the mass media a "prophecy" of Nietzsche's is fulfilled: in the end the true world becomes a fable. If we, in late modernity, have an idea of reality, it cannot be understood as the objective given lying beneath, or beyond, the images we receive of it from the media. How and

where could we arrive at such a reality "in itself"? For us, reality is rather the result of the intersection and "contamination" (in the Latin sense) of a multiplicity of images, interpretations and reconstructions circulated by the media in competition with one another and without any "central" coordination." (TS 7)

When considering the current diversity of the media, it becomes clear that we have freed ourselves from the "metaphysical-objectivist heritage"[19] of metaphysics, even in our concrete "life world" (*Lebenswelt*). In this sense, Vattimo can speak of hermeneutics as well as the "*koine*" of postmodernity.

> [Hermeneutics] is not concerned with freeing itself from interpretations, but much more with freeing interpretations from the dominance of the one, "true" truth, and from the demand for it—because the latter would call for being entrusted to the scientists, the religious gerontocracy, the political central committees, or another category of "unspoiled" intelligence, along with all the risks to freedom that such a step would carry. The world of medial communication can therefore appear as a world characterized by the freedom of interpretation.[20]

Indeed, Vattimo even goes so far as to suppose that the "twisting" (*Verwindung*) of "metaphysics, as aspired to by the philosophy of Heidegger, only becomes possible under the new conditions of existence, which are determined by the technology of communication."[21]

In this sense, Vattimo's radical hermeneutics, which understands even the ascertainment of the interpretive character of all our experience as a mere interpretation, is the only possible philosophy of postmodernity characterized by the limitless pluralization of the media; this is so not because it truly represents an unchanging reality, but because it alone is in a position to enter into a dialogue with our "life world." As Vattimo writes:

> If hermeneutics indeed wishes to be a philosophy of dialogue as a moment that cannot be reduced to a pure instrument, which is provisional and basically does not essentially serve to uncover the one objective truth, it can only consequentially follow the "reality-dissolving" current that Nietzsche identified. Only on this condition will hermeneutics be able to present itself as a philosophy of the society of communication that has become general.[22]

For Vattimo, the pluralization of the media landscape constitutes not only the realization of the dissolution of the one truth in innumerable interpretations, but, as we will see, an eminently positive, emancipatory event, because in his view it creates plurality. Vattimo's media optimism stands in (conscious) opposition to the media chastising of the Frankfurt School. Whereas Adorno had interpreted the mass media as manipulative propaganda machinery that only serves to leave the masses in their "immaturity" (*Unmündigkeit*), Vattimo sees in the in principle totally uncontrolled possibilities of communication, that is, those offered by the internet—perhaps naively, perhaps simply provocatively exaggerated—the principal possibility of absolute freedom of opinion, insofar as every societal fringe group now has the means to express itself on an equal footing: "This giddy proliferation of communication as more and more subcultures 'have their say' is the most obvious effect of the mass media" (TS 6). Indeed, Vattimo knows of the basic danger of manipulation inherent in mass media Adorno warned about, but he believes that the situation of today is fundamentally different from that of the thirties of the twentieth century:

> When Adorno spoke of the mass media, he had the Nazi propaganda of Dr. Goebbels in the back of his mind—the voice of the "big brother" who could impress opinions, behavior patterns and assent on the masses in an almost hypnotic manner. But the media world, as it gradually crystallized out of the seventies, had more resemblance to Babylonian lingual confusion than to a monolithic structure ruled from a single center.[23]

If Baudrillard could characterize mass media as a unilateral movement from transmitter to receiver, which excluded all true communication, that is, all living dialogue, we must now, after the emergence of the internet at the latest, agree with Vattimo that medial events are today open to more "participants" than ever before:

> Even television advertising cannot manage without a certain reference to the audience, which regardless of how manipulable and manipulated it is, remains a conversation partner that is not totally predictable or conditionable. But it doesn't stop there. The possibility of becoming an active participant in the media "market," for instance by founding an independent radio and television station, is no longer the privilege of a small few—in any case, it depends more on political or legislative decisions than on purely economic factors.[24]

In Vattimo's concept of "weak thought" the total mediatization and pluralization of "reality," which appears in our media-dominated "lifeworld," is highly visible evidence that there is no existent "reality" as such; rather, all our seemingly immediate experience is always mediated, that is, interpreted: "Under the pressure of today's medial construction of reality we comprehend that reality was always a construction."[25]

The duplication of "world images" in the media can indeed be assessed as evidence that the model of an objective reality that would only need to be represented to derive its truth does not hold up. If reality in-itself were accessible, there would not be so many different representations, or interpretations, of it, but only one: "What could . . . the existence of more than one radio or TV channel mean in a world where the norm is the exact reproduction of reality, perfect objectivity, the complete identity of map and territory?" (TS 6–7).

In the duplication of reality in the media it becomes apparent that the *telos* of the theoretical notion of truth as correspondence or adequation is not realizable. Vattimo writes:

> Nietzsche showed the image of reality as a well-founded rational order (the perennial metaphysical image of the world) to be only the "reassuring" myth of a still primitive and barbaric humanity. Metaphysics is a violent response to a situation that is itself fraught with danger and violence. It seeks to master reality at a stroke, grasping (or so it thinks) the first principle on which all things depend (and thus giving itself an empty guarantee of power over events). Following Nietzsche in this respect, Heidegger showed that to think of being as foundation, and reality as a rational system of causes and effects, is simply to extend the model of "scientific" objectivity to the totality of being. All things are reduced to the level of pure presences that can be measured, manipulated, replaced and therefore easily dominated and organized—and in the end man, his interiority and historicity are all reduced to the same level. (TS 7–8)

With the omnipresence of the media this concept is finally demonstrated to be untenable. In the world of mass media it becomes apparent that objects always present themselves to us in interpretations. Empty (objective) facts do not exist, or at least they would have no "meaning." Whatever appears to us as something is always interpreted in some way. Modern mass media, in which the "*one* reality" appears as given only in its countless medial "world images," thereby becomes the demonstration of the phenomenon that the "truth" is accessible only in and as interpretations. In this liberation from unquestionable—and hence always repressive—objectivity or reality lies the emancipatory function of the media, according to Vattimo:

> The view I want to put forward is that in the media society, the ideal of emancipation modeled on lucid self-consciousness, on the perfect knowledge of one who knows how things stand (compare Hegel's Absolute Spirit or Marx's conception of man freed from ideology), is replaced by an ideal of emancipation based on oscillation, plurality and, ultimately, on the erosion of the very "principle of reality." (TS 7)

For Vattimo, "freedom" does not therefore consist in "having a perfect knowledge of the necessary structure of reality and conforming to it" (TS 7). Rather, the new emancipation, the new "freedom" of the foundationless post-metaphysical life world of "absolute meaning," or of generalized mediatization, consists in accepting the finiteness, and hence relativity, temporariness, and mutability of every position, especially one's own, and comprehending it as opportunity, which is very reminiscent of Nietzsche's "positive nihilism":

> If, in this multicultural world, I set out my system of religious, aesthetic, political and ethnic values, I shall be acutely conscious of the historicity, contingency and finiteness of these systems, starting with my own. Nietzsche, in *The Gay Science*, called this "continuing to dream knowing one is dreaming." But is such a thing possible? This is the essence of what Nietzsche called the "overman" (or beyond-man), the *Übermensch*: and he assigns the task of attaining it to mankind of the future, in the world of intensified communication. (TS 9–10)

Conclusion

What Vattimo suggests is a revaluation of science, technology, and media, which should no longer be seen as the realm of reification, but as outriders of the nihilistic, postmodern insight that the world has became a fable, that there is no objective truth but only interpretations. This is especially true if one looks at the astonishing possibilities given with biotechnologies. Thus the dissolution of (normative) human nature due to genetics, pharmacology, and prosthetics, can be interpreted as an aspect of the more general weakening of Being, which according to Vattimo characterizes postmodernity.

What is the effect of this attenuation of strong principles, which Vattimo sees in both technology and mass media? Vattimo identifies this attenuation with the weakening of concrete violence. According to Vattimo, violence is definable only as evident reason that excludes all contradictions. As the idea of unquestionable evidence dissolves, so does violence in the name of evident truth. Reference to evident, eternal, and true reasons makes it at least easier to legitimate violence, Vattimo claims. Conversely, the insight that every position represents only one of many possible positions makes it impossible to practice violence in the name of eternal truth, and leads to a form of *pietas* toward other positions and to an ironic and critical attitude toward one's own position. In this way, Vattimo's philosophy is not exhausted by theoretical considerations, but offers the beginnings of a post-metaphysical ethics.

Notes

1. Friedrich Nietzsche, *Götzen-Dämmerung, Kritische Studienausgabe*, vol. 6, ed. Giorgio Colli and Mazzino Montinari (München: Walter de Gruyter, 1988), 80.
2. See Martin Weiss, *Hermeneutik des Unerschöpflichen. Das Denken Luigi Pareysons* (Würzburg: Lit, 2004).
3. See Rudolf Boehm, *Husserl und Nietzsche,* in Rudolf Boehm, *Vom Gesichtspunkt der Phänomenologie* (The Hague: Martinus Nijhoff, 1968), 217–236.
4. Friedrich Nietzsche, *Nachlass*, in *Kritische Studienausgabe* vol. 12, p. 7.
5. See Günter Figal, *Der Sinn des Verstehens. Beiträge zur hermeneutischen Philosophie* (Stuttgart: Reclam, 1996).
6. Francis Fukuyama, *Our Posthuman Future: Consequences of the Biotechnology Revolution* (New York: Picador, 2002), 130.
7. Ibid., 157.
8. Gregory Stock, *Redesigning Humans: Choosing Our Genes, Changing Our Future* (New York: Mariner Books, 2003).
9. Nick Bostrom, "In Defense of Posthuman Dignity," *Bioethics* 19, 3 (2005): 202–214.
10. www.maxmore.com/extprn3.htm (July 22, 2007).
11. Stock, *Redesigning Humans*, 40.

12. See Kurt Bayeritz, "Die menschliche Natur und ihr moralischer Status," in *Die menschliche Natur. Welchen und wie viel Wert hat sie?*, ed. Kurt Bayeritz (Paderborn: Mentis, 2005), 9–32.
13. Stock, *Redesigning Humans*, 197.
14. See Max Horkheimer and Theodor W. Adorno, *Dialectic of Enlightenment*, ed. Gunzelin Schmid Noerr, trans. Edmund Jephcott (Stanford: Stanford University Press, 2002).
15. See Martin Heidegger, *The Basic Problems of Phenomenology*, revised trans. with introduction Albert Hofstadter (Bloomington: Indiana University Press, 1982).
16. See also Martin Weiss, *Gianni Vattimo. Einführung. Mit einem Interview mit Gianni Vattimo* (Vienna: Passagen, 2006).
17. See Bruno Latour, *Politics of Nature—How to Bring the Sciences into Democracy* (Cambridge: Harvard University Press, 2004).
18. Martin Heidegger, "The Age of the World Picture," in *Off the Beaten Path*, ed. and trans. Julian Young and Kenneth Haynes (Cambridge: Cambridge University Press, 2002), 57–71.
19. Gianni Vattimo and Wolfgang Welsch, *Medien-Welten Wirklichkeiten* (Munich: Fink, 1998), 17. All passages from this work are the author's translation.
20. Ibid.
21. Ibid., 20.
22. Ibid., 19.
23. Ibid., 16.
24. Ibid., 16.
25. Ibid., 7.

Contributors

LUCA BAGETTO is Associate Professor of Theoretical Philosophy at the University of Pavia, Italy. A former student of Vattimo's at the University of Turin, he is the author of *Decisione ed effettività. La via ermeneutica di Dietrich Bonhoeffer* (1991), *Il pensiero della possibilità. La filosofia torinese come storia della filosofia* (1995), *Etica della comunicazione. Che cos'è l'ermeneutica filosofica* (1999), *La figura della parola. Visione e comunicazione nella* Fenomenologia dello spirito (2000), and *L'espressione del servo muto. Mente e mondo dopo Kant* (2005).

SILVIA BENSO is Professor of Philosophy at Rochester Institute of Technology. She is the author of *Pensare dopo Auschwitz: Etica filosofica e teodicea ebraica* (1992), *The Face of Things: A Different Side of Ethics* (2000), and *Pensare ambientalista. Tra filosofia e ecologia* (2000) with Brian Schroeder, with whom she is also the coeditor of *Contemporary Italian Philosophy: Crossing the Borders of Ethics, Politics, and Religion* (2007) and *Levinas and the Ancients* (2008).

GIOVANNA BORRADORI is Professor of Philosophy at Vassar College. The author of *Il Pensiero Post-Filosofico* (1988), she is also editor of *Recoding Metaphysics: The New Italian Philosophy* (1988), *The American Philosopher: Conversations with Quine, Davidson, Putnam, Nozick, Danto, Rorty, Cavell, MacIntyre, and Kuhn* (1994), and *Philosophy in a Time of Terror: Dialogues with Jürgen Habermas and Jacques Derrida* (2003).

PETER CARRAVETTA is Alfonse M. D'Amato Professor of Italian and Italian American Studies at Stony Brook University. He is the founding editor of *Differentia: Review of Italian Thought* (nine issues 1986–1999), and author of *Prefaces to the Diaphora. Rhetorics, Allegory and the Interpretation of Postmodernity* (1991), *Il Fantasma di Hermes. Saggio su metodo retorica interpretare* (1996), *Dei parlanti. Studi e ipotesi su metodo e retorica dell'interpretare* (2002), and *Del postmoderno. Critica e cultura in America all'alba del duemila* (2009). He has recently completed *The Elusive Hermes: Method, Discourse, and the Critique of Interpretation* and his translation of Vattimo and Rovatti's *Weak Thought* is forthcoming.

GAETANO CHIURAZZI is Assistant Professor in the Department of Philosophy at the University of Turin, Italy. In addition to several articles on themes of deconstructionism and hermeneutics, he is the author of *Scrittura e tecnica. Derrida e la metafisica* (1992), *Hegel, Heidegger e la grammatica dell'essere* (1996), *Il postmoderno* (1997), *Modalità ed esistenza* (2001), published in German as *Modalität und Existenz* (2006), and *Teorie del giudizio* (2005). He is also the coeditor, with Gianni Vattimo, of the journal *Trópos: Rivista di ermeneutica e critica filosofica*.

CLAUDIO CIANCIO is Professor of Theoretical Philosophy at the Università del Piemonte Orientale in Vercelli, Italy. In addition to various publications on classical German philosophy (especially early Romanticism and Schelling) and hermeneutic ontology, especially on themes of freedom, evil, and the relation between philosophy and religion, he is the author of *Friedrich Schlegel: Crisi della filosofia e la rivelazione* (1984), *Il paradosso della verità* (1999), *Del male e di Dio* (2006) and *Libertà e dono dell'essere* (2009).

FRANCA D'AGOSTINI teaches philosophy of science at the University of Turin, Politecnico, and Analysis of Public Language at the University of Piemonte Orientale, Vercelli, Italy. The author of *Analitici e continentali* (1997), *Breve storia della filosofia nel Novecento* (1999), *Logica del nichilismo* (2000), *Disavventure della verità* (2002), *The Last Fumes. Nihilism and the Nature of Philosophical Concepts* (2008), and *Paradossi* (2009), she is a regular contributor to the Italian newspapers *La Stampa* and *Il Manifesto*.

EDISON HIGUERA AGUIRRE, OFM, holds a doctorate in philosophy from the Pontificia Universitas Antonianum in Rome. His doctoral dissertation was titled *Hermeneutics and Nihilism in Gianni Vattimo*. Presently he teaches philosophical anthropology at the Studium Theologicum Franciscanum "Cardenal Echeverría" in Quito, Ecuador.

EDUARDO MENDIETA is Professor of Philosophy at Stony Brook University. His most recent publications are *Global Fragments: Globalizations, Latinamericanisms, and Critical Theory* (2007), an edited volume of interviews with Richard Rorty titled *Take Care of Freedom and Truth Will*

Take Care of Itself (2006), and a collection of interviews with Angela Davis titled *Abolition Democracy: Beyond Empire, Torture, and Prisons* (2005).

JAMES RISSER is Professor of Philosophy and Director of the Honors Program at Seattle University. He is the author of *Hermeneutics and the Voice of the Other: Re-Reading Hans-Georg Gadamer's Philosophical Hermeneutics* (1997), editor of *Heidegger Toward the Turn: The Work of the 1930s* (1999), and coeditor of *American Continental Philosophy: A Reader* (2000).

BRIAN SCHROEDER is Professor and Department Chair of Philosophy and Director of Religious Studies at Rochester Institute of Technology. He is the author of *Altared Ground: Levinas, History and Violence* (1996) and with Silvia Benso of *Pensare ambientalista. Tra filosofia e ecologia* (2000). He is the coeditor of *Thinking Through the Death of God: A Critical Companion to Thomas J. J. Altizer* (2004) and *Japanese and Continental Philosophy: Conversations with the Kyoto School* (2010), and with Silvia Benso of *Contemporary Italian Philosophy: At the Threshold of Ethics, Politics, and Religion* (2007) and *Levinas and the Ancients* (2008).

ROBERT T. VALGENTI is Assistant Professor of Philosophy at Lebanon Valley College. He has studied with Vattimo as a Fulbright Scholar at the University of Turin and is currently translating Luigi Pareyson's *Truth and Interpretation*.

ERIK M. VOGT is Professor of Philosophy at Trinity College (CT) and Universitäts-Dozent of Philosophy at University of Vienna, Austria. He is the author of *Sartre's Wieder-Holung* and *Zugänge zur politischen Ästhetik*, and also coeditor of volumes on American continental philosophy, Derrida and politics, Žižek, Sartre, and Adorno/Derrida. He is the general editor of the philosophical book series *Neue Amerikanische Philosophie*.

DAVID WEBB is Senior Lecturer in Philosophy at Staffordshire University, United Kingdom. His writings include *Heidegger: Ethics and the Practice of Ontology* (2009) and several papers on Heidegger, Foucault, and Serres. He is currently working on the influence of the mathematical sciences on Foucault's *The Archaeology of Knowledge*. He has also translated several of Vattimo's books into English.

MARTIN G. WEISS teaches at the University of Klagenfurt, Austria, and is director of the project "The Dissolution of Human Nature: The Philosophical Discourse on Biotechnologies between Substantialism and Emancipation" at the Life-Science-Governance Research Platform of the University of Vienna, Austria. He is the author of *Gianni Vattimo. Einführung. Mit einem Interview mit Gianni Vattimo* (2003) and *Bios und Zoë. Die menschliche Natur im Zeitalter ihrer technischen Reproduzierbarkeit* (2009).

Index

Abbagnano, Nicola, 185, 199
Abraham, 127, 144, 146, 229
Actuality, 8, 23, 30, 53, 63, 69, 117, 118, 139, 140, 145, 163, 168–170, 172, 174, 176, 179, 188, 192, 204, 205, 211, 218, 221, 229, 234, 235, 244
Adikia, 22–24
Adorno, Theodor W., 6, 49, 72, 101, 116, 209, 221–224, 226, 235, 239, 248, 252, 256, 259
Agreement, 3, 4, 23, 33, 172, 177, 179, 184, 207
Aletheia, 50, 178
Ambiguity, 26, 156, 157
Anarchism, 176, 184
Anaximander, 22, 23, 30
An-denken, 72, 217
Antiseri, Dario, 110, 113
Apel, Karl-Otto, 64, 231
Arendt, Hannah, 180, 196
Aristotle, 1, 4, 29, 32, 33, 79, 105
Art, 15, 19, 28, 29, 34, 37, 38, 44, 115, 117, 170, 172, 176, 177, 203, 225, 226, 236, 238
Artifact, 110
Artwork, 223
Atheism, 7, 150, 151, 154, 162, 163, 184

Bacon, Francis, 20, 29, 209
Badiou, Alan, 206, 236
Barth, Karl, 96
Baudrillard, Jean, 244, 252
Being-in-the-world, 52, 92, 138

Benjamin, Walter, 72, 217, 227
Benveniste, Emile, 147
Bergson, Henri, 24, 30
Biotechnology, 10, 241, 245, 248–250, 255
Bloch, Ernst, 72, 151, 162, 209, 211, 219
Bostrom, Nick, 247, 255

Campanella, Tommaso, 209
Cassirer, Ernst, 187, 190, 194, 199, 200
Charity, 6, 43, 44, 89, 114, 124, 127, 133, 151, 160–162, 206
Chiodi, Pietro, 77, 199
Christ, 5, 6, 90, 94, 126, 194
Christian(ity), 4–7, 33, 44, 61, 80, 81, 89, 90, 93, 94, 96, 106, 113, 123–126, 128, 134, 137, 138, 140, 144–148, 150, 151, 156, 158, 159, 161–164, 193, 194, 204, 206, 236, 248
Cohen, Hermann, 187, 200
Communication, 49, 59, 60, 75, 191, 221, 227–229, 231–233, 235, 251, 252
Communism, 215
Community, 5, 39, 60, 88, 90, 92, 147, 172, 175, 204, 206, 209
Conscience, 72, 189, 202
Consciousness, 8, 16, 19, 21, 41, 52, 68, 71, 87, 140–143, 160, 188, 189, 192, 195–199, 209, 229, 242, 254
Consensus, 115, 179, 208, 228
Contingency, 87, 114, 124, 133, 170, 191, 192, 211, 230, 235, 254

261

Continuity, 2, 8, 9, 15, 19, 23, 62, 81, 97, 170, 178, 183–185, 188, 190–195, 197, 199, 200, 203, 206, 208, 209, 212, 214, 216–218
Croce, Benedetto, 138
Custom, 190, 216
Cyberspace, 233, 238, 239

Dasein, 19, 20, 51–54, 72, 86–88, 92, 93, 105, 106, 108, 109, 111, 114, 117, 155, 186
Davidson, Donald, 32, 96, 257
Deconstruction, 2, 68, 146, 181, 210, 213, 258
Deduction, 74, 76, 77
Deleuze, Gilles, 16, 36, 61, 236
Democracy, 7, 8, 136, 137, 147, 168–173, 175, 178, 180, 184, 201, 206, 208, 211, 217, 230, 234–237, 246, 247, 256, 259
Derrida, Jacques, 6, 7, 16, 31, 64, 68, 101, 137, 138, 144, 146–148, 182, 190, 204, 211, 219, 239, 257–259
Destination, 52, 53, 92, 143, 169, 208, 214
Destiny, 5, 36, 37, 41, 42, 63, 68, 69, 74, 76, 77, 91–93, 107–110, 112, 127, 139, 189, 191, 208, 214, 218
Dewey, John, 185, 208
Dialectic(al), 5, 65, 67, 70–74, 81, 82, 89, 90, 116, 119, 132, 175, 177, 183, 184, 186, 197, 199, 222, 223, 232, 235, 248, 256
Dialogue, 6, 7, 17, 27, 43, 44, 57, 58, 87, 94, 104, 105, 114, 115, 176, 179, 181, 204, 206, 208, 251, 252, 257
Dilthey, Wilhelm, 41, 138, 186, 194, 206
Discontinuity, 9, 81, 184, 194, 211, 212, 217
Discourse, 8, 29, 37, 47, 55, 57, 61, 64, 72, 90, 94, 95, 97, 106, 112, 131, 138, 146, 147, 161, 172–174, 178, 180, 188, 212, 213, 244, 245, 248–250

Disjunction, 22, 23
Distortion, 22–24, 72, 74, 82, 95, 145, 191, 213, 215, 217, 237. See also *Verwindung*
Dogmatism, 18, 21, 57, 68, 75, 141, 171, 185, 190
Donation, 23
Dostoevsky, Fyodor, 184

Economics, 191, 195, 201, 231, 237
Einstein, Albert, 187, 200
Emancipation, 5, 8, 9, 21, 24, 40, 42, 43, 55, 65, 89, 124, 145, 168, 180, 182, 184, 190, 194, 196, 203, 205–208, 214, 216, 237, 247–249, 254, 260
Enlightenment, 48, 80, 81, 90, 94, 105, 130, 137, 141, 142, 146, 147, 190, 201, 209, 222, 229, 237, 248
Eschatology, 89, 129, 217
Eternal return, 24–27, 30, 31
Ethics, 2, 4, 5, 30, 47–49, 51, 55, 56, 61, 62, 75, 76, 80, 81, 83, 91, 93, 94, 97, 114, 115, 179, 214, 216, 231, 234, 255
Euripides, 173
Event, 3, 8, 17, 18, 28, 37, 50, 57, 59, 65, 85, 90, 92, 94, 108, 112, 122–125, 158, 161, 170, 171, 204, 224, 227, 228, 249, 253
Evidence, 19, 40, 83, 156, 194, 249, 255
Evil, 125, 126, 129, 130, 135, 258
Experience, 3, 15–19, 21–27, 34, 56–58, 74, 75, 128, 130, 131, 140, 143, 164, 169, 175, 187, 189, 194, 222, 224, 227, 229

Factuality, 25, 26, 69, 142
Faith, 7, 94, 105, 136–138, 143–147, 156, 157, 159, 163, 173, 193, 194, 229
Figal, Günter, 97, 244, 255
Finitude, 19, 21, 29, 48, 55, 56, 62, 71, 76, 84, 92, 111, 112, 114, 122, 124, 130, 204, 205, 214

Foucault, Michel, 47, 61, 139, 169, 172, 174–176, 178, 179, 181, 259
Foundationalism, 44, 65, 83, 168, 207, 230
Frankfurt School (the), 141, 197, 252
Frege, Gottlob, 25, 31, 32, 186
Friendship, 3, 4, 33, 40, 41, 43, 44, 55, 180
Fukuyama, Francis, 245, 246, 255
Fundamentalism, 141, 193, 234
Future (the), 3, 7–9, 21, 23, 26, 54, 71, 122, 123, 125, 127–131, 136, 179, 185, 203, 208–210, 212, 214, 216, 217, 223, 232, 246

Gadamer, Hans-Georg, 1, 8, 15, 17–19, 21, 28, 29, 41, 44, 58, 64, 68, 71, 72, 77, 84, 87, 88, 139, 144, 163, 167, 171, 172, 176–179, 183–185, 242, 259
Gelassenheit, 224–226, 228
Ge-stell, 9, 74, 75, 108, 109, 191, 222–228
Girard, René, 81, 95, 145
Globalization, 7, 147, 148, 193, 195, 201, 231, 237, 258
Gramsci, Antonio, 136

Habermas, Jürgen, 7, 47, 59, 64, 75, 88, 151, 160, 161, 164, 196, 231, 245–247, 257
Habit, 86, 190, 191, 243
Hardt, Michael, 198, 202, 231, 237
Hegel, Georg Wilhelm Friedrich, 8, 15, 19, 29, 37, 38, 40, 65, 67, 70, 71, 73, 127, 132, 147, 184, 186, 188, 190, 195, 196, 199, 201, 204, 205, 209, 213, 218, 254, 258
Historicism, 39, 70, 71, 139, 160, 204, 205
Historicity, 15, 19, 37, 38, 50, 84, 87, 105, 106, 111, 112, 116, 123, 124, 148, 161, 171, 185, 186, 188, 190, 191, 204, 205, 208, 216, 230, 253, 254

Historiography, 80
History of Being, 39, 40, 50, 51, 69, 76, 103, 107, 118, 132, 155, 157, 158, 204
History of metaphysics, 5, 63, 65, 66, 72, 74, 75
Honneth, Axel, 197, 201
Hope, 93, 148, 176, 194, 210, 216
Human sciences/humanities, 17, 18, 24, 75, 182, 228, 242
Hume, David, 93, 190
Husserl, Edmund, 9, 19, 186, 242, 255

Identity, 22, 55, 58–61, 89, 108, 115, 129, 132, 133, 137, 149, 160, 180, 218, 230, 232, 234, 253
Ideology, 67, 72, 95, 105, 142, 181, 212, 231–233, 254
Incarnation, 80, 90, 94, 124, 125, 144, 145, 151, 159, 161, 214, 249
Irrationalism, 64, 68, 91

James, William, 185
Jünger, Ernst, 22, 30

Kant, Immanuel, 9, 21, 26, 31, 63, 65, 67, 70–77, 93, 111, 141, 144, 146, 147, 185–188, 190, 241
Kenosis, 6, 80, 145, 151, 159, 214
Kierkegaard, Søren, 229
Kuhn, Thomas, 188, 200, 257

Language, 1, 25, 27, 32, 43, 80, 82, 85, 88, 89, 94, 97, 104, 111, 114, 123, 139, 140, 154, 161, 171, 186–190, 199, 203, 204, 228
Latour, Bruno, 250, 256
Leibniz, Gottfried Wilhelm, 187
Levinas, Emmanuel, 6, 62, 64, 101, 102, 116, 122, 123, 204, 218, 257, 259
Liberation, 16, 19, 49, 102, 124–127, 132, 149, 197, 199, 207, 208, 215, 230, 245, 247–249, 254
Local(ity), 58–61, 217, 230

Logicism, 187
Logos, 25, 36, 91, 170, 172, 177
Love, 6, 131–133, 146, 151, 214
Löwith, Karl, 1, 210
Lyotard, Jean-François, 89

Marcuse, Herbert, 36, 49, 236
Marx, Karl, 31, 95, 147, 161, 184, 215, 235, 254
Marxism/Marxist, 95, 105, 136, 137, 184, 195, 197, 198
Media, 9, 49, 191, 193, 223, 228, 232, 236, 241, 245, 250–255
Memory, 81, 86, 89, 91, 92, 94, 106, 169, 216, 217
Mentalism, 185, 187, 189, 193
Messianism, 9, 211, 212, 214
Moltmann, Jürgen, 216
More, Max, 247
More, Thomas, 211
Mortality, 19, 92, 97, 114, 138, 174
Multiculturalism, 234
Multiplicity, 1, 68, 79, 87, 91, 102, 128, 170, 196, 214, 228, 229, 231, 233, 251

Nancy, Jean-Luc, 150, 162
Natural sciences, 10, 18, 20, 48, 242, 250
Negri, Antonio (Toni), 198, 202, 231, 237
Neo-Kantian(ism), 8, 49, 185–192, 194, 196, 199, 200
New Testament, 121, 125, 144, 191
Nonviolence, 81, 142, 231, 234

Ontology of actuality, 8, 63, 139, 145, 168–170, 172, 174, 176, 179, 188, 192, 204, 205, 218, 221, 229, 234, 235
Ontology of freedom, 127
Ontology of weakening (weak ontology), 81, 83, 124, 131, 145, 190, 230, 250
Opening, 1, 4, 18–21, 43, 49–51, 57, 74, 88, 105, 109, 110, 114, 127, 170, 171, 177, 185, 188, 189, 194, 198, 203, 204, 227, 233
Origin, 6, 42, 50, 52, 70, 76, 82, 96, 117, 121–133, 137, 143, 144, 147, 151, 160, 180, 206, 209, 217, 218, 227, 242, 247
Overcoming, 22, 48, 71, 74, 80–82, 105–108, 121, 122, 124, 145, 159, 191, 213, 227, 243, 248
Overman, 24, 26, 80, 157, 160, 215, 254. See also *Übermensch*

Pareyson, Luigi, 1, 64, 129, 134, 142, 185, 199, 204, 206, 242, 255, 259
Parmenides, 105, 119
Past (the), 23, 25, 26, 55, 68, 76, 131, 139, 140, 169, 170, 208, 214, 216, 217
Peirce, Charles Sanders, 34
Perniola, Mario, 117, 232, 238
Persuasion, 39, 40, 172, 178, 205
Pietas, 5, 33, 44, 72, 73, 80, 83, 97, 124, 214, 255
Plato, 2, 26, 88, 103, 105, 152, 156, 157, 171, 173, 176, 177, 206, 211, 241, 243, 248
Pluralism, 7, 58, 59, 164, 168, 172, 230
Poetry, 203, 226, 236
Popper, Karl, 106, 110, 119
Positivism, 26, 49, 105
Poststructuralism, 2, 36
Pragmatism, 4, 28, 33, 34, 44, 185
Praxis, 3, 27, 32, 160
Presence, 6, 22, 23, 72, 82, 86, 91, 107, 108, 112, 126, 184, 186, 188, 190, 199, 212, 230, 233, 237, 249, 250, 253
Present (the), 23, 24, 26, 56, 123, 136, 139, 169, 198, 206, 214, 216, 232
Proletariat, 197, 198
Provenance, 22, 50, 55, 56, 58, 62, 89, 112, 121, 122, 124, 125, 127, 130, 143, 145, 183, 189, 190, 194, 204, 214, 221

Quine, Willard Van Orman, 40, 45, 257

Racism, 234
Rationalism, 64, 68, 104, 110, 201, 208, 209
Rationality, 64, 65, 67–70, 74–76, 83, 103, 104, 160, 177, 208, 222–224, 226
Recognition, 191, 195–197, 230, 231
Recollection, 51, 54, 143, 169–172, 176, 180, 181
Redemption, 23, 81, 124, 126, 129, 223
Reformism, 9, 212, 214
Relativism, 64, 66, 87, 88, 125, 242
Religion, 3, 5, 6, 11, 20, 48, 80, 81, 83, 84, 90, 93, 94, 96, 121, 126, 130, 131, 135–147, 149, 151, 159, 161, 170, 184, 193, 207
Representation, 8, 20, 127, 159, 187–194, 197, 198, 200, 209, 211, 216, 231, 244, 253
Resistance, 9, 48, 61, 126, 137, 140, 198, 202, 216, 217
Responsibility, 8, 65, 70, 76, 89, 93, 137, 141, 153, 160, 192, 194, 198, 205, 218
Revolution, 9, 127, 150, 184, 194, 196–198, 201–203, 212, 214, 217, 219, 236, 237, 246
Rhetoric(al), 3, 4, 33, 34, 37, 39, 66, 73, 83, 84, 111, 136, 148, 172, 176–178, 257
Ricoeur, Paul, 58, 64
Rorty, Richard, 6–8, 28, 38, 40, 42, 47, 56, 57, 64, 65, 68, 139, 148, 185, 208, 215, 216, 239, 257, 258
Rovatti, Pier Aldo, 1, 10, 95, 117, 258

Sartre, Jean-Paul, 71, 72, 87, 92, 259
Schelling, Friedrich Wilhelm Joseph, 6, 90, 132–134, 258
Schleiermacher, Friedrich, 122
Schmitt, Carl, 159, 191, 192, 201
Science, 10, 20, 34, 37–39, 43, 69, 74, 75, 88, 90, 102, 103, 106, 110, 141, 164, 170, 177, 187, 215, 223, 228, 236, 242, 245, 247, 250, 254
Scientism, 68, 70, 91

Secularism, 136, 143, 146
Secularization, 6, 7, 48, 89, 90, 96, 109–111, 113, 138, 143–147, 149–152, 159, 161–163, 207, 214, 236
Serres, Michel, 47, 59, 61, 62, 259
Shock, 17, 19, 29, 34, 135, 227
Silence, 7, 114, 175
Silencing, 103–105, 114, 188, 190, 191, 244
Skepticism, 48, 68, 75
Socialism, 168, 193, 196, 197, 201, 215, 231
Society, 10, 35, 42, 71, 87, 111, 115, 127, 147, 169, 171, 177, 189, 195, 197, 198, 205, 209, 210, 212, 216, 222, 223, 226, 254
Socrates, 104, 105, 173–175, 178, 180
Solidarity, 40, 41, 43, 44, 172, 177–179
Stock, Gregory, 247, 248, 255

Tarski, Alfred, 25, 32
Taylor, Mark, 64
Technics, 103, 104, 108, 108, 116
Technology, 3, 7, 9, 10, 49, 51, 54, 75, 83, 108, 109, 141, 221–228, 231–234, 236, 239, 242, 245, 247, 248, 251, 254, 255
Technoscience, 142
Temporality, 23, 24, 90, 94, 155, 161, 186
Terrorism, 93, 148, 195, 197, 199, 215
Testimony, 8, 133, 139, 193, 195, 197, 198
Theology, 6, 7, 96, 110, 121, 146, 149, 163, 164, 212
Thucydides, 173
Totalitarian(ism), 9, 91, 105, 223, 226, 228, 230
Totality, 72, 75, 122, 139, 209, 210, 223, 253
Totalization, 71, 81, 90
Trace, 22, 65, 97, 107, 121, 123, 138–140, 144, 145, 152, 158, 159, 162, 169, 214, 239
Transcendence, 52, 53, 62, 133, 177, 199

Transcendental(ism), 21, 38, 54, 65, 70, 72–76, 80, 111, 155, 185, 186, 190, 225
Transformation, 2, 3, 8, 16, 17, 21, 24, 26, 51, 54, 61, 70, 75, 85, 88, 122, 133, 144, 195, 197, 206, 208, 212, 219, 224, 230
Transparency, 221, 228, 231, 233
Trinity (the), 125
Tugendhat, Ernst, 40, 45

Übermensch, 36, 152, 154, 162, 218, 229, 254. *See also* Overman
Ungrounding, 15, 16, 19, 21
Utopia(n), 8, 9, 82, 179, 203, 208–218, 223, 229

Verification, 18, 70, 83, 187
Verwindung, 3, 21–23, 30, 72–74, 76, 82, 95, 145, 159, 191, 212–214, 216, 217, 236, 251. *See also* Distortion

Vico, Giambattista, 88
Violence, 5, 6, 47, 57, 60, 61, 65, 101–107, 113–116, 125–127, 141, 145, 147, 159, 183, 191, 194, 207, 215, 219, 230, 231, 237, 244, 246, 253, 255
Vocation, 7, 16, 27, 109, 111, 112, 128, 129, 144, 147, 149, 150, 160, 205, 206, 218

Weak thought, 1–8, 11, 63, 64–67, 70, 73, 79, 81–83, 89, 104, 110, 125, 130, 160, 167, 183–190, 193–200, 214, 253
Weber, Max, 144
Witness, 8, 20, 79, 93, 101, 105, 113, 153, 194, 198
Wittgenstein, Ludwig, 44

Žižek, Slavoj, 9, 225, 233, 235, 237–239, 259